PRIVACY, REGULATIONS, AND CYBERSECURITY

PRIVACY, REGULATIONS, AND CYBERSECURITY

THE ESSENTIAL BUSINESS GUIDE

Chris Moschovitis

WILEY

Published by John Wiley & Sons, Inc., Hoboken, New Jersey.
Published simultaneously in Canada.

For general information on our other products and services or for technical support, please contact our Customer Care Department within the United States at (800) 762-2974, outside the United States at (317) 572-3993, or fax (317) 572-4002.

Wiley publishes in a variety of print and electronic formats and by print-on-demand. Some material included with standard print versions of this book may not be included in e-books or in print-on-demand. If this book refers to media such as a CD or DVD that is not included in the version you purchased, you may download this material at http://booksupport.wiley.com. For more information about Wiley products, visit www.wiley.com.

Library of Congress Cataloging-in-Publication Data is Available:

ISBN 9781119658740 (hardback)
ISBN 9781119660118 (ePub)
ISBN 9781119660149 (ePDF)

Cover image: © Yuichiro Chino / Getty Images, © dem10 / Getty Images
Cover design: Wiley

SKY10023964_011221

CONTENTS

FOREWORD

You will never do anything in this world without courage.
It is the greatest quality of the mind, next to honor.

—*Aristotle*

Businesses today are faced with increasing demands for privacy protections, ever-more complex regulations, and ongoing cybersecurity challenges that place heavy demands on scarce resources. During these difficult times it is important that we have the courage to proactively deal with these imperatives. This book is an essential tool for any business executive who needs to orchestrate the "handshake" between privacy, security, and ongoing regulations. Oh yes, and courage.

A few years ago, I returned to one of my passions—security—when I took over as the leader of a business in the eastern US. These last three years have been challenging but exciting, and I have seen an unprecedented level of interest by business executives in privacy and security. I have made more board presentations and been in more meetings with the C-suite on these topics in the last three years than the ten years before that combined. When I was appointed to the board of the ISACA (Information Systems Audit and Controls Association), I was thrilled at the opportunity to make significant change in the security profession. But I expected too much too soon, and the board's message after my first presentation was clear: "We need more research on the concept of information security management and how security is viewed by executives before we make any investments."

It was early in the new millennium, and security was becoming a topic of conversation in the executive suite. Even though the first CISO had been appointed at Citi in 1995, the body of knowledge for security was defined by technical and product-specific certifications with no frameworks to support organizations, and privacy regulations such as GDPR were still just a distant thought.

At that time, I had made my recommendation to the board of the ISACA to drive the setting of "common body of knowledge" of the future CISO. I had a strong belief that there was wider acceptance of the role and its importance in protecting the organization.

Maybe it was a turning point, but several events came together early in the new millennium to reinforce this belief. "I LOVE YOU" infected millions of computers, followed by the first criminal conviction of a hacker, the widespread disruption caused by denial-of-service attacks on Microsoft systems (and Bill Gates's decree that Microsoft products would embed security as part of the product), and a series of other high-profile hacks. This was exacerbated by the financial collapse of Enron and its impact on the trust in the US economic system. Regulation followed with the Sarbanes-Oxley Act and many others around the globe. It was a new world, and the continued regulation around security and privacy gained momentum.

That year I became chairman of the board of ISACA, and the new body of knowledge accompanied by a certification (CISM) was launched. The founding group was made up of four dedicated CISOs, and the certification is still the standard for security management professionals.

Which brings me back to my good friend Chris, with whom I have formed a terrific bond over mutual interests. Fine food and wine and a connection as first-generation Greeks cemented our friendship. Recently, we discussed and debated many topics, including the need for those executives who understand security risks to transform that knowledge into action around privacy and security around regulation.

I have found Chris's intellectual curiosity and sense of humor to be both compelling and engaging. These traits are a perfect vehicle to take the reader on this journey, from the fundamentals of privacy to the ongoing regulatory pressures and how companies can be better prepared at the executive level to tackle these changes.

Chris is able to interpret complex principles and distill them into a natural flow, where the reader is taken on a journey. In Homer's *Odyssey*, Circe warned Odysseus of the impending perils so that he would be prepared. Likewise, Chris's book prepares the executive to be aware of the perils and opportunities ahead and provides a roadmap on how to act with courage as security and privacy regulations continue to proliferate.

Be prepared and do the right thing and not just because of regulation—do it for your customers, employees, shareholders, and everyone who places trust in you and your company. Use the step-by-step approach from this book, so you and your company can be ready for whatever challenges the future might hold.

It is time to act, and with this guide in hand, you are well on your journey.

Marios Damianides
Cyber Security Leader, Ernst & Young LLP
Chair of the Board, ISACA (2003–2005)

PREFACE

"What? I've been working like this all my life! Now, you're telling me that I have to be GDP … umm … GD-whatever compliant?"

My friend and client, an immigration attorney from way back when "immigration" was not a dirty word, was angry. Her practice had been very successful over the years, dealing with all sorts of immigration issues across continents. The problem is that she is doing business with citizens of the European Union (EU). Worse, she has a partner in Athens, Greece, an EU-member country.

Fabulous! She must comply with the General Data Protection Regulation of the EU, better known by its acronym, GDPR. For those of you blissfully unaware of GDPR, it is a law passed by the European Union in 2016. It has far-reaching consequences to businesses worldwide, including yours!

If you are a businessperson who, like my friend, has no idea where to begin with GDPR, then this book is for you! It is the sequel to *Cybersecurity Program Development for Business: The Essential Planning Guide* (Wiley, 2018), and just like that book, this one is designed with you, a businessperson, in mind. In *Cybersecurity*, my goal was to give you enough information so that you wouldn't be at the mercy of experts talking over your head and around your business when it came to cybersecurity. In its introduction, I wrote:

> *What if there was a book that put the whole cybersecurity thing into perspective, using simple, direct language? What if there were sections and chapters explaining what is going on, what the risks are, and what all the technobabble really means? And, what if the book had a step-by-step, actionable approach on what you can do about all this? A book that aggregated the current best practices, put them in perspective, injected my experience and my own point of view, and how I applied all this across all our clients?*
>
> *All the while poking a little fun at ourselves, too?*

The goal, approach, and style remain the same—only this time, the aim is to transform your hard-earned cybersecurity awareness into one that is privacy-centric and regulation-aware. If you're one of the many businesspeople out there who are new to all this, just starting to confront the new cyberwar realities, concerned about yours and your business' privacy, and worried that some regulation will descend to levy God knows what kind of fine, then you're in luck!

This book will guide you through all this step-by-step, section-by-section: privacy, regulations, and cybersecurity. We'll work through the basics together, as well as reviewing case studies and examples of best practices across different industries and different size companies.

Just like in the first book, which I will be referencing frequently, especially in Part Three, we need a case-study disclaimer: The case studies and examples presented throughout both books are aggregated from my own work and from the work of many colleagues who were gracious enough to share their experiences. As you would expect, all names, industries, and geographies have been changed to protect the anonymity of these clients. In some of the cases, multiple problems were combined into one. In others, many assignments were broken out into a single one. The goal has been to distill the essential lesson from each case while protecting the identity and respecting the privacy and confidentiality of every client.

There is a fundamental difference, though, between the first book and this one. The first book dealt strictly with the practical and pragmatic design of a cybersecurity program with the goal of protecting your business. This book synthesizes two distinct, diverse, and complex segments into a privacy-first and regulation-focused cybersecurity program. If you already have a cybersecurity program in place, then this book will help you hone what's already there into a privacy-centric and regulation-compliant cybersecurity program.

If you don't have a cybersecurity program in place, then … where have you been?

Nevertheless, I am glad you're with us now! This is your opportunity to start building a cybersecurity program from the bottom up that, from inception, will be privacy- and regulation-compliant-focused.

One more thing before we dive right in: Just as it is important to understand what this book is, and who it is for, it is equally important to know what it is not. This is especially true since we will be dealing with topics that are at once scholarly, legal, and technical in nature. This book is not intended to be an academic analysis, a legal brief, or a technical how-to manual, although it will borrow and reflect work from all these disciplines.

If you're looking for the latest scholarly book on privacy, an in-depth legal treatment of the California Consumer Privacy Act, or how to configure your firewall, this book is not for you!

This book is intended as a practical, pragmatic, and actionable business guide for people across industries and business sizes who need to understand what all this talk about privacy really means, what the effect of all these laws and regulations are, and how to put it all together in a cybersecurity program to protect what's of value to them.

It relies heavily on the outstanding work of numerous scholars, lawyers, and information technology and cybersecurity professionals, without whom it would not have been possible to write it. You will find a detailed bibliography of sources at the end of the book, and I urge you to use it and dig deeper as you see fit.

For me, each one of these topics, and especially privacy, represent fascinating areas of study. Privacy and cybersecurity force us to confront questions of how we as people manage difficult, complex concepts and how we translate those concepts into actionable laws and ways of doing business.

ABOUT THE AUTHOR

I was born in Athens, Greece. After high school, I chose to come to the United States to study physics and computer science. I did that at the State University of New York, the College at Brockport, in upstate New York. My years at Brockport were formative to me as a person, a scientist, and as a professional. Words for the gratitude and respect I have for the dedicated faculty that shaped my life can easily fill a couple of books, but that is for another time.

After graduating with my bachelor's degree in science, I became an instructor of computer science and a computer systems manager at the Stratford School in Rochester, New York. Following brief graduate work stints at the Rochester Institute of Technology and the University of Rochester, I moved to New York City to serve as the director of academic computing at Pratt Institute. There, under the direction of the vice president of information technology (there were no "chief information officers" back then), I was responsible for the building and management of four computing centers of excellence, each focusing on a specific discipline (art, architecture, engineering, and information science). From there, I was recruited to be the vice president of information technology at the O'Connor Group, a real estate manager and developer in New York City. Then, in the middle of the Reagan Recession, I decided that there was no better time than the present to start my own company, which I did in 1989.

I have been running my own firm ever since, surrounded by partners and colleagues who teach me more and more every single day, and together we deliver a broad spectrum of IT consulting services. I have been privileged to partner with great clients, to engage in fantastic projects of business and technology transformation, and to collaborate with teams that push boundaries and develop incredible business solutions. I lived through the amazing advances in computer science that are now the stuff of lore: I was there during BitNet, sending email messages and watching the message hop from node to node. I was amazed at formatting the first 10 MB hard disks of IBM's new personal computer. I've fed endless floppies in and out of the first Macs. I've built muscles carrying the Compaq "Portable," which was nicknamed "luggable" for good reason. I've carried pagers and cell phones the size of suitcases. I subscribed to CompuServe and AOL and still have a working Hayes 14.4 modem.

Throughout it all, I have always been fascinated by security, privacy, and the protection of data. Even before "cybersecurity" was a word, I insisted that the sites we designed and managed implemented business-appropriate computer security and disaster recovery. Maybe it was because George Whelan, a partner of mine at the time, was a computer virus collector (he still has them). Maybe, because I remain culturally Greek, naturally cautious and private. Whatever the reason, I always asked, "What happens if 'this' gets out?" or "How fast can we be back up and running?" Any of my consultants will tell you that even now, the first thing they are taught when they start working for me is that "not checking the backup is a career-ending mistake."

Following decades as a practitioner of both IT governance and cybersecurity management, I decided to make it official and joined Information Systems Audit and Control Association (ISACA), an independent, nonprofit, global association that was founded in 1969, engaging in "The development, adoption and use of globally accepted, industry-leading knowledge and practices for information systems." Joining ISACA was one of the smartest things I ever did. Through IASCA, I got certified in three areas: First in cybersecurity, becoming a Certified Information Security Manager (CISM), then in IT governance, becoming Certified in Governance of Enterprise IT (CGEIT), and finally as a Certified Data Privacy Solutions Engineer (CDPSE).

Not one to stand still, and always fascinated by the beauty in complexity, I decided in 2018 to study privacy and its implications on our society, business, and systems. I subsequently joined the International Association of Privacy Professionals (IAPP). Just like ISACA, the IAPP is an incredible community of privacy experts that have dedicated their life to the study and implementation of sound privacy principles. I found a welcome home there and endless resources to help me in my journey that has led me here, to this book, that I am humbled to share with you.

I am privileged to be able to continue my journey, running my firm tmg-emedia, inc., and to be surrounded by incredible professionals, clients, and friends that teach me the value of hard work, dedication, and love every day.

ACKNOWLEDGMENTS

Every book is a labor of love. This one is no different. After I finished my first baby, *Cybersecurity Program Development for Business: The Essential Planning Guide*, I knew I wanted to write a second, one specifically focused on Privacy. The initial idea was unformed but persistent. Privacy intrigued me. The "P" word was used practically daily; legislators were passing laws pretending to preserve it while businesspeople were at a loss about what to do with it.

I was clear from the beginning that I did not want to write a scholarly treatment on privacy. Better-equipped scholars of many stripes have produced, and continue to produce, great works on the subject. My approach was to be similar to the first book: What do we need to know on privacy so that we can be informed as citizens and enabled as professionals? More to a pragmatic point, how does all this privacy legislation affect our capacity to design and deliver an effective cybersecurity program?

To answer all these questions, I came up with the format for this book. It would have three distinct parts: one on privacy; one on regulations, worldwide; and one on privacy-centric cybersecurity program development. The latter would be based on the previous book but enhanced by our understanding of privacy, not just as a concept but as a set of concrete regulatory requirements. The result is in your hands!

Books are never solitary efforts. Yes, the image of the writer toiling away at her desk day-in, day-out is true, but the author brings a universe of people to paper. Same with me. Over the course of 31-plus years in the information technology industry, I have had the privilege to meet hundreds of professionals, experts, partners, clients, and vendors who have shaped my thinking, formed my experiences, and honed my expertise. Their influence is reflected in the pages that follow. They wrote the book with me.

From my original partner in the business, George Whelan, who religiously collected and kept live computer viruses on floppy disks, to instructors such as Jay Ranade, who has forgotten more than I'll ever know, to clients who partnered with me and staff who tirelessly worked to solve problems, I owe each one a debt of gratitude that no acknowledgment can do justice.

Still, I must start somewhere, and the right place to start is with an apology for my omissions. They are entirely my own.

Next, I want to acknowledge a debt of gratitude to my clients, my true partners to success. Every day, I am honored and privileged to be your ally and to contribute to your goals. I am constantly humbled by all the things that you teach me every day. I would be remiss if I didn't single out the Hoffman family, Andrew, Mark, and Steve, who have been loyal supporters and mentors since I started the firm 31 years ago; the founding partners at Allegaert Berger and Vogel, Chris, David, and Michael, for their trust in me, their loyalty, and wise counsel through thick and thin; the amazing team at Kapitus for teaching me and my team how to jump onto a rushing freight train; and to Vigdis Eriksen at Eriksen Translations for her trust in us and for her feedback that makes us better every day!

In the same breath, I want to thank my own partners and associates, whose incredible expertise, loyalty, dedication, skills, empathy, and personal engagement make my and our clients' success possible. They are, alphabetically: Anna Murray, Atsushi Tatsuoka, Danielle Chianese, Doel Rodriguez, Frank Murray, Greg Andrews, James Rich, Justin Schroeder, Leon Tchekmedyian, Pedro Garrett, Thomas Hussey, Tyler Raineri, and Yeimy Morel. Thank you for the privilege of working with you, for all you do, day and night, and for allowing me to shut my door and write, write, write! You made this possible!

Whenever there is a book, there is an editor and a publisher. I have been the luckiest of authors to have the best in both. First, my eternal gratitude to the one-and-only, walk-on-water-on-her-bad-days, amazing Hilary Poole, my editor, coauthor, and friend of countless years and just as many books. Hilary, you are amazing! I absolutely refuse to go next to a keyboard unless I am reassured that you'll edit the outcome. Thank you!

Deepest thanks to everyone at John Wiley & Sons, one of the most professional and exceptional publishers in the world, and especially to my executive editor, Sheck Cho, captain and commander extraordinaire and Susan Cerra, the project's managing editor! This book is as much yours as it is mine, and I am grateful for all your help, guidance, and support.

To all the privacy, cybersecurity, and governance professionals around the world, working tirelessly in the field, in academia, in research institutions, in government agencies, and militaries, this book pales in comparison to your achievements every day. I cannot emphasize this enough: Without your endless efforts in breaking new ground, expanding and enhancing our scientific understanding, and guiding us through the maze, we would be lost. All your works represent the lighthouses that helps us navigate, and if I aspire to anything, it is for this book to aid in reflecting your light, interpreting your guidance, and adding wind to the sails.

To the many international organizations that help all practitioners learn, hone, and apply their craft, as well as develop the frameworks we depend on, my gratitude for your ongoing contributions, tireless curation, and unending support. I must particularly single out CERT, ENISA, IAPP, ISACA, (ISC)^2, ISECOM, ISO, ISSA, NIST, NSA, OECD, OWASP, and SANS, with my apologies for omitting the many other deserving organizations worldwide. My specific thanks to IAPP and ISACA for their continuous support and endless resources. The ISACA New York chapter remains a home away from home for me and countless professionals in the New York metro area.

To the many friends who supported me in so many ways, through encouragement, advice, and love: Jeanne Frank, I know you're watching from Heaven! You were right about the book! Alex and Mari, Richie and Charlene, Sherryl, Sotos, Dimitris and Koralia, and last but not least, Madina, my princess Indira, and my prince Kamron: I don't know what I did to deserve any of you, but I can't imagine life without you! Thank you!

Finally, to Anna Murray, a name that keeps on repeating in these acknowledgments but from where I sit, not enough! You are the most brilliant, expert, capable, tenacious, fierce, loving, accepting, and giving person, amazing professional, and talented writer I know! Every day I thank my lucky stars that brought you to my life as my partner in the business and my partner in life. You are, and always will be, the brightest star in the dark of night, guiding me home. Thank you!

PART ONE
Privacy

What man art thou that, thus bescreened in night, so
stumblest on my counsel?
—William Shakespeare, *Romeo and Juliet*

CHAPTER 1

Understanding Privacy

Bene vixit, bene qui latuit.
—Ovid, *Tristia*

In case your Latin is rusty, Ovid's quote above translates to: "To live well is to live concealed." My interpretation is different: "To live well is to live in privacy."

But let's not get ahead of ourselves here. What, exactly, is *privacy*? What does it mean? What do we understand when we describe something as "private"?

Do we mean *secret?* Is something private also secret? Certainly, the reverse is not true: we can have many secrets that are not private! They may be secrets of others, secret negotiations, secret deals, and so on.

Do we mean *personal?* Is it data coupled with our personhood? If so, is all personal data private? What about our name? Are there degrees of privacy?

Defining privacy has puzzled minds far greater than mine, and the definitions for privacy have been just as grand and diverse. Let's start with our perennial friends at Merriam-Webster. They define privacy as:

1. a: the quality or state of being apart from company or observation: SECLUSION
   b: freedom from unauthorized intrusion
2. a: SECRECY
   b: a private matter: SECRET
3. archaic: a place of seclusion

The *Oxford English Dictionary*, on the other hand, defines privacy as:

1. A state in which one is not observed or disturbed by other people.
   1.1 The state of being free from public attention.

And, one of my favorites, Wiktionary's definition, covers all the bases, albeit sometimes cyclically:

1. The state of being secluded from the presence, sight, or knowledge of others.
2. Freedom from unwanted or undue disturbance of one's private life.
3. Freedom from damaging publicity, public scrutiny, surveillance, and disclosure of personal information, usually by a government or a private organization.
4. (obsolete) A place of seclusion.
5. (obsolete, law) A relationship between parties seen as being a result of their mutual interest or participation in a given transaction, contract, etc.; Privity.
6. (obsolete) Secrecy.
7. (obsolete) A private matter; a secret.

Not to be left out, of course, is the legal definition of privacy. *Black's Law Dictionary* defines privacy as:

> The right that determines the nonintervention of secret surveillance and the protection of an individual's information. It is split into 4 categories:
>
> 1. Physical: An imposition whereby another individual is restricted from experiencing an individual or a situation;
> 2. Decisional: The imposition of a restriction that is exclusive to an entity;
> 3. Informational: The prevention of searching for unknown information; and
> 4. Dispositional: The prevention of attempts made to get to know the state of mind of an individual.

It's worthwhile to pay attention to those four categories: physical, decisional, informational, and dispositional. We'll be returning to those in more detail when we take on the meanings of privacy for your business.

**It's not that I have something to hide,
I have nothing I want you to see.**

—Amanda Seyfried

Definitions of privacy have evolved over time, and our understanding of the concept is constantly changing. Therefore, it would be naive to assume that Privacy with a capital P can be rendered via a legal definition, complex or not, or a dictionary entry.

Privacy has been, and remains, the subject of rigorous academic study. Anthropology, sociology, psychology, history, and other disciplines have been looking into the concept and developing their own definitions and models to describe Privacy.

It is clearly out of scope for this book to get into details on the academic research on privacy or do a literature review. For our purposes a few drops from the ocean will suffice.

The two giants in privacy research are considered to be Alan Westin (1929–2013), professor of public law and government at Columbia University, and Irwin Altman (1930), professor and chairman of the Psychology Department of the University of Utah, now emeritus.

Westin's book *Privacy and Freedom* (1968) is considered to be the foundational text on the subject. Westin defines privacy as follows:

> Privacy is the claim of individuals, groups, or institutions to determine for themselves when, how, and to what extent information about them is communicated to others.

Westin goes on to describe four states of privacy, and four functions or purposes of privacy. He defines the privacy states as solitude, intimacy, anonymity, and reserve, and the purposes as personal autonomy, emotional release, self-evaluation, and limited and protected communication.

Westin's position is that privacy operates at three levels: The individual, the group, and the organizational level. He also constrains his theory of privacy as applicable to western societies only. In 2002, Westin proposed what's known as the Westin segmentation, classifying the public into three groups: the privacy fundamentalists, who place a premium on privacy and make up about 25 percent of the population; the privacy unconcerned, who couldn't care less about privacy and make up about 20 percent of the population; and the privacy pragmatists, the remaining 55 percent, who are aware of the trade-off between privacy and external offerings.

For his part, Altman outlined his privacy regulation theory in *The Environment and Social Behavior* (1975). Put very simply, privacy regulation theory has to do with the fact that people have different privacy standards at different times and in different contexts. For example, your definition of what constitutes "private information" in your relationship with your spouse is clearly different than in your relationship with your children, and it's also different with your boss and yet again with your coworkers.

According to Altman, this phenomenon is due to "the selective control of access to the self," which has five properties:

- Temporal dynamic process of interpersonal boundaries (feelings about privacy change based on context);
- Desired and actual levels of privacy (what we hope for and what we get can differ);
- Non-monotonic function of privacy (what constitutes the "optimal" amount can increase or decrease);
- Bi-directional nature of privacy (privacy involves both "inputs" and "outputs"); and
- Bi-level nature of privacy (individual privacy is different from group).

Altman went on to describe additional features of privacy, including units of privacy, its dialectic nature, and desired versus achieved privacy.

Altman and Westin share a view of privacy as a very dynamic state with multiple inputs and outputs—essentially a system in constant state of rebalancing, depending on the environment. Their work has spurred both vigorous academic debates and hundreds of researchers moving the field forward by expanding on these theories, adding and elaborating on the privacy features, as well as driving a lot of experimental work all over the world. The majority results of this research to date seem to validate Westin and Altman, building on their solid foundational work.

Also of note is Nancy Marshall's work, for instance her article "Privacy and Environment" (1972). Marshall developed the Privacy Preference Scale, the first of its kind, based on her identification of six privacy states: intimacy, solitude, anonymity, reserve, seclusion, and not neighboring. Communication studies scholar Virginia Kupritz helped introduce objective environmental measurements of privacy, further expanding Altman's work by reorganizing it and introducing additional psychological and cognitive variables. Kuptritz also did significant research on the architectural effect on privacy.

Most recently, Tobias Dienlin, a scholar in communications science and media psychology at the University of Hohenheim, has proposed a Privacy Process Model that attempts to integrate all major work on privacy into one cohesive model. It integrates the work of Westin, Altman, and numerous others, and differentiates between "factual privacy context and subjective privacy perceptions," a distinction that Dienlin posits as important both online and offline. His model has four privacy dimensions—informational, social, psychological, and physical—that he argues are equally applicable to both physical and digital worlds.

As you would expect, these debates and work on privacy are far from over. For that matter, they may never be over. Not only does technology continue to evolve, but so do we, across cultures and geographies. The end result is a constantly changing landscape in which we must navigate carefully, constantly challenging our values and protecting what we think, at the time, is near and dear to our identity as people, community members, and value-creating citizens.

CHAPTER 2

A (Very) Brief History of Privacy

The right to be let alone is indeed the beginning of all freedom.

—William O. Douglas

(Dissenting opinion, *Public Utilities Commission v. Pollak* [1952])

Having a grasp on the concept of privacy is useful, but it's not enough for our purposes. We will soon have to confront regulations governing privacy that directly impact the way we do business. It is paramount that we understand not only privacy as a concept but privacy *in context*.

In other words, how did we get here?

Since time immemorial, all cultures, all over the world, have had some understanding of privacy as a concept. Some codified it into laws, while others integrated it with religious beliefs. There is substantial scholarship on the subject, and you'll find selected entries in the bibliography to kick off your in-depth review. For our purposes here, a few snippets will suffice to give as a sense of history and scope.

The ancient Greeks, borrowing from the Egyptians, venerated the God of Silence and Secrets, Harpokrates. He is usually pictured as a mischievous little boy with his finger to his lips as if he is saying "Shhh!" (You've got to start somewhere, I guess!) But the Greeks, being geometry savvy, didn't just include a secretive god in their pantheon. They also designed their living spaces by placing what we would consider window openings in such a way that it would limit the view of an outside observer peering in.

9

The ancient Chinese, meanwhile, had—and still have—a very different and complex understanding of privacy. In broad terms, the word for privacy, *yin-si*, is a composite of two meanings: yin for "hidden" and si for "not for public disclosure." As such, yin-si was meant to describe the concept of privacy, but in a negative light—the term carries the sense of a shameful secret.

According to scholars of ancient Chinese culture, the Chinese were more focused in the governance of the state, and in protecting the governance structure, than protecting the individual. This was ultimately codified in a collection of morality-driven laws governing behavior across many levels, eventually compiled by none other than Confucius. In his *Analects*, he wrote, "Do not watch what is improper. Do not listen to what is improper. Do not speak nor act improperly." He also wrote that that gossip and hearsay were improper and urged everyone to double-check their Internet sources before forwarding their mother-in-law's conspiracy theory emails. (Yes, Gladys! We did land on the moon, the earth is not flat, and vaccines do save lives! Move on! Let it go!)

As tempting as it is to go through each ancient empire one by one (Egyptians, Babylonians, Greek, Assyrian, Persian ...), I'll spare you the individual details and focus on the one thing they had in common with regards to privacy: they didn't have any! Certainly not as we understand—or struggle to understand—privacy today.

Until the Middle Ages, privacy was not particularly possible. Most houses had one room. Most common spaces were open. To be sure, some cultures more than others took some steps to preserve what we today would identify as privacy, but in general, it was a time of communal living with little consideration of individual privacy.

I am not suggesting that this was necessarily by choice. But it was the reality for the vast masses of people, all over the world. To be sure, one would expect that they would rather have their own individual rooms, and so forth, but that was not possible, mostly for socioeconomic reasons. For that matter, Clellan Ford and Frank Beach in their *Patterns of Sexual Behavior* (1951) demonstrated that pretty much universally and irrespective of culture, humans would prefer their intimate moments to be private—even if that means taking them outside. (I suppose this is the reverse of "get a room," back when rooms were not an option!)

The ones who did "have a room," as we got closer and closer to the Renaissance, were the rich, living in their castles and palaces. It's around this time that the notion of privacy starts getting some traction. In fact, the historian Peter Smith declared that "Privacy (is) the ultimate achievement of the Renaissance!" Interestingly, privacy was made possible by the intersection of technology (namely, Gutenberg's press) and the Catholic Church. It might seem counterintuitive, but a mandatory one-on-one confession between the individual and God (as decreed in the Great Council's declaration of 1215), was a dramatic departure from the communal way of enforcing morality. Then, once printed bibles became commonplace, the devout could study and contemplate in private isolation, further distancing themselves from the community. A dramatic shift was underway, one that would take a couple of centuries to take hold, away from the "community" and toward individual privacy.

The fun started in 1604 with England's attorney general Sir Edward Coke and his famous ruling in Semayne's Case. The ruling has become popularly known as "The Castle Doctrine," because it starts with " … the house of every one is to him as his Castle and Fortress as well for defence against injury and violence, as for his repose." But in fact Coke's writing is substantially more complex than just that notion. He went on to clarify the specifics of how this fortress is to be used and also set limits on how the authorities (at the time, the Sheriff) could gain access. Think warrants! A good start!

For the next two and a half centuries, the western world was busy doing everything from establishing the slave trade, to publishing the King James Bible, mourning the death of Shakespeare, completing the Taj Mahal, chopping off the head of Charles the First, developing calculus, establishing trade with China, printing the first daily newspaper, losing 30,000 souls in the Lisbon earthquake, signing the US Declaration of Independence, starting the French Revolution, painting portraits of Napoleon, watching Charles Babbage invent the first computer, reading Lincoln's Emancipation Proclamation, covering their ears when Nobel set off his first dynamite, and saying "cheese" to George Eastman's perfected Kodak box camera.

The Legal Case for Privacy (the Big Print)

It is at this point where our review of privacy history takes on a different focus: Privacy's legal status. I, personally, find all these foundational privacy law cases and opinions absolutely fascinating, and wanted to include them all here, exuberantly sharing them with you! But my editor reminded me that I also love eating raw sea urchins, which—like my choice of reading—may be an acquired taste.

Therefore, I have taken her wise advice and split the legal case section in two: the Big Print section (here), and the Fine Print section (Chapter 3). In the first section, we'll go over the legal review on a high level, discussing why and how these cases and opinions shaped our thinking and led to the regulations we all deal with today. In the Fine Print section that follows in Chapter 3, I will present more detailed excerpts of the opinions for those that want to revel in the original writing of these great legal minds.

With that in mind, let's begin!

If I were to pick the major milestones for privacy law evolution in the western world, I would select the ones enumerated in Table 2.1.

Slouching toward Privacy

It is no surprise that privacy law is culture dependent. European cultures tend to reflect a stronger community identity, and privacy laws reflect that difference. American culture, by contrast, tends toward the individualistic, and the development of privacy laws reflect that.

A hugely significant moment was an 1890 article in the *Harvard Law Review*, "The Right to Privacy" by Samuel Warren and Louis Brandeis. Extensive quotes from the article are included in the Fine Print section; for now, a quick overview.

Warren and Brandeis were writing in the context of then-recent inventions of photography and audio-recording devices, which the authors claimed, "have invaded the sacred precincts of private and domestic life." Warren and Brandeis wrote, "The press is overstepping in every direction the obvious bounds of propriety and of decency." Their article was a defense of, as they called it, "the right to be let alone."

"The Right to Privacy" was the first attempt at pulling together accepted US standards into some kind of coherent legal standing for privacy. The argument is essentially that a right to privacy, while not spelled out in the Constitution literally, nonetheless exists in common law. They cite the Fourth Amendment as a strong undergirding for the right, specifically, "to be secure

Table 2.1 Milestones in the Evolution of Privacy Law

Year	Milestone
1888	Thomas M. Cooley, Justice and later Chief Justice of the Michigan Supreme Court, writes: *"A Treatise on the Law of Torts or the Wrongs Which Arise Independently of Contract."*
1890	Samuel D. Warren and Louis Brandeis publish "The Right to Privacy" in the *Harvard Law Review*.
1902	*Roberson v. The Rochester Folding Box Company* antiprivacy judgment gives rise to Section 50 and 51 of New York State's Civil Rights Law.
1905	The Georgia Supreme Court accepts Warren and Brandeis unanimously in *Pavesich v. New England Life Ins. Co.*
1939	The American Law Institute's first revision of Restatement of Torts to include privacy concepts.
1948	The Universal Declaration of Human Rights is adopted, including Article 12: The Right to Privacy.
1950	The European Convention on Human Rights is adopted, including Article 8, an expanded right to privacy.
1967	The Freedom of Information Act (FOIA) is enacted in the Unites States.
1977	The American Law Institute revises again the Restatement of Torts to include modern privacy concepts.
1980	The Organization for Economic Co-operation and Development (OECD) issues its first guidelines on data privacy protection.
1981	The Council of Europe adopts Treaty 108: Convention for the protection of individuals with regard to automatic processing of personal data.
1983	The Federal Constitutional Court of Germany (Bundesverfassungsgericht) strikes down the Personal Identifiable Information component of the German census, marking a milestone in individual privacy rights.
1995	The European Data Protection Directive 95 is adopted, the predecessor to today's General Data Protection Regulation (GDPR).
2014	The European Union Court of Justice rules that EU law grants EU citizens "the right to be forgotten" from search engines.
2018	The European Union adopts the General Data Protection Regulation (GDPR).
2020	California passes the strictest privacy law in the United States, the California Consumer Protection Act (CCPA).

in their persons, houses, papers and effects." The article also cites the Fifth Amendment, which comes into play because, just as people shouldn't be forced to say things they don't want to, they should not be forced to share information, either.

Today, "The Right to Privacy" is recognized as a foundational moment in American jurisprudence. But it certainly didn't start out that way! The New York Court of Appeals, for example, defied the arguments of Warren and Brandeis, in their ruling for the defendant in *Roberson v. The Rochester Folding Box Company*. That case was brought when Ms. Roberson objected to her image being used by the defendant without her permission in flour packaging boxes.

On the other hand, in the case of *Pavesich v. New England Life Ins. Co*, the Georgia Supreme Court unanimously accepted Warren and Brandeis's pro-privacy arguments and found for the plaintiff. (As with the Warren/Brandeis article, you can find a lot more detail on the Georgia case in the Fine Print section.)

What's more, even though the New York Court of Appeals hadn't found Brandeis persuasive, some sense that he had a point must had begun to take root in the public consciousness. The Court's decision sparked such a strong public outcry on Ms. Robeson's behalf that the New York State Legislature passed a law (section 50 and 51 of New York State's Civil Rights Law, still in the books, albeit amended) prohibiting anyone from using images of individuals without their consent.

The law was the first to specifically enumerate privacy as a right.

Right of privacy. A person, firm or corporation that uses for advertising purposes, or for the purposes of trade, the name, portrait or picture of any living person without having first obtained the written consent of such person, or if a minor of his or her parent or guardian, is guilty of a misdemeanor.

You may have noticed that New York's courts had one response to Warren and Brandeis, while Georgia's courts had the opposite. This brings us to a key point: privacy legislation in the United States is initiated by the states and, as you would expect, reflects the individual state priorities. This makes for a hodge-podge of laws that companies that do business in multiple states have to follow, giving rise to substantial lobbying efforts in Washington for passage of a federal privacy law that can preempt the state ones. I suspect, and hope, that federal law will be enacted, but for now ... don't hold your breath!

But while the US legislature dithers, more cohesive, and far more protective/restrictive privacy laws continue to be enacted by the Europeans. The consequence, given the market size of the European Union, is that EU rules are—basically by default—setting the tone for all business, worldwide. After all, if you must comply with GDPR for Europe, you might as well comply with GDPR globally. It makes no sense to implement GDPR for only your European operations, while maintaining a separate data governance environment for your US operations. Too expensive to maintain, and it takes one mistake to have you found in violation of GDPR, so why risk it?

Debating Privacy in the US

Mostly in the US, and to a lesser extent around the world, privacy legislation is fiercely debated. These debates have been going on since Warren and Brandeis, and they reflect both ideological, cultural, and legal disagreements on what privacy is, and to what degree it requires protection.

For example, Professor Frederick Davis in his 1959 essay "What Do We Mean by 'Right to Privacy'?" writes:

> The concept of a right to privacy was never required in the first place, and that is whole history is an illustration of how well-meaning but impatient academicians can upset the normal development of law.

A few years later, Professor Harry Kalven, in his 1966 "Privacy in Tort Law—Were Warren and Brandeis Wrong?" wrote:

The lack of legal profile and the enormity of the counterprivilege converge to raise for me the question of whether privacy is really a viable tort remedy. The mountain, I suggest, has brought forth a pretty small mouse.

Finally, in 1983 Diane L. Zimmerman's "Requiem for a Heavyweight: A Farewell to Warren and Brandeis's Privacy Tort" in the *Cornell Law Review* concludes in part:

After ninety years of evolution, the common law private-facts tort has failed to become a usable and effective means of redress for plaintiffs. Nevertheless, it continues to spawn an ever-increasing amount of costly, time-consuming litigation and rare, unpredictable awards of damages. In addition, this "phantom tort" and the false hopes that it has generated may well have obscured analysis and impeded efforts to develop a more effective and carefully tailored body of privacy-protecting laws.

Many of the most troubling privacy questions today arise not from widespread publicizing of private information by the media, but from electronic eavesdropping, exchange of computerized information, and the development of data banks. Much of this information, which individuals supply as a necessary prerequisite to obtaining important benefits like credit, medical care, or insurance, can cause serious harm, even if circulated only to one or two unauthorized recipients. Privacy law might be more just and effective if it were to focus on identifying (preferably by statute) those exchanges of information that warrant protection at their point of origin, rather than continuing its current, capricious course of imposing liability only if the material is ultimately disseminated to the public at large.

Today, the debate is far from over, and it rages on worldwide. That said, there is no question that with the explosion of big data, artificial intelligence, increased data processing capacity, and a constant hunger for analysis, everyone from consumers to industry and constituents to legislators recognize that they need to do "something."

The *what* and *how* remain elusive.

Confidentiality vs. Privacy

We started this journey with the various definitions of privacy. We went on to get a feel on how privacy concepts and law evolved over time. As intellectually fascinating all this has been, we need to get back to today's business reality! What does all this mean for us, exactly?

For one, we now know that the definition of privacy is—at best—elastic and will change over time. We know, as per *Black's Legal Dictionary*, that it has multiple dimensions (let's review: the dimensions are physical, decisional, informational, and dispositional).

We need to be able to synthesize what we know about privacy at the conceptual level, what we know our business needs to be, what regulations we need to comply with, and conjure our own "business" definition of privacy, so that we can use it to implement our cybersecurity program around it. This definition must be a living definition of privacy—one we look at carefully and frequently, and one that we must be willing to modify as our society and laws change.

Let's start with what cybersecurity is. In my previous book on *Cybersecurity Program Development*, I defined cybersecurity as:

> ... the ongoing application of best practices intended to ensure and preserve confidentiality, integrity, and availability of digital information as well as the safety of people and environments.

Confidentiality, integrity, and availability are known as the three pillars of cybersecurity; safety is added to account for the real-life impact of cybersecurity on people and ecosystems.

It is easy to note that at least one of the pillars, confidentiality, is inferred through the use of "secrecy" again and again in multiple privacy definitions.

Those two words are functionally synonymous. The problem with secrecy (aka confidentiality), though, is that it rests in the eyes of the beholder!

To better understand this, we'll need to take a few paces into the rabbit hole!

Like we discussed, the easiest way people understand something *confidential* is by its synonym: *secret*. The issue, of course, is with who gets to decide what is secret?

Edward Snowden, for example, had some … let's say, serious disagreements … with what his employer, the US government's National Security Agency, was doing to collect secrets: namely collecting, storing, and cataloguing every single phone call, text message, and email, essentially worldwide. Whether this "disagreement" is treachery or heroism depends in great part on your definition of what is (or should be) secret. Obviously, the US government considers Mr. Snowden to be a traitor, while the International League of Human Rights granted him one of their most prestigious honors, the Carl von Ossietzky Medal.

Irrespective of your feelings on Snowden, the fact remains: the definition of confidentiality (secrecy) rests with the person defining it. Complicating matters further, that definition can change over time! The examples are numerous:

- A happily married couple considers their partner's emails and texts as confidential, until … the divorce proceedings where they serve each other subpoenas to enter into evidence all the alleged love letters and sexting.
- Two nations happily exchange intelligence until … the day the newly elected leader of one decides to align with someone else. Then, all of a sudden, what was shared becomes top secret!
- Two companies are partnered to offer a product or service and they share all kinds of data to increase efficiency until … the partnership falls apart, and they acrimoniously sue each other for patent infringement, intellectual theft, and serving bad coffee at board meetings.

It gets worse!

Not only is there ambiguity as to who decides what is confidential, but there is question on the degree of confidentiality, and how this degree of confidentiality changes over time. Also, the degree of control on these definitions is increasingly being removed from the hands of the individual and transferred, via legislation from our duly elected representatives, to the hands of regulatory agencies that have the right to come knocking on your door asking questions about your treatment of confidential data.

To bring all these hypotheticals into the real world, let's quickly look to Europe. In 2013, the European Union's council outlined four levels, or degrees, of confidentiality. They are (emphasis added):

1. TRÈS SECRET UE (EU TOP SECRET): information and material the unauthorized disclosure of which could cause **exceptionally grave prejudice to the essential interests** of the European Union or of one or more of the Member States;
2. SECRET UE (EU SECRET): information and material the unauthorized disclosure of which **could seriously harm the essential interests** of the European Union or of one or more of the Member States;
3. CONFIDENTIEL UE (EU CONFIDENTIAL): information and material the unauthorized disclosure of which **could harm the essential interests** of the European Union or of one or more of the Member States;
4. RESTREINT UE (EU RESTRICTED): information and material the unauthorized disclosure of which **could be disadvantageous to the interests** of the European Union or of one or more of the Member States.

Why do we care about what the EU nation-states classify as degrees of confidentiality?

We care because the same body that wrote the 2013 document also came up with 2018's General Data Protection Regulation (GDPR)—aka, the standard-bearer on electronic privacy rights. The same concepts and degrees of severity were picked up from the 2013 document reworked and reworded to apply to individual data, and voila! *Le GDPR nouveau est arrivé!*

When we were talking cybersecurity program development, we took these types of confidentiality degrees and translated them directly to our corporate data. My suggestion was, and remains, to keep things simple!

Classify your data only with the absolutely necessary degrees of confidentiality. After all, you'll be the one that will need to manage all this metadata for your corporate assets, and you'll need to do this quickly and effectively. If possible, use the following confidentiality degrees:

Top Secret:	Board of directors eyes only
Secret:	Board and executive committee's eyes only
Confidential:	Board, executives, and management team's eyes only
Public:	Everyone, and the horse they rode in on

That's enough for now. Let's get out of the rabbit hole and see how this affects our implementation of a privacy-first cybersecurity program.

First things first: Where are the similarities, and differences, between confidentiality and privacy. How do we translate the individualistic attributes of privacy to the concrete attributes of confidentiality? What do their definitions have in common? Where do they diverge?

Privacy is all about people's rights and expectations. Privacy is an "individual" right. Confidentiality, on the other hand, is all about data. The Table 2.2 should help clarify this.

Table 2.2   Privacy vs. Confidentiality

Privacy is …	Confidentiality is …
a right of people	a property of data, any data, not just PII
a right to control access across a person's physical, decisional, informational, and dispositional dimensions	an agreement on the rating of data
a right protected by law around the world	an attribute of data that can be regulated

Our job in developing a privacy-first cybersecurity program is to make sure that we are protecting people's privacy through the proper governance of the confidentiality of their data.

As luck would have it, the four pillars of cybersecurity are: confidentiality, integrity, availability, and safety! All these go together, hand in hand. You can't just protect people's confidential data but ignore aspects of their data availability and integrity. And, certainly, you can't protect people's privacy if you can't ensure their safety!

The good news? We have frameworks for that! NIST, ISO, and so forth. We're all over confidentiality, integrity, availability, and safety! And, that's exactly what we will do in the chapters that follow! We'll start with understanding what the major privacy regulations are impacting our business, and then we'll walk down the path of a privacy-first cybersecurity program implementation.

CHAPTER 3

The Legal Case for Privacy (the Finer Print)

> I stared up at the sky and raised my middle finger, just in case God was watching. I don't like being spied on.
>
> —Annabel Pitcher
> *My Sister Lives on the Mantelpiece*

This is the fun chapter! I mean, who doesn't want to read legal opinions? It's like suggesting that you don't enjoy reading the various user agreements and consent forms before hitting "Accept!" Silly, I know! But, just in case this is not your cup of tea, you can go right ahead and skip this section, and go directly to Part 2: "Regulations."

For those, clearly superior, intellects who stayed on, I will start with professor's Thomas M. Cooley, Justice and later Chief Justice of the Michigan Supreme Court, writing: *A Treatise on the Law of Torts or the Wrongs Which Arise Independently of Contract* (emphasis added):

> **§ 101. Violating right of privacy.** Within the past few years, the existence of a right of privacy, or right to be let alone, has been considerably discussed in the courts and legal periodicals. The question
>
> *(continued)*

(*continued*)

has arisen mostly in the suits to enjoin or recover damages for the unauthorized use of one's name or likeness for advertising purposes. So far, we believe, the question has been squarely presented and squarely decided by but two courts of last resort. The New York court of appeals has decided against the right by a bare majority of four to three. In a more recent case the supreme court of Georgia has unanimously affirmed the existence of the right. In the New York case the opinion of the court was rendered by Chief Justice Parker and is based upon the lack of any precedent, the failure of the great commentators on the common law to even mention such a right, and especially upon the evil consequences that would attend the judicial establishment of such a right. Upon the latter point the learned judge says: "If such a principle be incorporated into the body of the law through the instrumentality of a court of equity, the attempts to logically apply the principle will necessarily result, not only in a vast amount of litigation, but in litigation bordering upon the absurd, for the right of privacy once established as a legal doctrine, cannot be confined to the restraint of the publication of a likeness, but must necessarily embrace as well the publication of a word picture, a comment upon one's looks, conduct, domestic relations or habits. And were the right of privacy once legally asserted it would necessarily be held to include the same things if spoken instead of printed, for one, as well as the other, invades the right to be absolutely left alone. An insult would certainly be in violation of such a right and with many persons would more seriously wound the feelings than would the publication of their picture. And so we might add to the list of things that are spoken and done day by day which seriously offend the sensibilities of good people to which the principle which the plaintiff seeks to have imbedded in the doctrine of the law would seem to apply. I have gone only far enough to barely suggest the vast field of litigation which would necessarily be opened up should this court hold that privacy exists as a legal right enforceable in equity by injunction, and by damages where they seem necessary to give complete relief."

The suit was brought by a young woman to enjoin the use of her likeness by the defendants in advertising their wares. The supreme court sustained the motion and granted the relief. This decision was reversed by the court of appeals in the case referred to. The dissenting opinion was rendered by Mr. Justice Gray and was not only concurred in by his two associates but has been fully approved and adopted by the supreme court of Georgia. We quote from this opinion on the nature of the right and the grounds upon which it is based. **"Security of person is as necessary as the security of property; and for that complete personal security, which will result in the peaceful and wholesome enjoyment of one's privileges as a member of society, there should be afforded protection, not only against the scandalous portraiture and display of one's features and person, but against the display and use thereof for another's commercial purposes or gain.** The proposition is to me an inconceivable one, that these defendants may, unauthorizedly, use the likeness of this young woman upon their advertisement, as a method of attracting widespread public attention to their wares, and that she must submit to the mortifying notoriety, without right to invoke the exercise of the preventive power of a court of equity. It seems to me that the principle, which is applicable, is analogous to that upon which courts of equity have interfered to protect the right of privacy, in cases of private writings, or of other unpublished products of the mind. The writer or the lecturer, has been protected in his right to a literary property in a letter, or a lecture, against its unauthorized publication; because it is property, to which the right of privacy attaches. I think that this plaintiff has the same property in the right to be protected in the use of her face for defendant's commercial purposes, as she would have, if they were publishing her literary compositions. The right would be conceded if she had sat for her photograph; but if her face or her portrait has a value, the value is hers exclusively; until the use be granted away to the public."

The Georgia case was a suit for damages for the unauthorized publication of the plaintiff's picture in a life insurance advertisement. The court unanimously decided that the action was maintainable.

(*continued*)

(continued)

The right of privacy, conceding it to exist, is a purely personal one, that is it is a right of each individual to be let alone, or not to be dragged into publicity. One has no right of privacy with respect to his relatives, living or dead. Thus a parent may not enjoin the publication of the picture of his infant child. And the widow, children or other relatives of a deceased person cannot enjoin the use of such person's likeness for advertising purposes, the erection of a statue of such deceased, or the publication of a memoir of his life.

This is truly exceptional because of two key statements. The first: "Security of person is as necessary as the security of property and [...] there should be afforded protection..." and the second: "The right of privacy, conceding it to exist, is a purely personal one, that is it is a right of each individual to be let alone..." Remember, this is being discussed in 1888, and it reads as if it were right out of the Congressional Record in 2019!

Part of what makes these entries visionary for their time and particularly useful for our purposes is that they tie the concept of "security of person" to the understanding of privacy. We'll be getting back to that in some detail as we start integrating the prevailing concept of privacy, the regulations affecting it, and translating all this into an actionable, business-pragmatic cybersecurity program. For now, back to the lessons of history!

On December 15, 1890, two years after Cooley's writings, two brilliant young lawyers, Samuel D. Warren and Louis D. Brandeis, who would eventually become a Supreme Court Justice, published in the *Harvard Law Review* an article titled "The Right to Privacy."

Today, the article is still considered to be one of the most important works on the subject of privacy, with accolades such as "Nothing less than adding a chapter to our law" (Roscoe Pound) and "Perhaps the most famous and certainly the most influential law review article ever written" (Melville B. Nimmer). Professor Neil Richards, one of the world's leading experts in privacy law, wrote in his "The Puzzle of Brandeis, Privacy, and Speech" that "two short texts by Louis D. Brandeis are the foundation of American Privacy Law—his coauthored *Harvard Law Review* article 'The Right to Privacy' and his dissent in *Olmstead v. United States*."

It is tempting to include the whole article here; it is that good and that important! Nevertheless, and as much as I urge you to read it in its entirety, for our purposes, a few key entries will suffice.

The first entry I'd like you to consider is the matter of *Principle*. Warren and Brandeis write:

The principle which protects personal writings and any other productions of the intellect or of the emotions, is the right to privacy, and the law has no new principle to formulate when it extends this protection to the personal appearance, sayings, acts, and to personal relation, domestic or otherwise.

If the invasion of privacy constitutes a legal injuria, the elements for demanding redress exist, since already the value of mental suffering, caused by an act wrongful in itself, is recognized as a basis for compensation.

The right of one who has remained a private individual, to prevent his public portraiture, presents the simplest case for such extension; the right to protect one's self from pen portraiture, from a discussion by the press of one's private affairs, would be a more important and far-reaching one. If casual and unimportant statements in a letter, if handiwork, however inartistic and valueless, if possessions of all sorts are protected not only against reproduction, but against description and enumeration, how much more should the acts and sayings of a man in his social and domestic relations be guarded from ruthless publicity. If you may not reproduce a woman's face photographically without her consent, how much less should be tolerated the reproduction of her face, her form, and her actions, by graphic descriptions colored to suit a gross and depraved imagination.

Warren and Brandeis go on to establish boundaries to this right of privacy:

It remains to consider what are the limitations of this right to privacy, and what remedies may be granted for the enforcement of the right.

1. The right to privacy does not prohibit any publication of matter which is of public or general interest.

(continued)

(continued)

In determining the scope of this rule, aid would be afforded by the analogy, in the law of libel and slander, of cases which deal with the qualified privilege of comment and criticism on matters of public and general interest. There are of course difficulties in applying such a rule, but they are inherent in the subject-matter, and are certainly no greater than those which exist in many other branches of the law,—for instance, in that large class of cases in which the reasonableness or unreasonableness of an act is made the test of liability.

2. The right to privacy does not prohibit the communication of any matter, though in its nature private, when the publication is made under circumstances which would render it a privileged communication according to the law of slander and libel.

Under this rule, the right to privacy is not invaded by any publication made in a court of justice, in legislative bodies, or the committees of those bodies; in municipal assemblies, or the committees of such assemblies, or practically by any communication made in any other public body, municipal or parochial, or in any body quasi public...

3. The law would probably not grant any redress for the invasion of privacy by oral publication in the absence of special damage.

The same reasons exist for distinguishing between oral and written publications of private matters, as is afforded in the law of defamation by the restricted liability for slander as compared with the liability for libel.

4. The right to privacy ceases upon the publication of the facts by the individual, or with his consent.

This is but another application of the rule which has become familiar in the law of literary and artistic property.

5. The truth of the matter published does not afford a defence. Obviously this branch of the law should have no concern with the truth or falsehood of the matters published. It is not for injury to the individual's character that redress or prevention is sought, but for injury to the right of privacy.

6. The absence of "malice" in the publisher does not afford a defence.

Personal ill-will is not an ingredient of the offence, any more than in an ordinary case of trespass to person or to property.

Warren and Brandeis close the article with these remarks and final plea:

The remedies for an invasion of the right of privacy are also suggested by those administered in the law of defamation, and in the law of literary and artistic property, namely:—

1. An action of tort for damages in all cases. Even in the absence of special damages, substantial compensation could be allowed for injury to feelings as in the action of slander and libel.
2. An injunction, in perhaps a very limited class of cases.

It would doubtless be desirable that the privacy of the individual should receive the added protection of the criminal law, but for this, legislation would be required. Perhaps it would be deemed proper to bring the criminal liability for such publication within narrower limits; but that the community has an interest in preventing such invasions of privacy, sufficiently strong to justify the introduction of such a remedy, cannot be doubted. Still, the protection of society must come mainly through a recognition of the rights of the individual. Each man is responsible for his own acts and omissions only. If he condones what he reprobates, with a weapon at hand equal to his defence, he is responsible for the results. If he resists, public opinion will rally to his support. Has he then such a weapon? It is believed that the common law provides him with one, forged in the slow fire of the centuries, and to-day fitly tempered to his hand. The common law has always recognized a man's house as his castle, impregnable, often, even to its own officers engaged in the execution of its commands. Shall the courts thus close the front entrance to constituted authority, and open wide the back door to idle or prurient curiosity?

Although now this article is considered seminal in the field, it was not immediately accepted by legal scholars, nor was it—or currently is it—devoid of controversy.

Twelve years later, in 1902, a case reached New York's Court of Appeals that seemed designed to test the popularity of Brandeis's views. The case, *Roberson v. The Rochester Folding Box Company*, was in some senses a repeat of the case discussed by Justice Cooley earlier: a woman named Abigail Roberson objected when the Rochester Box company used her image without permission in packaging materials for Franklin Mills Flour.

Roberson alleged that the use of her image had caused damage to her reputation that was so severe, she'd actually become ill from the stress of it all. The initial court ruling found in Roberson's favor but admitted that there was no firm precedent for doing so. The box company appealed, and not only did the Court reverse the decision, it even mocked Brandeis's article in its finding for the defendant!

An examination of the authorities leads us to the conclusion that the so-called "right of privacy" has not as yet found an abiding place in our jurisprudence, and, as we view it, the doctrine cannot now be incorporated without doing violence to settled principles of law by which the profession and the public have long been guided.

While New York's highest court was anti-Brandeis, the Supreme Court of Georgia took a very different view of the matter. On March 3, 1905, in *Pavesich v. New England Life Ins. Co*, they unanimously accepted Warren and Brandeis's position. Cherry-picking from their decision:

2. A right of privacy is derived from natural law, recognized by municipal law, and its existence can be inferred from expressions used by commentators and writers on the law as well as by judges in decided cases.
3. The right of privacy is embraced within the absolute rights of personal security and personal liberty.

And:

5. Personal liberty includes not only freedom from physical restraint, but also the right "to be let alone," to determine one's mode of life, whether it shall *[191] be a life of publicity or of privacy, and to

order one's life and manage one's affairs in a manner that may be most agreeable to him, so long as he does not violate the rights of others or of the public.

6. Liberty of speech and of the press, when exercised within the bounds of the constitutional guaranties, are limitations upon the exercise of the right of privacy.

7. The constitution declares that the liberty of speech and of the press must not be abused; and the law will not permit the right of privacy to be asserted in such a way as to curtail or restrain such liberties. The one may be used to keep the other within lawful bounds, but neither can be lawfully used to destroy the other.

Closing, in part, with:

So thoroughly satisfied are we that the law recognizes within proper limits, as a legal right, the right of privacy, and that the publication of one's picture without his consent by another as an advertisement, for the mere purpose of increasing the profits and gains of the advertiser, is an invasion of this right, that we venture to predict that the day will come when the American bar will marvel that a contrary view was ever entertained by judges of eminence and ability.

As you can already see from the New York opinion versus the Georgia one, the road of recognizing privacy as a right was, and remains, far from straight and smooth. The next big case came in 1928, when the US Supreme Court was asked to rule on the government's warrantless wiretapping of Roy Olmstead, an alleged bootlegger. Olmstead had been convicted based on the evidence collected from a wiretap of his office. His conviction was upheld in a 5-to-4 majority decision delivered by William Howard Taft, which included such interesting statements like:

The common law rule must apply in the case at bar. Nor can we, without the sanction of congressional enactment, subscribe to the suggestion that the courts have a discretion to exclude evidence the admission of which is not unconstitutional because unethically secured.

Louis Brandeis, also a member of the Court, wrote a now-famous, scathing dissent. In it, Brandeis firmly defined "the right to be let alone" as "the most comprehensive of rights, and the right most valued by civilized men." He wrote (emphasis added):

The makers of our Constitution undertook to secure conditions favorable to the pursuit of happiness. They recognized the significance of man's spiritual nature, of his feelings, and of his intellect. They knew that only a part of the pain, pleasure and satisfactions of life are to be found in material things. They sought to protect Americans in their beliefs, their thoughts, their emotions and their sensations. **They conferred, as against the Government, the right to be let alone – the most comprehensive of rights, and the right most valued by civilized men**. To protect that right, every unjustifiable intrusion by the Government upon the privacy of the individual, whatever the means employed, must be deemed a violation of the Fourth Amendment. And the use, as evidence in a criminal proceeding, of facts ascertained by such intrusion must be deemed a violation of the Fifth.

By 1939 so many state courts had adopted some interpretation of the Warren and Brandeis positions on privacy that it made it in the American Law Institute's 1939 Restatement of Torts:

A person who unreasonably and seriously interferes with another's interest in not having his affairs known to others or his likeness exhibited to the public is liable to the other.

The floodgates had opened. More privacy-based lawsuits followed, and by 1977 the American Law Institute had to revise its Restatement of Torts again. This time they added four distinct torts:

1. Unreasonable intrusion upon the seclusion of another
2. Appropriation of the other's name or likeness
3. Unreasonable publicity given to the other's private life
4. Publicity that unreasonably places the other in false light before the public.

From 1977 to today, most of these torts have been recognized by most courts in the United States.

International Privacy Legislation

The first modern international privacy law appeared in 1948, as Article 12 of the Universal Declaration of Human Rights. It was proclaimed on December 10 in Paris, with the wounds of the Second World War still fresh. It is a powerful document, drafted by representatives from all over the world hoping for a fresh, and less bloody start. It starts with:

Preamble

Whereas recognition of the inherent dignity and of the equal and inalienable rights of all members of the human family is the foundation of freedom, justice and peace in the world,

Whereas disregard and contempt for human rights have resulted in barbarous acts which have outraged the conscience of mankind, and the advent of a world in which human beings shall enjoy freedom of speech and belief and freedom from fear and want has been proclaimed as the highest aspiration of the common people . . . .

(continued)

(*continued*)

Now, Therefore THE GENERAL ASSEMBLY proclaims THIS UNIVERSAL DECLARATION OF HUMAN RIGHTS as a common standard of achievement for all peoples and all nations, to the end that every individual and every organ of society, keeping this Declaration constantly in mind, shall strive by teaching and education to promote respect for these rights and freedoms and by progressive measures, national and international, to secure their universal and effective recognition and observance, both among the peoples of Member States themselves and among the peoples of territories under their jurisdiction.

Of interest to us are Articles, 1, 2, 3, and the privacy-specific Article 12:

Article 1.

All human beings are born free and equal in dignity and rights. They are endowed with reason and conscience and should act towards one another in a spirit of brotherhood.

Article 2.

Everyone is entitled to all the rights and freedoms set forth in this Declaration, without distinction of any kind, such as race, colour, sex, language, religion, political or other opinion, national or social origin, property, birth or other status. Furthermore, no distinction shall be made on the basis of the political, jurisdictional or international status of the country or territory to which a person belongs, whether it be independent, trust, non-self-governing or under any other limitation of sovereignty.

Article 3.

Everyone has the right to life, liberty and security of person.

Article 12.

No one shall be subjected to arbitrary interference with his privacy, family, home or correspondence, nor to attacks upon his honour and reputation. Everyone has the right to the protection of the law against such interference or attacks.

This aspirational and hopeful declaration was the first to bring out privacy as a human right. In that way, and framed around the rest of the articles, the Declaration of Human Rights is considered seminal in its role in elevating privacy to a legally protected right.

It was quickly followed in 1950 by the European Convention of Human Rights, with its own Article 8 addressing privacy:

ARTICLE 8

Right to respect for private and family life

1. Everyone has the right to respect for his private and family life, his home and his correspondence.
2. There shall be no interference by a public authority with the exercise of this right except such as is in accordance with the law and is necessary in a democratic society in the interests of national security, public safety or the economic well-being of the country, for the prevention of disorder or crime, for the protection of health or morals, or for the protection of the rights and freedoms of others.

The European version is more specific, both in terms of what privacy means (e.g., spelling out "correspondence") and the limits of claims to privacy (e.g., introducing legal exceptions to the right "as necessary").

It will not be for another 23 years that Sweden passes the Data Act ("Datalagen," 1973), considered to be the first national data protection law. This law, which was fairly conservative by today's standards, governed how personally identifiable information was processed in computerized registers. It established a data protection authority with the ominous name "The Data Inspection Board," which would issue permits before a new personal data register could operate and determine specific conditions for its operation. The law has since been superseded by the European General Data Protection Regulation.

By 1980, and with data processing blindly obeying Moore's Law, the Organization for Economic Cooperation and Development (OECD) issued the first international guidelines on data privacy protection. It is in these guidelines that the world first gets a glimpse of what's to come in the years ahead. Terms such as "Data Controller" and "Data Subject" are introduced and defined, along with the concept of transborder data flows.

The OECD was very careful to respect domestic law—framing its document as voluntary guidelines—while at the same time trying to be firm by calling them "The minimum standards" to be supplemented by additional legislation to protect personal data.

The eight OECD principles, as currently revised, are:

Collection Limitation Principle

There should be limits to the collection of personal data and any such data should be obtained by lawful and fair means and, where appropriate, with the knowledge or consent of the data subject.

Data Quality Principle

Personal data should be relevant to the purposes for which they are to be used, and, to the extent necessary for those purposes, should be accurate, complete and kept up-to-date.

Purpose Specification Principle

The purposes for which personal data are collected should be specified not later than at the time of data collection and the subsequent use limited to the fulfilment of those purposes or such others as are not incompatible with those purposes and as are specified on each occasion of change of purpose.

Use Limitation Principle

Personal data should not be disclosed, made available or otherwise used for purposes other than those specified in accordance with Paragraph 9 except:

a. with the consent of the data subject; or
b. by the authority of law.

Security Safeguards Principle

Personal data should be protected by reasonable security safeguards against such risks as loss or unauthorised access, destruction, use, modification or disclosure of data.

Openness Principle

There should be a general policy of openness about developments, practices and policies with respect to personal data. Means should be readily available of establishing the existence and nature of personal data, and the main purposes of their use, as well as the identity and usual residence of the data controller.

Individual Participation Principle

Individuals should have the right:

a. to obtain from a data controller, or otherwise, confirmation of whether or not the data controller has data relating to them;
b. to have communicated to them, data relating to them
   i. within a reasonable time;
   ii. at a charge, if any, that is not excessive;
   iii. in a reasonable manner; and
   iv. in a form that is readily intelligible to them;
c. to be given reasons if a request made under subparagraphs (a) and (b) is denied, and to be able to challenge such denial; and

(continued)

(continued)

d. to challenge data relating to them and, if the challenge is successful to have the data erased, rectified, completed or amended.

Accountability Principle

A data controller should be accountable for complying with measures which give effect to the principles stated above.

These guidelines would serve as the backbone for the countless additional guidelines and—ultimately—laws that would be enacted around the planet. The race was on!

On the heels of the OECD guidelines, the Council of Europe adopted Treaty 108: Convention for the protection of individuals with regard to automatic processing of personal data. This is a significant piece of legislation, exclusively dedicated to data processing and privacy governance and, at the time, represented "the only legally binding multilateral agreement in the field of personal data protection." Key highlights from the Treaty include:

Article 1 – Object and purpose

The purpose of this Convention is to secure in the territory of each Party for every individual, whatever his nationality or residence, respect for his rights and fundamental freedoms, and in particular his right to privacy, with regard to automatic processing of personal data relating to him ("data protection") … .

Article 5 – Quality of data

Personal data undergoing automatic processing shall be:

a. obtained and processed fairly and lawfully;
b. stored for specified and legitimate purposes and not used in a way incompatible with those purposes;

c. adequate, relevant and not excessive in relation to the purposes for which they are stored;
d. accurate and, where necessary, kept up to date;
e. preserved in a form which permits identification of the data subjects for no longer than is required for the purpose for which those data are stored.

Article 6 – Special categories of data

Personal data revealing racial origin, political opinions or religious or other beliefs, as well as personal data concerning health or sexual life, may not be processed automatically unless domestic law provides appropriate safeguards. The same shall apply to personal data relating to criminal convictions.

Article 7 – Data security

Appropriate security measures shall be taken for the protection of personal data stored in automated data files against accidental or unauthorised destruction or accidental loss as well as against unauthorised access, alteration or dissemination.

The next major milestone in privacy law was the 1983 decision of the German Federal Constitutional Court, which struck down the requirement that the 1983 German census gather personally identifiable data such as name, religious affiliation, educational background, profession, housing situation, and the like. The decision includes the following gem:

The general right of personality encompasses, based on the notion of self-determination, the power conferred on the individual to, in principle, decide themselves whether and to what extent to disclose aspects of their personal life.

If individuals cannot, with sufficient certainty, determine what kind of personal information is known to their environment, and if it is

(continued)

(continued)

difficult to ascertain what kind of information potential communication partners are privy to, this may seriously impair the freedom to exercise self-determination. In the context of modern data processing, the free development of one's personality therefore requires that the individual is protected against the unlimited collection, storage, use and sharing of personal data.

The next main event in privacy law was, of course, the 1995 European Data Protection Directive 95. We will, nonetheless, completely ignore it, even though it has some great stories, including a lawsuit that blew up the safe harbor agreement between the United States and the European Union, sending thousands of executives running in a mad spree down hallways with their hair on fire. But Directive 95 has since been superseded and can safely be ignored in favor of the General Data Protection Regulation (GDPR), which followed in 2018.

Before getting to that, we'll briefly leave Europe, and talk about the 2004 Asia-Pacific Economic Cooperation (APEC) introduction of their first Privacy Framework that was voluntarily adopted by 21 countries. This represented the first major Asia-Pacific effort in privacy regulations, work that started when the APEC ministers endorsed the original 1998 Blueprint for Action on Electronic Commerce.

The APEC Privacy Framework includes the following principles:

I. Preventing Harm
Recognizing the interests of the individual to legitimate expectations of privacy, personal information protection should be designed to prevent

II. Notice
Personal information controllers should provide clear and easily accessible statements about their practices and policies with respect to personal information that should include:

a. the fact that personal information is being collected;
b. the purposes for which personal information is collected;
c. the types of persons or organizations to whom personal information might be disclosed;
d. the identity and location of the personal information controller, including information on how to contact them about their practices and handling of personal information;
e. the choices and means the personal information controller offers individuals for limiting the use and disclosure of, and for accessing and correcting, their personal information.

III. Collection Limitation

The collection of personal information should be limited to information that is relevant to the purposes of collection and any such information should be obtained by lawful and fair means, and where appropriate, with notice to, or consent of, the individual concerned.

IV. Uses of Personal Information

Personal information collected should be used only to fulfill the purposes of collection and other compatible or related purposes except:

a. with the consent of the individual whose personal information is collected;
b. when necessary to provide a service or product requested by the individual; or,
c. by the authority of law and other legal instruments, proclamations and pronouncements of legal effect.

V. Choice

Where appropriate, individuals should be provided with clear, prominent, easily understandable, accessible and affordable mechanisms to exercise choice in relation to the collection, use and disclosure of their personal information. It may not be appropriate for personal information controllers to provide these mechanisms when collecting publicly available information.

(continued)

(continued)

VI. Integrity of Personal Information

Personal information should be accurate, complete and kept up-to date to the extent necessary for the purposes of use.

VII. Security Safeguards

Personal information controllers should protect personal information that they hold with appropriate safeguards against risks, such as loss or unauthorized access to personal information, or unauthorized destruction, use, modification or disclosure of information or other misuses. Such safeguards should be proportional to the likelihood and severity of the harm threatened, the sensitivity of the information and the context in which it is held, and should be subject to periodic review and reassessment.

VIII. Access and Correction

Individuals should be able to:

a. obtain from the personal information controller confirmation of whether or not the personal information controller holds personal information about them;
b. have communicated to them, after having provided sufficient proof of their identity, personal information about them;
   i. within a reasonable time;
   ii. at a charge, if any, that is not excessive;
   iii. in a reasonable manner;
   iv. in a form that is generally understandable; and,
c. challenge the accuracy of personal information relating to them and, if possible and as appropriate, have the information rectified, completed, amended or deleted.

IX. Accountability

A personal information controller should be accountable for complying with measures that give effect to the Principles stated above.

> When personal information is to be transferred to another person or organization, whether domestically or internationally, the personal information controller should obtain the consent of the individual or exercise due diligence and take reasonable steps to ensure that the recipient person or organization will protect the information consistently with these principles.

If you're thinking this all sounds familiar, you're not wrong. By this time, frameworks and legislations across the world are borrowing from one another liberally.

By 2011, APEC introduced the APEC Cross-Border Privacy Rules (CBPR) as a "government-backed data privacy certification." This takes the APEC Framework and essentially creates a legal standard that both governments and companies can use to regulate cross-border data flows.

And this brings us to 2018 and the enactment of the European Union's General Data Protection Law. The legislation, considered by many to be the gold standard of privacy regulation, built on years of experience, not only within the EU but from all over the world. We will be looking at the regulation in detail in its own chapter, but for those hungry to get a glimpse of what's to come, its salient points, as published by the EU itself and excerpted here, are:

What is the Aim of the Regulation?
- It allows European Union (EU) citizens to better control their personal data. It also modernises and unifies rules allowing businesses to reduce red tape and to benefit from greater consumer trust.
- The general data protection regulation (GDPR) is part of the EU data protection reform package, along with the data protection directive for police and criminal justice authorities.

(continued)

(continued)

Key Points

Citizens' rights

The GDPR strengthens existing rights, provides for new rights and gives citizens more control over their personal data. These include:

- easier access to their data — including providing more information on how that data is processed and ensuring that that information is available in a clear and understandable way;
- a new right to data portability — making it easier to transmit personal data between service providers;
- a clearer right to erasure ('right to be forgotten') — when an individual no longer wants their data processed and there is no legitimate reason to keep it, the data will be deleted;
- right to know when their personal data has been hacked — companies and organisations will have to inform individuals promptly of serious data breaches. They will also have to notify the relevant data protection supervisory authority.

Rules for businesses

The GDPR is designed to create business opportunities and stimulate innovation through a number of steps including:

- a single set of EU-wide rules — a single EU-wide law for data protection is estimated to make savings of €2.3 billion per year;
- a data protection officer, responsible for data protection, will be designated by public authorities and by businesses which process data on a large scale;
- one-stop-shop — businesses only have to deal with one single supervisory authority (in the EU country in which they are mainly based);
- EU rules for non-EU companies — companies based outside the EU must apply the same rules when offering services or goods, or monitoring behaviour of individuals within the EU;

- innovation-friendly rules — a guarantee that data protection safeguards are built into products and services from the earliest stage of development (data protection by design and by default);
- privacy-friendly techniques such as pseudonymisation (when identifying fields within a data record are replaced by one or more artificial identifiers) and encryption (when data is coded in such a way that only authorised parties can read it);
- removal of notifications — the new data protection rules will scrap most notification obligations and the costs associated with these. One of the aims of the data protection regulation is to remove obstacles to free flow of personal data within the EU. This will make it easier for businesses to expand;
- impact assessments — businesses will have to carry out impact assessments when data processing may result in a high risk for the rights and freedoms of individuals;
- record-keeping — SMEs are not required to keep records of processing activities, unless the processing is regular or likely to result in a risk to the rights and freedoms of the person whose data is being processed.

I hope and expect you've now had your fill of privacy history! Just in case, you will find all the references in the bibliography, and you can spend hours of uninterrupted fun digging through all the original texts and revel in the wordsmithing capabilities of legislators worldwide!

This will do it, though, for us. Next up: Regulations. There we will visit the regulations, region by region, that affect your business. We'll leave the legalese behind in favor of substance, and we'll focus on business impact. We'll need to know all this so that when we start diving into creating our privacy-first cybersecurity program, we know which laws we must comply with and which risks we can accept.

PART TWO
Regulations

The only way to stop big data from becoming big brother is introduce privacy laws that protect the basic human rights online.

—Arzak Khan

CHAPTER 4

Introduction to Regulations

> If, however, a government refrains from regulations and allows matters to take their course, essential commodities soon attain a level of price out of the reach of all but the rich, the worthlessness of the money becomes apparent, and the fraud upon the public can be concealed no longer.
>
> —John Maynard Keynes

Now that we have a sense of what privacy is and how we narrowly apply it to our world of data, let's see what legislators have come up with to address it.

Our approach will be limited in scope. We are only interested in privacy regulations that are specific to our data at rest (data storage), in motion (data transfer), and during data processing. Bodily and territorial privacy, while critical topics requiring your attention as a world citizen, are beyond the scope of this book.

As always, we will start with a definition! What does the term *regulation* mean? My favorite definition comes from our perennial friends at Merriam-Webster:

Regulation (noun)

1. The act of regulating: the state of being regulated
2. a: an authoritative rule dealing with details or procedure
   b: a rule or order issued by an executive authority or regulatory
   agency of a government and having the force of law

Across the world, the "executive authority or regulatory agency" described above has been either legislative bodies, governmental agencies, or various flavors of decrees coming from some supreme leader or another.

Of course, there are other ways to define *regulation*. After all, one government's "regulation" is another businessperson's "threat"! Many businesspeople view regulations as a threat to profitability, even calling them an impediment to value creation. To some degree this may depend on a particular political view, but for a risk manager, it's more black-and-white: what do you call anything that requires you deploy controls? A threat!

Of course, regulations are not a literal threat because they, as a rule, do not harm the assets. But they may represent a serious business risk. If there is a regulation that applies to your business, failure to comply can result in penalties, which may be significant. You—or more precisely your board of directors—must decide on one of two approaches:

You will either deploy controls so that you're in compliance with the regulation or the board (aka the legal representative of the shareholders) will accept the risk of noncompliance and pay any necessary penalties. The latter, as crazy as it may sound, can be a valid strategy for dealing with regulations. Boards accept this risk when the cost of compliance far outweighs the expense of the controls. For example, if the fine is going to be $10,000 for violating the regulation, but it will cost you $1,000,000 to comply, it's cheaper to pay the fine! Obviously, this is not a sustainable strategy, given that the "executive authorities or regulatory agencies" tend to take a dim view of repeat offenders, but it at least buys you some runway to either become compliant or to move your operations to some tropical island away from peering eyes.

Speaking of tropical islands, this is a good point to discuss the geographical scope of this book. When it comes to data, we're one big happy data-sharing planet, and so this book will endeavor to cover as much literal and metaphorical ground as possible. After all, e-commerce is a global business. Clients, vendors, partners come from everywhere, landing on your website and engaging with your brand. In that process, there will be the inevitable data exchange. If data is exchanged, you can be certain that there is some regulation that governs it.

That being said, it is impossible for this book to cover data regulation of every country on earth. You, and only you, can tell for certain which country's regulations apply to your business, and it will ultimately be your responsibility to research them and make sure you're in compliance.

I can tell you this: as of this writing the United Nations Conference on Trade and Development reports that 58 percent of the world's countries have privacy legislation in place and an additional 10 percent have draft legislation. (Of the remainder, 21 percent currently have no legislation, and 12 percent don't answer the phone to tell us one way or another.)

What can this book do for you? We will survey the world and discuss the main pieces of privacy legislation you need to understand. We will look at the major Internet hubs across continents and hemispheres and also provide you with the necessary resources for you to dig further on any country of interest as your business demands it.

Our journey will start in the United States, then head north to Canada, east to Europe, continue on to Asia, dip south to Oceania, head northwest to Africa, jump over to South America, and make our way back via Central America to New York for bagels. Pack lightly, we're doing this only with a carry-on.

Preparing to Take Charge

Before we plunge into the country-specific regulations on privacy, we need to do some homework. This homework is not geography dependent. You'll need to do this no matter where you do business.

The assignment is simple! You need to answer one question: What business are we in?

This is not an "industry" or "sector" question. This, and all other questions that follow, are privacy-centric. We need to know exactly the type of business we're engaging from a data privacy point of view.

For example, if your business collects personally identifiable information (PII), it doesn't matter if you're a widget maker, a dating service, or a trucking company. The fact that you collect PII is enough to tell us that you're likely under regulatory scrutiny from someone, somewhere, and that we need to address this.

Now, you might argue that there is no business that does not collect PII. How can you be in business and not collect some personally identifiable information? How do you bill your client? Obviously, you have the client's PII.

You are right! We all collect some form of PII in the course of doing business. For that matter, we collect PII even if we're not doing business with someone. If you meet someone at a networking function and exchange cards, you just exchanged PII. So does this mean we're all liable under God-knows-how-many different privacy statutes? If my phone gets stolen, am I liable under some privacy law for all the stored contacts?

As an individual you will not be prosecuted under the various privacy laws. In the US you could be sued for negligence or failure of fiduciary duty in civil court (if you were storing obviously sensitive data for others, e.g., medical or financial records of friends or relatives), but even in those cases the burden of proof is significant and varies from jurisdiction to jurisdiction. To be safe, you need to demonstrate that you have taken reasonable steps to protect your equipment that stores PII, even if that PII is just a friend's records. Leaving an unlocked phone on the coffee counter with all sorts of data and (potentially compromising?) photographs of several of your closest naked friends is asking for trouble—so be careful and keep your lawyer's number memorized!

As a business, on the other hand, your liability—including personal liability—is very different. Regardless of the type of business, and regardless of the volume of PII collected, the expectation is that you will be able to prove that you've taken reasonable, prudent steps to prevent unauthorized access. You must also demonstrate that you took immediate action in the case of a breach: notifying those affected, notifying the appropriate authorities, and taking all the steps necessary to respond to the incident. More on that in later chapters, as we develop a privacy-centric incident response plan.

So back to the "What business are we in?" question. You need to know the volume and type of PII that you collect, store, and process (put more simply, what kind and how much). You also will need to know how long you keep this data and how the data will ultimately be disposed of.

You need to perform this exercise, region by region wherever you do business. Then, you need to assess any privacy laws that may apply to your specific industry. Are you in health care? Are you working with children's PII? Are you in financial services? Each industry, across geographies, has specific regulations governing privacy and data security.

Sounds like a maze? You're right—it is, and we need a way to navigate it. We need a tool that can help us find our way through this labyrinth of regulations, something that we can maintain over time, as both our business and the regulations will change.

There are commercial tools that can help, but be prepared to bring your wallet. They are expensive, time consuming, and frequently require dedicated teams to install, run, and maintain. As a result, these are not a viable option for most companies. Yet, the need remains!

Still, there is good news: where budgets may fall short, innovation and creativity flourish. In the chapters that follow, we'll create our own tool using various spreadsheets. I'll show you how to link them and use them in your own privacy practice. You can even transfer them to your neighborhood-friendly database, if you're so inclined. I have had clients who took them and built their own SharePoint application that's just perfect for their needs.

The bottom line is this: You will need to take ownership of this issue, partner with the right professionals within your company, and retain outside expertise only as you need it, for specific "surgical" assignments. To do this, you'll need to get familiar with the regulations that apply to your company specifically, based on your location, industry, business size, and data exchange between parties and then apply that knowledge to a privacy-by-design cyber-security program.

Can you do this? You bet. You're already halfway there by reading this book. We'll do it together, and I will be guiding you step-by-step.

Creating Your Privacy Profile

But let's not get ahead of ourselves. What we need to do at this point is pretty simple: It's a one-pager: our Executive Summary Company Privacy Profile.

You will need to collect the following data:

1. What is your company's annual revenue? How much money are you making, subsidiaries included, please.
2. Where are you doing business? (e.g., country, regions, states, cities.)
3. PII Profile:

    a. Do you collect PII in any form (organically, through purchase, through exchange, etc.)? If yes:

        i. What kind of PII do you collect, store, and/or process? (e.g., children's records, health records, financial records, other protected classes?)
        ii. How much PII do you access (number of records)?
        iii. Do you store PII? If yes:

            1. How long is it stored for?
            2. How is it disposed of?

        iv. What do you do with the PII? (e.g., Do you sell it? Is it exclusive to your operations? Do you "enhance" it? Do you repurpose it? Do you aggregate it?)

How do you collect all this data? You ask questions! You review annual reports. You crash the executive committee's meeting. You go talk to (God help you) the IT folks. In short: Go out there, make friends, talk to people! Try it in person. Emails are nice, but they come with a "delete" option. You don't.

That's it. This is plenty for now. When you're done, this one-pager will be your preliminary company privacy profile, your first CPP. We'll do the heavy lifting later, when we get into the weeds of a privacy-centric cybersecurity program design. For now, this will give us a sense of what our regulatory exposure is. It should capture most of it, and later, when we do the detailed work, we can fill in any blanks during our asset discovery phase. By then, people at your company will have gotten to know this strange person walking around asking them all about PII!

Know before You Go: Using the Regulations Section

Before we dive into each region's regulations, it is important to take a minute to discuss what is included, what is not, and how to properly use this section so you can get the most out of it.

First and foremost, and perhaps most obvious, not all countries are included. I have included only the top three countries by region based on GDP. If your favorite country is not explicitly mentioned, do not despair. (I didn't include Greece either, which has me wondering if I can show my face back home this summer.) If the country you are interested in is not included, I recommend that you start your research at the International Association of Privacy Professionals (IAPP) at www.iapp.org. They should always be your starting point. Another excellent starting resource is the online handbook *Data Protection Laws of the World* by DLA Piper. You will find it at https://www.dlapiperdataprotection.com. From there, you can dig further into country specifics, but always make sure that your sources are authoritative and independently confirmed.

Finally, depending on your business, you may only be interested in certain specific regions. It is perfectly fine to skip the rest and go to Part 3: Privacy and Cybersecurity. I will not be offended, because I know you care, and besides, you can always use this section as a future reference. It's a win-win!

Depending on your appetite for reading regulatory text, you should either feel free to skim over the sections that are directly quoted from the regulations or relish in their language. Obviously, the book does not include the full text of any of the regulations (that, again, would result in a multi-thousand-page book). Instead, excerpts are introduced, and even those, when possible, are edited and formatted for clarity.

For all the regulations that are presented in this section the following format is followed:

Jurisdiction

Which geographical jurisdiction does this law apply to?

Background

Any pertinent background information, either directly taken from the law itself or put in context by synthesizing from multiple sources.

Intent and Major Provisions

What does the law try to achieve? What are the major provisions? To the degree possible, excerpted text directly from the legislation will appear here.

PII Definition

How is personal information defined under this law? Also, there may be entries when the law divides personal information from "sensitive" personal information. Again, to the degree possible, excerpted (and edited) text directly from the legislation will appear here.

Inclusion Criteria

Who's on the hook for this law?

Exclusions

Who gets a "get out of jail free" card?

Enforcement Agency

Who are the "men in black" enforcing the law?

Penalties

How much will it cost if you violate the law?

Complete Text

A link to the complete text of the legislation.

Impact

What is the impact of the law? Country-specific? Regional? Global?

Even with all this said, I forgive you if you glaze over some of the language that is by necessity quoted. Try to plow through, or alternatively, rejoice in knowing that there is a good reason why God made lawyers, and refer the matter to them.

One Last Thing before We Go!

Irrespective of whether you plow through every single entry that follows or you immediately skip to Part 3, there is one thing that you cannot ignore: Europe's General Data Protection Regulation (GDPR).

The reasons you can't ignore it have nothing to do with whether it applies to your business or not. It has everything to do with the global impact that this regulation has had on every privacy regulation, guideline, legislation (enacted or aspired to). This was obvious even before the GDPR was enacted, when Article 95 was "the law of the land" and was already setting the privacy tone worldwide.

In 2012, Graham Greenleaf, a professor of law and information systems at the University of New South Wales, wrote a paper titled: "The influence of European data privacy standards outside Europe: Implications for globalisation of Convention 108?" In it, he rightly concluded:

> 39 countries outside Europe have now enacted data privacy laws covering most of their private sectors (and most of those also cover their public sectors), and this growth outside Europe is accelerating. Examination of 33 of those 39 laws shows that, to a surprising extent, these laws share most (average 7/10) of the factors that are distinctive of European data privacy laws.

For me, it is clear that this trend has continued and increased. It's safe to say that, as of this writing, the GDPR represents the gold standard against which all other data protection laws will be measured. And the European Union is not done yet! They are constantly trying to improve and innovate in privacy and data protection, in part because of their brutal history and in part because of what they see as the erosion of privacy due to the onslaught of information technologies from outside their shores.

My suggestion, therefore, is this: Get to know this eight-hundred-pound privacy gorilla. Her influence will be felt both globally and locally, and that should be a welcome relief from the confusion and noise that all the varied interests create in their own self-service.

A worldwide GDPR is not as far-fetched as once thought (we're almost there as it is), and the faster we get there, the better we will all be. Not only because this elusive concept of privacy will finally be protected as well as possible but because we would all be able to speak a single, common, privacy language. In the words of the recent Nobel laureate Mr. Bob Dylan, "Privacy is something you can sell, but you can't buy it back."

Now, grab your boarding pass, get your passport ready, and we're off!

CHAPTER 5

North American Regulations

> You already have zero privacy. Get over it!
> —Scott McNealy, CEO Sun Microsystems, 1999

United States

If your business is located in the United States or does business there, pay close attention, and memorize the following. (There will be a quiz!)

ADA, ADEA, APA, BCR, BITAG, BSA, CALEA, CALOPPA, CAN-SPAM, CARU, CCPA, CFPB, CISA, CMIA, COBRA, COPPA, CPBR, CPEA, CPNI, CRA, DAA, DMA, DNC, DNT, DODD-FRANK, DPA, EBR, ECOA, ECPA, EEOC, EHR, EPIC, EPPA, ERISA, ESI, ESRB, FACTA, FATCA, FBI, FCC, FCRA, FDCPA, FERPA, FINCEN, FIPP, FIRREA, FISA, FISC, FLSA, FMLA, FOIA, FTC, GINA, GLBA, GPEN, HHS, HIPAA, HITECH, HITRUST, ICRAA, IRCA, IRS, MSCM, NHTSA, NIH, NIST, NLRA, NLRB, NSA, NSF, NSL, NTIA, PCI-DSS, PCLOB, PHI, PI, PII, PPRA, QPO, RFPA, SAR, SCA, SCC, SOX, TCPA, TSR, UDAP, USA FREEDOM ACT, USA PATRIOT ACT, and VPPA.

Every acronym on this list has some direct or indirect regulatory effect or authority over data privacy. Of course, this is just the list as I write. By the time you're reading this, I suspect that the list will have grown! And that's just at the federal level. The fun *really* starts at the state level, where—in the absence of a federal preemptive privacy regulation—the local legislators have stepped in and created state-specific regulations. If you're doing business in multiple states, you can expect to spend hours of uninterrupted fun making sure that your business complies with each and every one of those as well.

So what do we do about this?

That is the exact same question that all companies have been asking. Tech giants in particular have been miffed, put out, and disappointed about having to deal with all these annoying state regulations. For once, they have been "begging" for a federal law to preempt them and simplify everything. Washington keeps promising (or threatening) to create one, but don't hold your breath—especially for the "preemptive" part. In general, federal regulations set a baseline but allow for stricter state versions to preempt them. So, yes, a federal US privacy law is coming, but it is unlikely to make anybody's life much easier. In cases where state regs are stronger, you will still need to deal with them.

For now, you need to think of regulation in the United States as having two distinct steps. First you have to ask, "Which federal regulations apply to my business?" and then, "Which state regulations do I also need to comply with?"

Federal Regulations

When you confront federal regulations, what you're confronting are industry-specific, or legal-area-specific rules. The main ones are listed in Table 5.1. Using the table, identify the areas for federal regulation that may apply to your business.

Some of these regulations are intended to ensure that your company takes appropriate steps to protect PII, be it employee PII or consumer PII. Others clarify the extent of governmental power and reach when requesting PII from your company. Either way, you're on the hook.

One area that affects basically all businesses is employee privacy. Compliance with these laws is a company-wide responsibility, but the day-to-day nitty gritty of compliance rests primarily with your human resources department. They are a common denominator across all businesses in the United States. We will be working closely with HR when we get into the weeds of designing the privacy-first cybersecurity program later on.

Having set the employee privacy regulations to the side, now you can focus on the ones that specifically apply to the kind of business you're in. If you don't find any, great! But if you do, note them on the "Company Privacy Profile" ("CPP") that you started. They will become a "to-do" item when we generate our privacy program constraints list.

Table 5.1 Federal Regulations Affecting Personal Identifiable Information

Acronym	Description	Impact Areas
ADA	American with Disabilities Act	Employee privacy
ADEA	Age Discrimination in Employment Act	Employee privacy
APA	Administrative Procedure Act	Enforcement agency adjudication rules
BCR	Binding Corporate Rules	International data transfers
BSA	Bank Secrecy Act	Financial institutions
CALEA	Communications Assistance to Law Enforcement Act	Telecommunications industry
CAN-SPAM	Controlling the Assault of Non-Solicited Pornography and Marketing	Commercial emails
CISA	Cybersecurity Information Sharing Act	Cybersecurity information sharing
COBRA	Consolidated Omnibus Budget Reconciliation Act	Employee privacy
COPPA	Children's Online Privacy Protection Act	Children's online privacy
DODD-FRANK	Dodd-Frank Wall Street Reform and Consumer Protection Act	Financial services
ECPA	Electronic Communications Privacy Act	Employee privacy
EPPA	Employee Polygraph Protection Act	Employee privacy
ERISA	Employee Retirement Income Security Act	Employee privacy
FACTA	Fair and Accurate Credit Transactions Act	Financial services
FATCA	Foreign Account Tax Compliance Act	Tax evasion
FCRA	Fair Credit Reporting Act	Consumer financial privacy
FDCPA	Fair Debt Collection Practices Act	Consumer financial privacy
FERPA	Family Educational Rights and Privacy Act	Educational records access, control, and privacy
FIPP	Fair Information Privacy Practices	PII storing, processing, and managing guidelines
FIRREA	Financial Institutions Reform, Recovery, and Enforcement Act	Fraud prevention
FISA	Foreign Intelligence Surveillance Act	Foreign intelligence gathering and surveillance

Table 5.1 (*Continued*)

Acronym	Description	Impact Areas
FLSA	Fair Labor Standards Act	Employee privacy
FMLA	Family and Medical Leave Act	Employee privacy
FOIA	Freedom of Information Act	PII disclosure
GINA	Genetic Information Nondiscrimination Act	Anti-discrimination
GLBA	Gramm-Leach-Bliley Act	Financial institutions
HIPAA	Health Insurance Portability and Accountability Act	Health care
HITECH	Health Information Technology for Economic and Clinical Health	Health care
IRCA	Immigration Reform and Control Act	Employee privacy
NLRA	National Labor Relations Act	Employee privacy
NSL	National Security Letter	PII surveillance
PCI-DSS	Payment Card Industry Data Security Standard	Credit card processing
PPRA	Protection of Pupil Rights Amendment	Student PII
QPO	Qualified Protective Order	Health PII
RFPA	Right to Financial Privacy Act	Financial PII protection
SCA	Stored Communications Act	Employee privacy
SOX	Sarbanes–Oxley Act	Fraud prevention
TCPA	Telephone Consumer Protection Act	Telemarketing, advertising
TSR	Telemarketing Sales Rule	Fraud prevention
UDAP	Unfair and Deceptive Acts and Practices	Fraud prevention
USA FREEDOM ACT	USA Freedom Act	Surveillance and PII gathering
USA PATRIOT ACT	Uniting and Strengthening America by Providing Appropriate Tools Required to Intercept and Obstruct Terrorism Act	Surveillance and PII gathering
VPPA	Video Privacy Protection Act	Entertainment industry
WPA	Whistleblowers Protection Act	Employee privacy

State Regulations

Once that exercise is complete, you're ready for the next step: state regulations.

As we discussed, in the absence of federal law, the states have stepped in with their own legislation, most prominently California with the California Consumer Protection Act, Maine with the Maine Act to Protect the Privacy of Online Consumer Information, and Nevada with the Nevada Senate Bill 220 Online Privacy Law.

These are in addition to a slew of cybersecurity-specific legislation such as the Maryland Personal Information Protection Act, the Massachusetts Bill H.4806, the infamous New York State Department of Financial Services Cybersecurity Requirements for Financial Services Companies (23 NYCRR 500) Act, the New York Stop Hacks and Improve Electronic Data Security (SHIELD) Act, and the Oregon Consumer Information Protection Act (OCIPA).

But wait. There's more!

As I write, a whole slew of states are getting ready to pass privacy legislation. I recommend the International Association of Privacy Professionals (IAPP) website at https://iapp.org to get the most up-to-date information on privacy legislation status across each state and around the world.

MEET THE IAPP

This is an excellent opportunity to introduce you to one of the best privacy organizations in the world, the IAPP. As per the IAPP website:

> The International Association of Privacy Professionals (IAPP) is a resource for professionals who want to develop and advance their careers by helping their organizations successfully manage these risks and protect their data. In fact, we're the world's largest and most comprehensive global information privacy community. The IAPP is the only place that brings together the people, tools and global information management practices you need to thrive in today's rapidly evolving information economy.

I couldn't have said it better myself. I am a proud member of the IAPP, and I unreservedly urge you to become a member today.

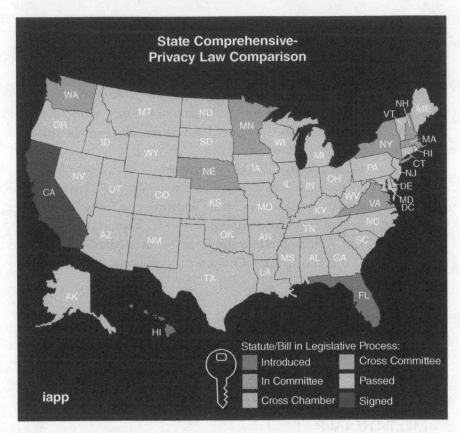

Figure 5.1 The IAPP's State Comprehensive Privacy Law Comparison (as of October 2020)
(Source: https://iapp.org/resources/article/state-comparison-table.) © International Association of Privacy Professionals

The IAPP maintains an up-to-date table (see Figure 5.1) of United States privacy legislation status (https://iapp.org/resources/article/state-comparison-table). My strong recommendation is to consult this resource frequently—not only during the design of the program but also once you've moved from program design to program maintenance.

As of this writing, only three states have privacy laws enacted: California, with their California Consumer Privacy Act; Maine, with their Act to

Protect the Privacy of Online Consumer Information; and Nevada, with their SB 220/Chapter 603A law.

More states are currently working on their own regulations: Illinois with their Data Transparency and Privacy Act, Massachusetts with their SD 341/S 120 law, Minnesota with their HF 2917 / SF 2912 law, New Jersey with their S2834 law, New York with their New York Privacy Act, Pennsylvania with their Consumer Data Privacy Act, and Rhode Island with their Consumer Privacy Protection Act. All these are "in committee," except Illinois, which is one step further in "cross committee review."

If you do business in any or all of these states, well, best get ready to hire a team of privacy professionals and figure out where is your exposure state-by-state, and what to do about it. I am told the line starts in Sacramento, and it's currently looping around downtown Boston!

All joking aside, this is a serious problem for any size business. It's not only the Fortune 5000 companies that need to be compliant to all these regulations. Hundreds of thousands of midmarket and small businesses interact with consumers, vendors, partners, freelancers, and traffic business-to-business data across state lines, and all of them are affected. Worse, even if they could find certified privacy professionals, the vast majority couldn't afford them or keep them for long.

Which brings us back to you and your allies. You will have to identify each state that you do business in, understand their privacy requirements, determine if your company is affected, and, if so, add this law to your Company Privacy Profile and to our eventual privacy program constraints list. (State regulations as of publication are summarized in Figure 5.2.)

Your allies are the resources in this book and your own research. The book, by the nature of the medium, is dated. I can only include summaries and guidance for what is current as of its writing. In the case of US state regulations, I have covered the three that are currently in place. Start with what is here, and then check with organizations such as the IAPP, who maintain the most up-to-date privacy regulations to fill in any blanks. Remember to keep your research focused to *your own company's* privacy profile. Avoid going down rabbit holes, and certainly don't follow any talking rabbits!

We'll go down the list alphabetically, starting with California.

State Comprehensive-Privacy Law Comparison

Bills introduced 2018-2020

				Consumer Rights	Business Obligations
State	Legislative Process	Statute/Bill (Hyperlinks)	Common Name		
Arizona		SB 1614			
Arizona		H52729			
California		**AB 375/SB 1121**	**California Consumer Privacy Act**		
Connecticut		RB 1108		Task force substituted for comprehensive bill.	
Florida		4-965			
Hawaii		H52872			
Hawaii		HCR 225		Task force substituted for comprehensive bill.	
Hawaii		SB 418			
Illinois		SB 2048	Data Privacy Act		
Illinois		SB 2330	Illinois Data Transparency and Privacy Act		
Illinois		H5 3863	Consumer Privacy Act		
Louisiana		HR 940		Task force substituted for comprehensive bill.	
Maine		**LD 946**	**An Act to Protect the Privacy of Online Consumer Information**		
Maryland		H5 949			
Maryland		HB 784	Online Consumer Protection Act		
Maryland		H5 1656			
Massachusetts		5 120		Study order issued.	
Minnesota		HF 3910	Minnesota Consumer Data Privacy Act		
Mississippi		HB 1253	Mississippi Consumer Privacy Act		
Nebraska		LB 746	Nebraska Consumer Data Privacy Act		
Nevada		**SB 220/Ch. 603A**			
New Hampshire		H5 1236			
New Hampshire		H5 1680			
New Jersey		A 2188			
New Jersey		A4255			
New Jersey		B3804			
New Mexico		SD 176	Consumer Information Privacy Act		
New York		S 224	Right to Know Act		
New York		S 642	New York Privacy Act		
North Dakota		H5 1485		Task force substituted for comprehensive bill.	
Pennsylvania		H51049	Consumer Data Privacy Act		
Rhode Island		H6094	Consumer Privacy Protection Act		
South Carolina		H4812	South Carolina Biometric Data Privacy Act		
Texas		HB 4390	Texas Privacy Protection Act	Task force substituted for comprehensive bill.	
Texas		HB 4518	Texas Consumer Privacy Act		
Virginia		HB 473	Virginia Privacy Act		
Washington		SB 6281	Washington Privacy Act		
Wisconsin		AB 870	Wisconsin Data Privacy Act (I)		
Wisconsin		AB 871	Wisconsin Data Privacy Act (II)		
Wisconsin		AB 872	Wisconsin Data Privacy Act (III)		

In Session: all above states.

Bold - passed law
Struck-through - bill died in committee or postponed

s - private right of action for security violations only
in - opt-in consent requirement
p - prohibition without consent

Arizona HB 2729's right of deletion only requires deletion if one of five requirements is satisfied (rather than an absolute right with exemptions, it's a conditional right).

Hawaii HR 2572 is the slimmed-down result of the comprehensive recommendations made by the HCR 225 task force, prohibits the sale of geolocation information and internet browser information without consent, updates parameters for government entity access to electronically stored data

Maine LD 946 applies only to internet service providers

Maryland HB 784 passed the Maryland House, but received an unfavorable report by the Senate Finance Committee, its continued progression is in doubt

Maryland HB 1656 prohibits the knowing sale to willfully disregarded disclosure of personal information of individuals under age 16 to third parties

New Hampshire HB 1236 creates a general private right of action for violations of an individual's expectation of privacy in personal information shared with third-party providers of information and services

New Jersey A3255 includes a right to opt-in for the sale of information and the collection of information

South Carolina H 4818 applies only to biometric information

Legislative Process: Introduced > In Committee > Crossed Chamber > Cross Committee > Passed > Signed

Last updated: 4/16/2020

Figure 5.2   State-by-State Comprehensive Privacy Law Comparison
(Source: https://iapp.org/resources/article/state-comparison-table).
(IAPP Westin Research Center – Used by permission).
© International Association of Privacy Professionals

California

The sweeping California Consumer Privacy Act ("CCPA") was passed in 2018; two years later it was amended and renamed as the California Privacy Rights Act ("CPRA").

Jurisdiction

State of California, effective January 1, 2020. The amended CPRA passed as California Proposition 24 with over 54% of the votes in the November 3, 2020 election.

Background

The first law (CCPA) was introduced in the California legislature in June 2018 and was signed into law a few days later by Governor Jerry Brown. It was rushed through the legislature for an interesting reason. If the legislature had not passed it in that session, the bill would have reappeared as a ballot initiative in November of the same year. Had it passed in ballot initiative form (as expected), the legislature would not be able to amend the law, because the state has a very convoluted process that governs changes to enacted ballot initiatives. By passing the law *as a law*, the legislature afforded themselves the ability to fine-tune it later. Indeed, numerous amendments were proposed very quickly.

After the law was passed, the same privacy advocates that pushed for CCPA, under the leadership of Alastair Mactaggart, pushed for additional measures intended to strengthen CCPA and make it immune to any "watering down" attempts by lobbyists. The result was Proposition 24, which essentially enshrines the CCPA in such a way that legislators can only make changes to strengthen the law, not weaken it.

Intent and Major Provisions

The CCPA established the following rights:

1. The right of Californians to know what personal information is being collected about them.

2. The right of Californians to know whether their personal information is sold or disclosed and to whom.
3. The right of Californians to say no to the sale of personal information.
4. The right of Californians to access their personal information.
5. The right of Californians to equal service and price, even if they exercise their privacy rights.

As modified into CPRA, CCPA established the following additional major provisions:

1. CPRA establishes the Right to Correction, whereby consumers can request that a business correct any PII that they have for errors or omissions.
2. CPRA creates a new class of PII: Sensitive Personal Information (SPI). SPI includes data such as biometric information, sexual information, geolocation, ethnicity, race, religion, content of communications such as email, and text messages, login credentials, and of course the usual social security numbers, financial account data, and the like. Additionally, CPRA includes the right to limit SPI sharing for secondary purposes.
3. Doubled that minimum required standard for the law's applicability from 50,000 to 100,000 PII records.
4. Establishes an expanded right of opt out, to include the ability to opt out from "automated decision-making technology," and the right to access the information used by such systems.
5. Establishes and funds a new agency to enforce the law: The California Privacy Protection Agency (CPPA).
6. Establishes mandatory risk assessments and cybersecurity audits for certain types of data processing and requires the findings to be submitted on a regular basis to the new CPPA.

PII Definition

Under the CCPA, personally identifiable information (PII) was defined as "information that identifies, relates to, describes, is capable of being associated with, or could reasonably be linked, directly or indirectly, with a particular consumer or household."

The act goes on to elaborate on PII, by defining such things as Identifiers, Biometrics, Protected Classifications, On-Line Activity, Geolocation, Educational data, and "Inferences drawn from any of the information identified in this subdivision to create a profile about a consumer reflecting the consumer's preferences, characteristics, psychological trends, preferences, predispositions, behavior, attitudes, intelligence, abilities, and aptitudes."

CPRA further expanded these definitions by creating the Sensitive Personal Information category discussed under the "Intent and Major Provisions" section above.

Inclusion Criteria

According to the CCPA, the law applies to:

1. A sole proprietorship, partnership, limited liability company, corporation, association, or other legal entity that is organized or operated for the profit or financial benefit of its shareholders or other owners, that collects consumers' personal information, or on the behalf of which such information is collected and that alone, or jointly with others, determines the purposes and means of the processing of consumers' personal information, that does business in the State of California, and that satisfies one or more of the following thresholds:
   a. Has annual gross revenues in excess of twenty-five million dollars ($25,000,000), as adjusted pursuant to paragraph (5) of subdivision (a) of Section 1798.185.
   b. Alone or in combination, annually buys, receives for the business' commercial purposes, sells, or shares for commercial purposes, alone or in combination, the personal information of 50,000 or more consumers, households, or devices (100,000 under the CPRA).
   c. Derives 50 percent or more of its annual revenues from selling consumers' personal information. This was amended by CPRA to include "sharing" the consumer's personal information.

(continued)

(continued)

2. Any entity that controls or is controlled by a business, as defined in paragraph (1), and that shares common branding with the business. "Control" or "controlled" means ownership of, or the power to vote, more than 50 percent of the outstanding shares of any class of voting security of a business; control in any manner over the election of a majority of the directors, or of individuals exercising similar functions; or the power to exercise a controlling influence over the management of a company. "Common branding" means a shared name, servicemark, or trademark.

Exclusions

The act excludes companies that do not do business in California, have collected data of California residents while the resident was outside the state, or if the PII is not being trafficked in California. Furthermore, non-profits, small businesses, and those that do not traffic significant volume of PII are excluded. Additional clarifications and guidance from Attorney General are expected to further clarify several of the law's provisions.

Enforcement Agency

CCPA provided for its enforcement by the California Attorney General, and also provided for a private right to action "in connection with certain unauthorized access and exfiltration, theft, or disclosure of a consumer's nonencrypted or nonredacted personal information."

CPRA, on the other hand, established the California Privacy Protection Agency, an independent agency that has powers of investigation, law enforcement, and the ability to draft additional regulations.

Penalties

CCPA provided for a $7,500 penalty per violation with a 30-day cure period. CPRA removed the cure period and tripled the maximum penalties for any violations concerning children.

Complete Text

The complete text for the CCPA can be found at: https://leginfo.legislature
.ca.gov/faces/billTextClient.xhtml?bill_id=201720180AB375

The complete text for CPRA can be found at: https://oag.ca.gov/
system/files/initiatives/pdfs/19-0021A1%20%28Consumer%20Privacy
%20-%20Version%203%29_1.pdf

Impact

California is the most-populated state and has the country's highest GDP, followed by Texas and New York. Therefore, it is no surprise that legislation
such as the CCPA and CPRA impacts business across the United States, as
well as the world. No business can afford to "fence off" from their California
operations. As a result, companies are likely to implement California's standards across the board, essentially making this law a de facto national standard,
pending any preemptive federal legislation.

The CPRA will go into effect on January 1, 2023. Businesses must continue to comply with the 2018 CCPA regulations until that time.

Maine

Maine's legislation—called the Act to Protect the Privacy of Online Consumer
Information—is much narrower that California's, both in scope and implementation.

Jurisdiction

State of Maine, effective July 1, 2020.

Background

The law was introduced to the Maine legislature in early 2019. Its focus
is in restricting the local broadband providers from trafficking PII, and it
imposes a more restrictive opt-in feature, as opposed to expansive opt-out
options.

Intent and Major Provisions

Under the Act to Protect the Privacy of Online Consumer Information, a Maine resident is ensured of the following rights:

2. Privacy of customer personal information. A provider may not use, disclose, sell or permit access to customer personal information, except as provided in subsections 3 and 4.
3. Customer consent exception. Consent of a customer is governed by this subsection.
   a. A provider may use, disclose, sell or permit access to a customer's customer personal information if the customer gives the provider express, affirmative consent to such use, disclosure, sale or access. A customer may revoke the customer's consent under this paragraph at any time.
   b. A provider may not:
      1. Refuse to serve a customer who does not provide consent under paragraph A;
         or
      2. Charge a customer a penalty or offer a customer a discount based on the customer's decision to provide or not provide consent under paragraph A.
   c. A provider may use, disclose, sell or permit access to information the provider collects pertaining to a customer that is not customer personal information, except upon written notice from the customer notifying the provider that the customer does not permit the provider to use, disclose, sell or permit access to that information.

PII Definition

Under the Act to Protect the Privacy of Online Consumer Information, PII is defined as:

1. Personally identifying information about a customer, including but not limited to the customer's name, billing information, social security number, billing address and demographic data; and
2. Information from a customer's use of broadband Internet access service, including but not limited to:
   a. The customer's web browsing history;
   b. The customer's application usage history;
   c. The customer's precise geolocation information;
   d. The customer's financial information;
   e. The customer's health information;
   f. Information pertaining to the customer's children;
   g. The customer's device identifier, such as a media access control address, 27 international mobile equipment identity or Internet protocol address;
   h. The content of the customer's communications; and
   i. The origin and destination Internet protocol addresses.

Inclusion Criteria

According to the Act to Protect the Privacy of Online Consumer Information, the law applies to Broadband service providers operating in Maine. More specifically:

"Broadband Internet access service" means a mass-market retail service by wire or radio that provides the capability to transmit data to and receive data from all or substantially all Internet endpoints, including any capabilities that are incidental to and enable the operation of the service, excluding dial-up Internet access service.

Exclusions

The act excludes companies that do not do business in Maine. Specifically, the Applicability section of the bill, reads:

> Applicability. The requirements of this section apply to providers operating within the State when providing broadband Internet access service to customers that are physically located and billed for service received in the State.

Enforcement Agency

Although no enforcement agency is explicitly specified in the bill, it is assumed that the Maine Attorney General would enforce it.

Penalties

No penalties are specified.

Complete Text

The complete text for the Act to Protect the Privacy of Online Consumer Information can be found at: https://mainelegislature.org/legis/bills/bills_129th/billtexts/SP027501.asp.

Effect

Limited to broadband companies serving Maine consumers.

Amendment to the Nevada Privacy of Information Collected on the Internet from Consumers Act via SB 220

Nevada's legislation is called the Privacy of Information Collected on the Internet from Consumers Act, SB 220.

Jurisdiction

State of Nevada, amendment effective October 1, 2019.

Background

This amendment was introduced to the original bill introduced in February 2019 to include the right of Nevada consumers to opt-out from the sale of their PII. The amendment further imposed additional verification requirements for commercial website operators in Nevada.

Intent and Major Provisions

Under the Nevada Privacy of Information Collected on the Internet from Consumers Act, a Nevada resident is ensured of the following rights:

2. Privacy of customer personal information. A provider may not use, disclose, sell or permit access to customer personal information, except as provided in subsections 3 and 4.
3. Customer consent exception. Consent of a customer is governed by this subsection.
   a. A provider may use, disclose, sell or permit access to a customer's customer personal information if the customer gives the provider express, affirmative consent to such use, disclosure, sale or access. A customer may revoke the customer's consent under this paragraph at any time.
   b. A provider may not:
      1. Refuse to serve a customer who does not provide consent under paragraph A;
      or
      2. Charge a customer a penalty or offer a customer a discount based on the customer's decision to provide or not provide consent under paragraph A.
   c. A provider may use, disclose, sell or permit access to information the provider collects pertaining to a customer that is not customer personal information, except upon written notice from the customer notifying the provider that the customer does not permit the provider to use, disclose, sell or permit access to that information.

PII Definition

Under the Nevada Privacy of Information Collected on the Internet from Consumers Act, PII is defined as:

1. "Personal information" means a natural person's first name or first initial and last name in combination with any one or more of the following data elements, when the name and data elements are not encrypted:
   a. Social security number.
   b. Driver's license number, driver authorization card number or identification card number.
   c. Account number, credit card number or debit card number, in combination with any required security code, access code or password that would permit access to the person's financial account.
   d. A medical identification number or a health insurance identification number.
   e. A user name, unique identifier or electronic mail address in combination with a password, access code or security question and answer that would permit access to an online account.

2. The term does not include the last four digits of a social security number, the last four digits of a driver's license number, the last four digits of a driver authorization card number or the last four digits of an identification card number or publicly available information that is lawfully made available to the general public from federal, state or local governmental records.

Inclusion Criteria

According to the Nevada Privacy of Information Collected on the Internet from Consumers Act, the law applies to "Operators" operating in Nevada:

1. "Operator" means a person who:

   a. Owns or operates an Internet website or online service for commercial purposes;

   b. Collects and maintains covered information from consumers who reside in this State and use or visit the Internet website or online service; and

   c. Purposefully directs its activities toward this State, consummates some transaction with this State or a resident thereof, purposefully avails itself of the privilege of conducting activities in this State or otherwise engages in any activity that constitutes sufficient nexus with this State to satisfy the requirements of the United States Constitution.

Exclusions

The act excludes the following from the definition of "operator."

The term does not include:

a. A third party that operates, hosts or manages an Internet website or online service on behalf of its owner or processes information on behalf of the owner of an Internet website or online service;

b. A financial institution or an affiliate of a financial institution that is subject to the provisions of the Gramm-Leach-Bliley Act, 15 U.S.C. §§ 6801 et seq., and the regulations adopted pursuant thereto;

c. An entity that is subject to the provisions of the Health Insurance Portability and Accountability Act of 1996, Public Law 104-191, as amended, and the regulations adopted pursuant thereto; or

d. A manufacturer of a motor vehicle or a person who repairs or services a motor vehicle who collects, generates, records or stores covered information that is:

(continued)

(continued)

1. Retrieved from a motor vehicle in connection with a technology or service related to the motor vehicle; or
2. Provided by a consumer in connection with a subscription or registration for a technology or service related to the motor vehicle.

Enforcement Agency

Nevada Attorney General's office.

Penalties

The Nevada Attorney General may seek temporary or permanent injunctions, and penalties of up to $5,000 per violation. No private right to action exists.

Complete Text

The complete text for the Nevada Privacy of Information Collected on the Internet from Consumers Act can be found at: https://www.leg.state.nv.us/App/NELIS/REL/80th2019/Bill/6365/Overview.

Effect

Limited to commercial website operators in Nevada.

Data Protection in the United States: Conclusions

When you review these three currently "live" laws, a few things emerge:

First, there *is* general consensus on the definition of PII. You should expect this to propagate into an eventual federal privacy statute.

Second, there is no consensus about "how long is this piece of string." That is to say, different states take different views on reach, what is included, what is excluded, and the penalties for violating the laws. This is likely to remain a strong point of contention between the warring factions of lobbyists in DC.

Third, the likelihood of a federal law preempting the state laws is not very great. To be sure, the federal law will fill the vacuum in states that do not have one, but the feds are likely to yield the right to the states to impose stricter conditions.

Fourth, the California Consumer Privacy Act is likely to serve as a federal template, expanded to include GDPR-like entries covering breach notification, cybersecurity requirements, and data transfer clauses, both to and from the United States.

What does this mean for you? Clearly, you'll need to ensure CCPA compliance. With that in place, you will be very well positioned to tackle any additional legislation coming your way in the months and years ahead.

Similarly, and this is a preview of things to come, if you are CCPA and GDPR compliant, there is very little doubt that you will exceed any federal requirements coming down the pike.

Canada

We must ensure that while we support the greater use of data, we are also protecting the trust and privacy of Canadians.
–Canada's Digital Charter in Action: A Plan by Canadians, for Canadians

Canada has two major pieces of legislation covering privacy. First is the Privacy Act, which governs how the Canadian Federal Government collects and uses personal information. The act applies only to Canadian Federal Institutions and specifies how the Canadian government can collect, use, disclose, keep, or dispose PII, all in the process of delivering government services to Canadian citizens. In other words, unless you are a member of the Canadian government, move along: this act doesn't apply to you.

The second piece of legislation is the Personal Information Protection and Electronic Documents Act (PIPEDA), enacted in early 2000. PIPEDA was amended by the Canadian Digital Privacy Act, which received Royal Assent in June of 2015.

As this book went to press in late 2020, the Trudeau government introduced Bill C11—a suite of legislation and amendments intended to modernize and strengthen the data protection for Canadian citizens. The proposed legislation included stiff fines for corporate violators, increased transparency, and strengthened rights of data erasure. But until Bill C11 goes into effect, PIPEDA is the law of the land, and it is this legislation we examine here.

Jurisdiction

Nation of Canada and foreign businesses doing business in Canada; came into force (as amended) November 1, 2018.

Background

The Privacy Act amendment was introduced such that PIPEDA, which governed how businesses could collect, use, and disclose PII, would be better aligned with the European Union's GDPR.

Intent and Major Provisions

PIPEDA establishes ten major principles for the protection of Personal Identifiable Information. These are:

Principle 1—Accountability

An organization is responsible for personal information under its control and shall designate an individual or individuals who are accountable for the organization's compliance with the following principles.

Principle 2—Identifying Purposes

The purposes for which personal information is collected shall be identified by the organization at or before the time the information is collected.

Principle 3—Consent

The knowledge and consent of the individual are required for the collection, use, or disclosure of personal information, except where inappropriate.

Principle 4—Limiting Collection

The collection of personal information shall be limited to that which is necessary for the purposes identified by the organization. Information shall be collected by fair and lawful means.

Principle 5—Limiting Use, Disclosure, and Retention

Personal information shall not be used or disclosed for purposes other than those for which it was collected, except with the consent of the individual or as required by law. Personal information shall be retained only as long as necessary for the fulfilment of those purposes.

Principle 6—Accuracy

Personal information shall be as accurate, complete, and up-to-date as is necessary for the purposes for which it is to be used.

Principle 7 — Safeguards

Personal information shall be protected by security safeguards appropriate to the sensitivity of the information.

Principle 8—Openness

An organization shall make readily available to individuals specific information about its policies and practices relating to the management of personal information.

Principle 9—Individual Access

Upon request, an individual shall be informed of the existence, use, and disclosure of his or her personal information and shall be given access to that information. An individual shall be able to challenge the accuracy and completeness of the information and have it amended as appropriate.

Principle 10—Challenging Compliance

An individual shall be able to address a challenge concerning compliance with the above principles to the designated individual or individuals accountable for the organization's compliance.

PII Definition

Under PIPEDA the definition of personal identifiable information is very broad. It states that:

Personal Information means information about an identifiable individual.

PIPEDA does give a little more definition to personal health information:

Personal Health Information, with respect to an individual, whether living or deceased, means

a. information concerning the physical or mental health of the individual;
b. information concerning any health service provided to the individual;
c. information concerning the donation by the individual of any body part or any bodily substance of the individual or information derived from the testing or examination of a body part or bodily substance of the individual;
d. information that is collected in the course of providing health services to the individual; or
e. information that is collected incidentally to the provision of health services to the individual.

Inclusion Criteria

PIPEDA's purpose and application, according to the act, is:

Purpose

The purpose of this (act) is to establish, in an era in which technology increasingly facilitates the circulation and exchange of information, rules to govern the collection, use and disclosure of personal information in a manner that recognizes the right of privacy of individuals with respect to their personal information and the need of organizations to collect, use or disclose personal information for purposes that a reasonable person would consider appropriate in the circumstances.

Application

This (act) applies to every organization in respect of personal information that:

a. the organization collects, uses or discloses in the course of commercial activities; or
b. is about an employee of, or an applicant for employment with, the organization and that the organization collects, uses or discloses in connection with the operation of a federal work, undertaking or business.

Exclusions

PIPEDA specifically excludes the following:

a. any government institution to which the Privacy Act applies;
b. any individual in respect of personal information that the individual collects, uses or discloses for personal or domestic purposes and does not collect, use or disclose for any other purpose; or
c. any organization in respect of personal information that the organization collects, uses or discloses for journalistic, artistic or literary purposes and does not collect, use or disclose for any other purpose.

Enforcement Agency

PIPEDA is administered by the Canadian Federal Privacy Commissioner, who can refer violations to the Canadian Federal Court.

Penalties

PIPEDA penalties can be as high as $100,000 (Canadian dollars).

Complete Text

The complete text for Personal Information Protection and Electronic Documents Act can be found at: https://laws-lois.justice.gc.ca/eng/acts/P-8.6/FullText.html.

Effect

All Canadian businesses and all businesses doing business in Canada.

Mexico

Following Mexico's constitutional reform in 2005, the legislators were able to focus on privacy passing the first Mexican privacy law: The Federal Law on the Protection of Personal Data held by Private Parties (*Ley Federal de Protección de Datos Personales en Posesión de los Particulares*). This law has since been enhanced by several additional regulations, recommendations, and guidelines, the most important of which is The General Law for the Protection of Personal Data in Possession of Obligated Subjects (*Ley General de Protección deDatos Personales en Posesión de Sujetos Obligados*).

The essential elements of these laws are:

Jurisdiction

The nation of Mexico and foreign businesses that process Mexican citizens' data.

Background

The goals of the Mexican legislature are clearly spelled out in Article 1 of the original law:

> This Law is of a public order and of general observance throughout the Republic, and has the purpose of protecting personal data held by private parties, in order to regulate its legitimate, controlled and informed processing, to ensure the privacy and the right to informational self-determination of individuals.

Intent and Major Provisions

The law explicitly defines the following principles of personal data protection and rights of data owners:

Principles of Personal Data Protection

Article 6. Data controllers must adhere to the principles of legality, consent, notice, quality, purpose, fidelity, proportionality and accountability under the Law.

Article 7. Personal data must be collected and processed in a lawful manner in accordance with the provisions established by this Law and other applicable regulations.

Personal data must not be obtained through deceptive or fraudulent means.

In all processing of personal data, it is presumed that there is a reasonable expectation of privacy, understood as the trust any one person places in another for personal data provided to be treated pursuant to any agreement of the parties in the terms established by this Law.

Article 8. All processing of personal data will be subject to the consent of the data owner except as otherwise provided by this Law.

Consent will be express when such is communicated verbally, in writing, by electronic or optical means or via any other technology, or by unmistakable indications.

It will be understood that the data owner tacitly consents to the processing of his data when, once the privacy notice has been made available to him, he does not express objection.

Financial or asset data will require the express consent of the data owner, except as provided in Articles 10 and 37 of this Law.

Consent may be revoked at any time without retroactive effects being attributed thereto. For revocation of consent, the data controller must, in the privacy notice, establish the mechanisms and procedures for such action.

(continued)

(continued)

Article 9. In the case of sensitive personal data, the data controller must obtain express written consent from the data owner for processing, through said data owner's signature, electronic signature, or any authentication mechanism established for such a purpose.

Databases containing sensitive personal data may not be created without justification of their creation for purposes that are legitimate, concrete and consistent with the explicit objectives or activities pursued by the regulated party.

Rights of Data Owners

Article 22. Any data owner, or, where appropriate, his legal representative, may exercise the rights of access, rectification, cancellation and objection under this Law. The exercise of any of these is not a prerequisite nor does it impede the exercise of another. Personal data must be preserved in such a way as to allow the exercise of these rights without delay.

Article 23. Data owners will have the right to access their personal data held by the data controller as well as to be informed of the privacy notice to which processing is subject.

Article 24. The data owner will have the right to rectify data if it is inaccurate or incomplete.

Article 25. The data owner will at all times have the right to cancel his personal data.

Cancellation of personal data will lead to a blocking period following which the data will be erased. The data controller may retain data exclusively for purposes pertaining to responsibilities arising from processing. The blocking period will be equal to the limitation period for actions arising from the legal relationship governing processing pursuant to applicable law.

Once the data is cancelled, the data owner will be notified.

Where personal data has been transmitted prior to the date of rectification or cancellation and continues to be processed by third parties, the data controller must notify them of the request for rectification or cancellation, so that such third parties also carry it out.

PII Definition

The law defines personal and sensitive personal data as follows:

> **Personal data:** Any information concerning an identified or identifiable individual.
>
> **Sensitive personal data:** Personal data touching on the most private areas of the data owner's life, or whose misuse might lead to discrimination or involve a serious risk for said data owner. In particular, sensitive data is considered that which may reveal items such as racial or ethnic origin, present and future health status, genetic information, religious, philosophical and moral beliefs, union membership, political views, sexual preference.

Inclusion Criteria

Any businesses that process Mexican citizens data.

Exclusions

None.

Enforcement Agency

The law is enforced by the Mexican National Institute of Transparency for Access to Information and Personal Data Protection—called "The Institute" for short—along with the Ministry of Economy and related administrative authorities.

Penalties

The penalties provisions of the law are interesting! Along with potential jail time for the offenders, the fines are based on multiples of the current minimum wage in Mexico City. The law spells out in details what is considered a violation of the law, and the associated penalties:

Article 63. The following acts carried out by the data controller are violations of this Law:

I. Failure to satisfy the data owner's request for personal data access, rectification, cancellation or objection without well-founded reason, in the terms of this Law;

II. Acting negligently or fraudulently in processing and responding to requests for personal data access, rectification, cancellation or objection;

III. Fraudulently declaring the inexistence of personal data where such exists in whole or in part in the databases of the data controller

IV. Processing personal data in violation of the principles established in this Law;

V. Omitting, in the privacy notice, any or all of the items referred to in Article 16 of this Law;

VI. Maintaining inaccurate personal data when such action is attributable to the data controller, or failing to perform legally due rectifications or cancellations where the data owner's rights are affected;

VII. Failure to comply with the notice referred to in section I of Article 64;

VIII. Breaching the duty of confidentiality established in Article 21 of this Law;

IX. Materially changing the original data processing purpose, without observing the provisions of Article 12;

X. Transferring data to third parties without providing them with the privacy notice containing the limitations to which the data owner has conditioned data disclosure;

XI. Compromising the security of databases, sites, programs or equipment, where attributable to the data controller;

XII. Carrying out the transfer or assignment of personal data outside of the cases where it is permitted under this Law;

XIII. Collecting or transferring personal data without the express consent of the data owner, in the cases where this is required;

XIV. Obstructing verification actions of the authority;

XV. Collecting data in a deceptive and fraudulent manner;

XVI. Continuing with the illegitimate use of personal data when the Institute or the data owners have requested such use be ended;

XVII. Processing personal data in a way that affects or impedes the exercise of the rights of access, rectification, cancellation and objection set forth in Article 16 of the Political Constitution of the United Mexican States;

XVIII. Creating databases in violation of the provisions of Article 9, second paragraph, of this Law, and

XIX. Any breach by the data controller of the obligations pertaining thereto as established in the provisions of this Law.

Article 64. Violations of this Law will be punished by the Institute as follows:

I. A warning instructing the data controller to carry out the actions requested by the data owner, under the terms established by this Law, in the cases described in section I of the preceding article;

II. A fine from 100 to 160,000 days of the Mexico City minimum wage, in the cases described in sections II to VII of the preceding article;

III. A fine from 200 to 320,000 days of the Mexico City minimum wage, in the cases described in sections VIII to XVIII of the preceding article; and

IV. In the event of repeated occurrences of the violations described in the preceding paragraphs, an additional fine will be imposed from 100 to 320,000 days of the current Mexico City minimum wage. With regard to violations committed in processing sensitive data, sanctions may be increased up to double the established amounts.

Complete Text

The full text for The Federal Law on the Protection of Personal Data held by Private Parties can be found at:

https://iapp.org/media/pdf/resource_center/2™percnt;20Regulations™percnt;20to™percnt;20the™percnt;20FLPPDHPP.pdf.

The full text for The General Law for the Protection of Personal Data in Possession of Obligated Subjects can be found at: http://www.dof.gob.mx/nota_detalle.php?codigo=5469949™fecha=26™percnt;2F01™percnt;2F2017.

Effect

The impact of this law is worldwide, in the sense that it affects any business that transacts in Mexico and deals with Mexican citizens' data.

***

Our North American trip is over. We're ready for our next stop in our journey: the European Union and GDPR. See you across the pond!

CHAPTER 6

European Regulations

Three quarters of us don't trust businesses to do the right thing with our emails, phone numbers, preferences and bank details.
I find that shocking!
—Elizabeth Denham, Information Commissioner
Speech to the Institute of Chartered Accountants in
England and Wales
January 17, 2017

European Union

The European Union consists of 27 countries: Austria, Belgium, Bulgaria, Croatia, Republic of Cyprus, Czech Republic, Denmark, Estonia, Finland, France, Germany, Greece, Hungary, Ireland, Italy, Latvia, Lithuania, Luxembourg, Malta, Netherlands, Poland, Portugal, Romania, Slovakia, Slovenia, Spain, and Sweden. There are a number of additional countries in negotiations to join, including Albania, Bosnia and Herzegovina, Montenegro, Turkey, and others. But EU expansion happens extremely slowly—people have been arguing about Turkey's potential membership since it first applied in 1987.

In 2018, the United Kingdom (England, Scotland, Wales, and Northern Ireland) voted to leave the European Union. As of this writing, the UK is in a transition period with the EU, with the new rules governing the relationship being worked out and expected to be in place on January 1, 2021. Scotland has strenuously objected to UK's exit from the EU and continues to press the UK government to find a way for Scotland to remain in the EU. Although that situation remains fluid, for our purposes, it doesn't matter. Even if all of the UK severs its bonds with the EU, they have stated that they plan to comply with GDPR.

Brussels, Belgium, is the capital of the European Union (EU), home to 60 percent of EU civil servants. It was here that in 1995 the first data protection directive was born, out of concern for EU residents' personal data trafficking. To put this in perspective: in 1995, Google.com was not a registered domain name.

The history, and drive, for data protection in Europe goes even further back, and it is worth a quick overview.

European sensitivity, and German sensitivity in particular, to data collection goes all the way back to before World War II. After taking power in 1933, the Nazi party collected an enormous amount of personal data, both during the census and when seizing various registries in occupied countries. They used this data to oppress and murder millions of people. The practice even continued after the war, when the Stasi, the East German "secret" police, continued to harvest data on East German citizens (and anyone else of interest).

The United Nations was formed after World War II, and the Universal Declaration of Human Rights was adopted in Paris on December 10, 1948. Article 12 reads:

> No one shall be subjected to arbitrary interference with his privacy, family, home or correspondence, nor to attacks upon his honour and reputation. Everyone has the right to the protection of the law against such interference or attack.

Two years later, Article 8 of The European Convention on Human Rights, took privacy concerns a step further:

> ARTICLE 8
>
> 1. Everyone has the right to respect for his private and family life, his home and his correspondence.

2. There shall be no interference by a public authority with the exercise of this right except such as is in accordance with the law and is necessary in a democratic society in the interests of national security, public safety or the economic well-being of the country, for the prevention of disorder or crime, for the protection of health or morals, or for the protection of the rights and freedoms of others.

That was the beginning of integrating privacy rights into European legislation, but it would take another 30 years for things to get really interesting! In 1981, in Strasbourg, Treaty 108 was brought forth for signature by the member States of the Council of Europe. The treaty, known as the "Convention for the Protection of Individuals with regard to Automatic Processing of Personal Data" built on the Organisation for Economic Co-operation and Development (OECD) guidelines of 1980, was the first binding instrument protecting PII, the first to outlaw the collection of sensitive PII (e.g. race, politics, health, sexuality, etc.), the first to introduce a redress method for the individual, and the first to regulate transborder data trafficking. This treaty became the foundational document for the many European regulations that follow.

Two short years later, in 1983, Germany's Supreme Court struck down the PII-collection component of that country's proposed census; this decision is widely acknowledged as _the_ precedent-setting victory for data privacy advocates. A few key points from the abstract submitted to the Venice Commission are worth noting:

1. The proceedings concerned several constitutional complaints lodged by citizens who directly challenged the 1983 Federal Census Act. The Act provided for a comprehensive data collection that went far beyond a population count, including personal information such as name, address, and religious affiliation, as well

(continued)

(*continued*)
   as information on the census subjects' educational background,
   professional occupation, and housing situation.
2. The Federal Constitutional Court found the constitutional complaints to be for the most part admissible; in part, the complaints
   were also well-founded.

And:

If individuals cannot, with sufficient certainty, determine what kind of
personal information is known to their environment, and if it is difficult to ascertain what kind of information potential communication
partners are privy to, this may seriously impair the freedom to exercise
self-determination. In the context of modern data processing, the free
development of one's personality therefore requires that the individual
is protected against the unlimited collection, storage, use and sharing
of personal data.

Scroll forward to 1995, and the ancestor to the General Data Protection
Regulation (GDPR) is born as the seductively named "Directive 95/46/EC on
the protection of individuals with regard to the processing of personal data and
on the free movement of such data," aka the Data Protection Directive. It was
the first comprehensive legislation in the EU, setting forth several principles
that survive in subsequent versions. It laid out definitions for PII, and processing transparency requirements, established a country-by-country supervisory
authority, as well as a public register for data processing operations, and regulated the cross-border trafficking of data to "third countries," that is, countries
outside the European Union.

The data transfer entries were particularly restrictive. The Directive prohibited the transfer of PII to any country that did not demonstrate that it
had an adequate level of protection, and established via Article 29 the "Working party on the Protection of Individuals with regard to the Processing of

Personal Data" commonly referred to as the "Article 29 Working Party" or the "Data Beasty Boyz" depending on who you talk to.

Needless to say, many American companies took a rather dim view of the legislation. In response, the United States and the folks from the Article 29 Working Party came up with the "Safe Harbour Principles." They revolved around seven principles: notice, choice, third-party transfer, cybersecurity, integrity, access, and enforcement. It may come as no surprise that a 2002 review found that a "substantial" number of companies that promised to adhere to the Safe Harbour Principles did not. The finding was confirmed in 2008.

Just as people were trying to make sense of who's doing what to who's data, the Snowden revelations hit!

In 2015 the European Court of Justice took on the case from the High Court of Ireland in what is known as *Schrems v Facebook*. Mr. Schrems, an Austrian citizen, complained that his data was being processed by Facebook in servers in the United States. Mr. Snowden had revealed that the NSA was spying on everything and everyone, and Schrems argued that therefore the US did not offer sufficient protection and surveillance. The court agreed, ordering that a new agreement be negotiated between the two countries. Safe Harbour 2.0 was born, and it held things in place for a few more years until the General Data Protection Regulation was ushered in with much fanfare on May 23, 2018. The world has not been the same since.

That's not to say that the GDPR rollout was completely smooth. To begin with, when GDPR was announced there was confusion about which businesses it applied to. Every business? EU businesses only? Does it apply to EU citizens? What about EU residents who aren't citizens? Many conversations and much guidance later, we found out that it applies to all businesses doing business in the EU, and to all residents (not just citizens), and that includes even noncitizens who happen to be traveling to the EU from all over the world. If you were in the EU, then GDPR applied to you, and, if you were doing business in the EU, no matter where headquartered, GDPR also applied to you.

To help everyone out, Siarhei Varankevich developed a document called "Territorial Scope of GDPR," which he published in LinkedIn in February 2017 and made available with a creative commons license. I have adapted his chart (see Figure 6.1).

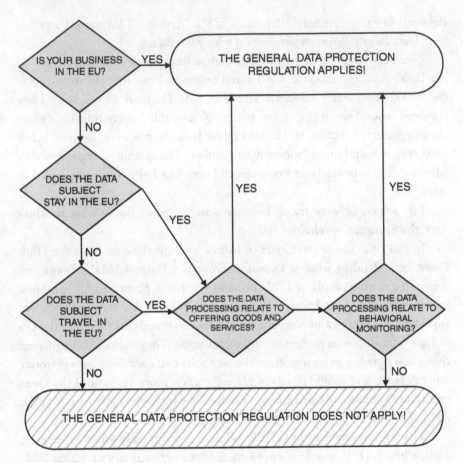

Figure 6.1   Does GDPR Apply to Your Business?

Jurisdiction

All EU businesses, as well as all companies doing business in the EU. The law was adopted in 2016 and took effect on May 25, 2018.

Background

The Privacy Act amendment was introduced such that PIPEDA, which governed how businesses could collect, use, and disclose PII, would be better aligned with the European Union's General Data Protection Regulation (GDPR).

Intent and Major Provisions

The GDPR established several principles governing the data processing of personal information. I have excerpted their salient points below:

Article 5: Principles relating to processing of personal data

1. Personal data shall be:
   a. processed lawfully, fairly and in a transparent manner in relation to the data subject ('lawfulness, fairness and transparency');
   b. collected for specified, explicit and legitimate purposes... ('purpose limitation');
   c. adequate, relevant and limited to what is necessary in relation to the purposes for which they are processed ('data minimisation');
   d. accurate and, where necessary, kept up to date... ('accuracy');
   e. kept in a form which permits identification of data subjects for no longer than is necessary for the purposes for which the personal data are processed... ('storage limitation');
   f. processed in a manner that ensures appropriate security of the personal data... ('integrity and confidentiality').
2. The controller shall be responsible for, and be able to demonstrate compliance with, paragraph 1 ('accountability').

Article 6: Lawfulness of processing

1. Processing shall be lawful only if and to the extent that at least one of the following applies:
   a. the data subject has given consent to the processing of his or her personal data for one or more specific purposes;
   b. processing is necessary for the performance of a contract to which the data subject is party or in order to take steps at the request of the data subject prior to entering into a contract;
   c. processing is necessary for compliance with a legal obligation to which the controller is subject;
   d. processing is necessary in order to protect the vital interests of the data subject or of another natural person;

(continued)

(continued)

    e. processing is necessary for the performance of a task carried out in the public interest or in the exercise of official authority vested in the controller;

    f. processing is necessary for the purposes of the legitimate interests pursued by the controller or by a third party ...

2. Member States may maintain or introduce more specific provisions to adapt the application of the rules of this Regulation ...

Article 7: Conditions for consent

1. Where processing is based on consent, the controller shall be able to demonstrate that the data subject has consented to processing of his or her personal data.

2. If the data subject's consent is given in the context of a written declaration which also concerns other matters, the request for consent shall be presented in a manner which is clearly distinguishable from the other matters, in an intelligible and easily accessible form, using clear and plain language. Any part of such a declaration which constitutes an infringement of this Regulation shall not be binding.

3. The data subject shall have the right to withdraw his or her consent at any time. The withdrawal of consent shall not affect the lawfulness of processing based on consent before its withdrawal. Prior to giving consent, the data subject shall be informed thereof. It shall be as easy to withdraw as to give consent.

4. When assessing whether consent is freely given, utmost account shall be taken of whether, inter alia, the performance of a contract, including the provision of a service, is conditional on consent to the processing of personal data that is not necessary for the performance of that contract.

Article 8: Conditions applicable to child's consent in relation to information society services

1. ... the processing of the personal data of a child shall be lawful where the child is at least 16 years old. Where the child is below

the age of 16 years, such processing shall be... authorised by the holder of parental responsibility over the child.

2. The controller shall make reasonable efforts to verify in such cases that consent is given or authorised by the holder of parental responsibility over the child...

Article 9: Processing of special categories of personal data

1. Processing of personal data revealing racial or ethnic origin, political opinions, religious or philosophical beliefs, or trade union membership, and the processing of genetic data, biometric data for the purpose of uniquely identifying a natural person, data concerning health or data concerning a natural person's sex life or sexual orientation shall be prohibited...

Article 10: Processing of personal data relating to criminal convictions and offences

Processing of personal data relating to criminal convictions and offences or related security measures based on Article 6(1) shall be carried out only under the control of official authority or when the processing is authorised by Union or Member State law...

Article 11: Processing which does not require identification

1. If the purposes for which a controller processes personal data do not or do no longer require the identification of a data subject by the controller, the controller shall not be obliged to maintain, acquire or process additional information in order to identify the data subject for the sole purpose of complying with this Regulation.
2. Where, in cases referred to in paragraph 1 of this Article, the controller is able to demonstrate that it is not in a position to identify the data subject, the controller shall inform the data subject accordingly, if possible.

What makes the GDPR regulation so important isn't the data protection requirements or even its international scope. Rather, it's the position of the

Data Protection Officer, and the extensive individual rights that were codified, including:

Article 12: Transparent information, communication and modalities for the exercise of the rights of the data subject

Article 13: Information to be provided where personal data are collected from the data subject

Article 14: Information to be provided where personal data have not been obtained from the data subject

Article 15: Right of access by the data subject

1. The data subject shall have the right to obtain from the controller confirmation as to whether or not personal data concerning him or her are being processed, and, where that is the case, access to the personal data and the following information:
   a. the purposes of the processing;
   b. the categories of personal data concerned;
   c. the recipients or categories of recipient to whom the personal data have been or will be disclosed, in particular recipients in third countries or international organisations;
   d. where possible, the envisaged period for which the personal data will be stored, or, if not possible, the criteria used to determine that period;
   e. the existence of the right to request from the controller rectification or erasure of personal data or restriction of processing of personal data concerning the data subject or to object to such processing;
   f. the right to lodge a complaint with a supervisory authority;
   g. where the personal data are not collected from the data subject, any available information as to their source;
   h. the existence of automated decision-making, including profiling … (and) meaningful information about the logic involved, as

well as the significance and the envisaged consequences of such processing for the data subject.

2. Where personal data are transferred to a third country or to an international organisation, the data subject shall have the right to be informed of the appropriate safeguards pursuant to Article 46 relating to the transfer.

3. The controller shall provide a copy of the personal data undergoing processing.

Article 16: Right to rectification

The data subject shall have the right to obtain from the controller without undue delay the rectification of inaccurate personal data concerning him or her. Taking into account the purposes of the processing, the data subject shall have the right to have incomplete personal data completed, including by means of providing a supplementary statement.

And the most famous Article of all:

Article 17: Right to erasure ('right to be forgotten')

1. The data subject shall have the right to obtain from the controller the erasure of personal data concerning him or her without undue delay and the controller shall have the obligation to erase personal data without undue delay where one of the following grounds applies:

   a. the personal data are no longer necessary in relation to the purposes for which they were collected or otherwise processed;
   b. the data subject withdraws consent on which the processing is based ... and where there is no other legal ground for the processing;
   c. the data subject objects to the processing ... and there are no overriding legitimate grounds for the processing ...

(continued)

(continued)

    d. the personal data have been unlawfully processed;

    e. the personal data have to be erased for compliance with a legal obligation in Union or Member State law to which the controller is subject;

    f. the personal data have been collected in relation to the offer of information society services referred to in Article 8(1).

2. Where the controller has made the personal data public and is obliged pursuant to paragraph 1 to erase the personal data, the controller, taking account of available technology and the cost of implementation, shall take reasonable steps, including technical measures, to inform controllers which are processing the personal data that the data subject has requested the erasure by such controllers of any links to, or copy or replication of, those personal data.

Article 18: Right to restriction of processing

Article 19: Notification obligation regarding rectification or erasure of personal data or restriction of processing

Article 20: Right to data portability

1. The data subject shall have the right to receive the personal data concerning him or her, which he or she has provided to a controller, in a structured, commonly used and machine-readable format and have the right to transmit those data to another controller without hindrance from the controller to which the personal data have been provided.

Insofar as the Data Protection Officer is a mandated position, the law added specific details on not only what is expected from the position but took the extra step of specifically establishing and protecting the position's independence. Article 38 reads, in part:

Position of the data protection officer

1. The controller and the processor shall ensure that the data protection officer is involved, properly and in a timely manner, in all issues which relate to the protection of personal data.
2. The controller and processor shall support the data protection officer in performing the tasks referred to in Article 39 by providing resources necessary to carry out those tasks and access to personal data and processing operations, and to maintain his or her expert knowledge.
3. The controller and processor shall ensure that the data protection officer does not receive any instructions regarding the exercise of those tasks. He or she shall not be dismissed or penalised by the controller or the processor for performing his tasks. The data protection officer shall directly report to the highest management level of the controller or the processor.
4. Data subjects may contact the data protection officer with regard to all issues related to processing of their personal data and to the exercise of their rights under this Regulation.
5. The data protection officer shall be bound by secrecy or confidentiality concerning the performance of his or her tasks, in accordance with Union or Member State law.
6. The data protection officer may fulfil other tasks and duties. The controller or processor shall ensure that any such tasks and duties do not result in a conflict of interests.

Article 39 has more to say about the officer's role:

Article 39: Tasks of the data protection officer

1. The data protection officer shall have at least the following tasks:
    a. to inform and advise the controller or the processor and the employees who carry out processing of their obligations

(continued)

(continued)

pursuant to this Regulation and to other Union or Member State data protection provisions;

b. to monitor compliance with this Regulation, with other Union or Member State data protection provisions and with the policies of the controller or processor in relation to the protection of personal data, including the assignment of responsibilities, awareness-raising and training of staff involved in processing operations, and the related audits;

c. to provide advice where requested as regards the data protection impact assessment and monitor its performance pursuant to Article 35;

d. to cooperate with the supervisory authority;

e. to act as the contact point for the supervisory authority on issues relating to processing, including the prior consultation referred to in Article 36, and to consult, where appropriate, with regard to any other matter.

2. The data protection officer shall in the performance of his or her tasks have due regard to the risk associated with processing operations, taking into account the nature, scope, context and purposes of processing.

The GDPR is the only law so far that both mandates and explicitly describes the tasks of a data protection officer, and then protect such a position within an enterprise. Previous regulations tended to discuss enforcement from the perspective of the government but remain silent on enforcement at the corporate level. Essentially, the GDPR mandates that an enforcement officer, hired by the business, should report directly to the highest management level, and be immune from termination of employment as a consequence of performing their duties under the law.

PII Definition

Under GDPR personal identifiable information is defined as:

any information relating to an identified or identifiable natural person ('data subject'); an identifiable natural person is one who can be identified, directly or indirectly, in particular by reference to an identifier such as a name, an identification number, location data, an online identifier or to one or more factors specific to the physical, physiological, genetic, mental, economic, cultural or social identity of that natural person.

Inclusion Criteria

The more specific inclusion criteria for the GDPR are laid out in Articles 1, 2, and 3. In summary:

Article 1: Subject-matter and objectives

1. This Regulation lays down rules relating to the protection of natural persons with regard to the processing of personal data and rules relating to the free movement of personal data.
2. This Regulation protects fundamental rights and freedoms of natural persons and in particular their right to the protection of personal data.
3. The free movement of personal data within the Union shall be neither restricted nor prohibited for reasons connected with the protection of natural persons with regard to the processing of personal data.

Article 2: Material scope

1. This Regulation applies to the processing of personal data wholly or partly by automated means and to the processing other than by automated means of personal data which form part of a filing system or are intended to form part of a filing system . . . .

Article 3: Territorial scope

1. This Regulation applies to the processing of personal data in the context of the activities of an establishment of a controller or a

(continued)

(continued)

    processor in the Union, regardless of whether the processing takes place in the Union or not.

2. This Regulation applies to the processing of personal data of data subjects who are in the Union by a controller or processor not established in the Union, where the processing activities are related to:

   a. the offering of goods or services, irrespective of whether a payment of the data subject is required, to such data subjects in the Union; or

   b. the monitoring of their behaviour as far as their behaviour takes place within the Union.

3. This Regulation applies to the processing of personal data by a controller not established in the Union, but in a place where Member State law applies by virtue of public international law.

Exclusions

There are very few exclusions under GDPR. Those that exist are enumerated under "Article 23: Restrictions" and revolve around data processed during an activity that is outside of EU jurisdiction, individual data processing for personal our household activity, law enforcement activities (investigation, prevention, detection, prosecution of criminal offenses), and when processing personal data under the scope of the Treaty on European Union.

Enforcement Agency

The GDPR is enforced by the EU member states' Supervisory Authority. In particular:

Article 51: Supervisory authority

1. Each Member State shall provide for one or more independent public authorities to be responsible for monitoring the application of this Regulation, in order to protect the fundamental rights and

freedoms of natural persons in relation to processing and to facilitate the free flow of personal data within the Union ('supervisory authority').

2. Each supervisory authority shall contribute to the consistent application of this Regulation throughout the Union. For that purpose, the supervisory authorities shall cooperate with each other and the Commission in accordance with Chapter VII.

3. Where more than one supervisory authority is established in a Member State, that Member State shall designate the supervisory authority which is to represent those authorities in the Board and shall set out the mechanism to ensure compliance by the other authorities with the rules relating to the consistency mechanism referred to in Article 63.

Penalties

Penalties in the GDPR were a matter of substantial controversy and intense lobbying. At the end of the day, the penalties began steep and remained that way in the final draft. As excerpted from Article 83, General Conditions for Imposing Administrative Fines, they are (emphasis added):

3. If a controller or processor intentionally or negligently, for the same or linked processing operations, infringes several provisions of this Regulation, the total amount of the administrative fine shall not exceed the amount specified for the gravest infringement.

4. Infringements of the following provisions shall, in accordance with paragraph 2, be subject to **administrative fines up to 10,000,000 EUR**, or in the case of an undertaking, **up to 2 % of the total worldwide annual turnover** of the preceding financial year, whichever is higher.

Bottom line: You definitely do not want to be found to be "a controller or processor intentionally or negligently" breaking this law. In the GDPR's case, compliance is not optional.

Complete Text

The complete text for the General Data Protection Regulation can be found at: https://eur-lex.europa.eu/legal-content/EN/TXT/HTML/?uri=CELEX: 02016R0679-20160504™from=EN.

Effect

The effect of the GDPR is truly global. The European market is one of the largest in the world, and as a result there are millions of companies doing business with European residents, and all of them, in one way or another, are affected by the GDPR. What's more, as you'll note as you read on, countries attempting to write their own regulation have begun to lean on GDPR as the gold standard. The principles and even the language of the GDPR will likely echo across all future regulations.

Non-EU Member European Countries

As much as the GDPR is the 800-pound gorilla in European data privacy regulations, there are countries that are currently outside of its direct reach, including: Albania, Belarus, Bosnia and Herzegovina, Kosovo, Liechtenstein, Macedonia, Moldova, Norway, Russia, Serbia, Switzerland, and Ukraine.

Of note, Norway, Iceland, and Liechtenstein are in the European Economic Area (EEA) allowing them to be part of EU's single market, while Switzerland, although not a member of the EEA, is also part of the single market. The EEA member countries are bound by the GDPR.

As of this writing, Russia's economy is ranked fifth, Switzerland is ranked ninth, and Norway is ranked twelfth. Given the constraints of this book, we will take a look at the privacy regulations in the first two of these countries only, since Norway is covered by the GDPR. You'll find additional resources to expand your research in the bibliography section, at the IAPP web site at www.iapp.org, and at the international law firm DLA Piper's compendium on "Data Protection Laws of the World" at dlapiperdataprotection.com.

Russia

The Russian Federal Law on Personal Data (No. 152-FZ) was enacted in 2006, and it has become the foundational piece of privacy legislation for the country. It has since been amended in 2014 (in force since 2015) to require that any Russian citizens' personally identifiable information must (first) be processed in facilities physically located in Russian Federation territory.

The Russian Data Protection Authority ("Roskomnadzor") has issued specific guidance since then to clarify a few key points, especially relating to post-processing activities.

Jurisdiction

Russian Federation.

Background

The stated goal of the law was to ensure the protection of freedom and human rights of Russian citizens in the course of data processing of their personally identifiable information, including the establishment of protections for Russian citizens' privacy rights.

Intent and Major Provisions

Under the Russian Federal Law on Personal Data, a Russian citizen is ensured of the following rights. (The translated text below has been edited, condensed as appropriate, and formatted for clarity):

Article 14. The Right of the Personal Data Subject to Access to His Personal Data

1. The personal data subject has the right to obtain information about the operator, its location, availability with the operator of personal data pertaining to the respective personal data subject also to get familiarized with such personal data except for the cases provided for by part 5 of this article.
2. The personal data subject is entitled to demand that the operator should keep his personal data current, block or destroy them if

(*continued*)

(continued)

the personal data are incomplete, outdated, unlawfully obtained, or not necessary for the stated purpose of processing (and) take measures provided for by the law in order to protect his rights.

3. Information about availability of personal data should be provided to the personal data subject in an understandable form and it should not contain personal data pertaining to other personal data subjects.

4. Access to one's personal data is granted to the personal data subject or his legitimate representative by the operator in case of communication or enquiry received from the personal data subject or his legitimate representative....

5. The personal data subject has the right to receive, in case of communication or enquiry received, the information concerning processing of his personal data containing, inter alia:

  a. a confirmation of the fact of personal data processing by the operator as well as the purpose of such processing;

  b. the methods of personal data processing applied by the operator;

  c. information about the persons who have access to the personal data or whom such access may be given to;

  d. the list of processed personal data and the source they were obtained from;

  e. the time limits of personal data processing including the time limits of their storage;

  f. information about the legal consequences the processing of personal data may entail to their subject.

The exclusions applicable to these rights include:

5. The personal data subject's rights to access to his personal data are restricted in case:

1. processing of personal data including the personal data obtained through special investigative techniques, counter-intelligence, and intelligence operations is performed for the purposes of defense of the country, security of the state, and law enforcement;
2. processing of personal data is performed by the agencies that detained the personal data subject on suspicion of offense or that brought a charge of crime against the personal data subject or that applied a measure of restraint to the personal data subject before a charge is brought, except for the cases provided for by the Russian Federation criminal procedure legislation if it is allowed for the suspect or indictee to get familiarized with such personal data;
3. provision of personal data infringes the constitutional rights and freedoms of other persons.

PII Definition

Under the Russian Federal Law on Personal Data, PII is defined as:

any information pertaining to a particular or identifiable, on the basis of such information, natural individual (the personal data subject), including his surname, first name, patronymic, year, month, date and place of birth, address, marital, social, property status, education, profession, income, other information

Ending with "other information" is not a misprint! That is exactly what is contained in the language, which as you can see is rather vague! This can present a real problem since it means the Roskomnadzor (the Russian Data Protection Authority) can wake up one morning and decide that a whole other list of attributes qualify for "personal data," making compliance a bit tricky!

Inclusion Criteria

Article 1 of the Russian Federal Law on Personal Data reads:

> This Federal Law regulates the relations connected with personal data processing carried out by federal state authorities, state authorities of Russian Federation constituents, other state bodies (hereinafter, state bodies), municipal bodies that are not part of local authorities (hereinafter, municipal bodies), legal entities, natural individuals with the help of automation aids or without them if personal data processing without such aids corresponds to the nature of actions (operations) done with personal data with the help of automation aids.

Essentially, any company that processes Russian citizen data is affected by this law. Additionally, if your company sports a Russian domain name, accepts payments in Russian rubles, delivers goods or services in the Russian Federation territories, or something as simple as having a Russian version of the website or, even, displaying Russian language advertisements, then you must comply with this law.

Exclusions

Similarly, Article 1 of the Russian Federal Law on Personal Data continues:

> This Federal Law does not cover the relations arising during:
>
> 1. personal data processing by natural individuals solely for personal and family needs if this does not infringe the rights of personal data subjects;
> 2. organization of storage, integration, accounting and use of the documents of the Archive Holding of the Russian Federation and other archive documents containing personal data, in accordance with the Russian Federation archiving legislation;

3. processing of data about natural persons subject to inclusion into the united state registry of individual entrepreneurs if such processing is performed in accordance with the Russian Federation legislation in connection with the natural individual's activities as an individual entrepreneur;
4. processing of personal data classified as data constituting state secret following the statutory procedures.

Enforcement Agency

The enforcement agency is the Russian Data Protection Authority ("Roskomnadzor").

Penalties

The Russian Data Protection Authority can take a variety of actions (such as shutting down your site, blocking your domain altogether, and so on). The Roskomnadzor has recommended legislation, which is currently moving through the Russian legislative process, that calls for fines of up to six million rubles (about $280,000) for the most egregious repeat offenders, plus a whole menu of fines covering different levels of violations ranging from $15,000 to $94,000. This legislation has not been finalized as of this writing, but you should expect the fines to be steep and their enforcement pursued vigorously.

Complete Text

The complete text for the Russian Federal Law on Personal Data (in English) can be found at: https://iapp.org/resources/article/english-translation-of-the-russian-federal-law-on-personal-data/.

Effect

Global. Anyone doing business in or with Russia is affected.

Switzerland

Switzerland has a long history with privacy going back well over a century, and it's a topic taken very seriously. Swiss laws are very strict when it comes to individual privacy, and through the nation's neutrality stance, Switzerland requires that all international information-sharing requests comply with local Swiss law, setting the bar very high. As an example, the Federal Supreme Court of Switzerland declared that Internet Protocol (IP) addresses are considered personally identifiable information and therefore subject to all pertinent privacy and disclosure laws.

The right to privacy is enshrined in the Swiss Constitution. Article 13 is unambiguous:

Article 13. Right to privacy

1. Every person has the right to privacy in their private and family life and in their home, and in relation to their mail and telecommunications.
2. Every person has the right to be protected against the misuse of their personal data.

In 1992, The Federal Assembly of the Swiss Confederation passed the Federal Act on Data Protection (FADP, or DPA). In 1993, they passed the Ordinance to the Federal Act on Data Protection (DPO), followed by the Ordinance on Data Protection Certification (DPCO) in 2007. Taken together, the act plus the ordinances set the tone for data privacy protection in Switzerland:

Jurisdiction

Switzerland.

Background

These laws are an extension of the Swiss privacy culture as it applies to personally identifiable information data processing. For that matter, the stated aim in Article 1 of the DPA is the protection of privacy and the fundamental rights of persons when their data is processed.

Intent and Major Provisions

The salient points of the DPA (as amended and in place from 2019) include:

Article 4. Principles

1. Personal data may only be processed lawfully.
2. Its processing must be carried out in good faith and must be proportionate.
3. Personal data may only be processed for the purpose indicated at the time of collection, that is evident from the circumstances, or that is provided for by law.
4. The collection of personal data and in particular the purpose of its processing must be evident to the data subject.
5. If the consent of the data subject is required for the processing of personal data, such consent is valid only if given voluntarily on the provision of adequate information. Additionally, consent must be given expressly in the case of processing of sensitive personal data or personality profiles.

Article 5. Correctness of the data

1. Anyone who processes personal data must make certain that it is correct. He must take all reasonable measures to ensure that data that is incorrect or incomplete in view of the purpose of its collection is either corrected or destroyed.
2. Any data subject may request that incorrect data be corrected.

Article 6. Cross-border disclosure

1. Personal data may not be disclosed abroad if the privacy of the data subjects would be seriously endangered thereby, in particular due to the absence of legislation that guarantees adequate protection.

According to the DPA, Swiss citizens have the following rights with regards to their PII:

Article 8. Right to Information

1. Any person may request information from the controller of a data file as to whether data concerning them is being processed.
2. The controller of a data file must notify the data subject:
   a. of all available data concerning the subject in the data file, including the available information on the source of the data;
   b. the purpose of and if applicable the legal basis for the processing as well as the categories of the personal data processed, the other parties involved with the file and the data recipient.
3. The controller of a data file may arrange for data on the health of the data subject to be communicated by a doctor designated by the subject.
4. If the controller of a data file has personal data processed by a third party, the controller remains under an obligation to provide information. The third party is under an obligation to provide information if he does not disclose the identity of the controller or if the controller is not domiciled in Switzerland.
5. The information must normally be provided in writing, in the form of a printout or a photocopy, and is free of charge. The Federal Council regulates exceptions.
6. No one may waive the right to information in advance.

PII Definition

Under the Swiss Federal Act on Data Protection, PII is defined as:

Article 3. Definitions

a. personal data (data): all information relating to an identified or identifiable person;
b. data subjects: natural or legal persons whose data is processed;

c. sensitive personal data: data on:
1. religious, ideological, political or trade union-related views or activities,
2. health, the intimate sphere or the racial origin,
3. social security measures,
4. administrative or criminal proceedings and sanctions

Inclusion Criteria

As per Article 2 of Swiss Federal Act on Data Protection:

Article 2. Scope

1. This Act applies to the processing of data pertaining to natural persons and legal persons by:
   a. private persons;
   b. federal bodies

Exclusions

Similarly, Article 2 of Swiss Federal Act on Data Protection excludes the following:

a. personal data that is processed by a natural person exclusively for personal use and which is not disclosed to outsiders;
b. deliberations of the Federal Assembly and in parliamentary committees;
c. pending civil proceedings, criminal proceedings, international mutual assistance proceedings and proceedings under constitutional or under administrative law, with the exception of administrative proceedings of first instance;
d. public registers based on private law;
e. personal data processed by the International Committee of the Red Cross.

If you find the exclusion of the Red Cross a little out of left field, remember that they are a Swiss organization, founded in 1863 in Geneva. The exclusion was a recognition of the Red Cross's humanitarian mission and a way to remove what the government considered an undue burden. In other words, even the infamously neutral Swiss play favorites sometimes. (At least it's a global humanitarian organization. I think we'll let them slide on this one.)

Enforcement Agency

The enforcement agency is the Swiss Federal Data Protection and Information Commissioner (FDPIC).

Penalties

The Swiss Federal Act on Data Protection stipulates penalties of up to 250,000 CHF.

Complete Text

The complete text for Swiss Federal Act on Data Protection (in English) can be found at: https://www.admin.ch/opc/en/classified-compilation/19920153/index.html.

The Ordinance to the Federal Act on Data Protection at: https://www.admin.ch/opc/en/classified-compilation/19930159/index.html.

The Ordinance on Data Protection Certification can be found at: https://www.admin.ch/opc/en/classified-compilation/20071826/201004010000/235.13.pdf.

Effect

Localized to Switzerland.

Coming Soon to a European Union Near You!

In closing the European regulations chapter, it is worth noting the current efforts to strengthen the GDPR further through what is called the ePrivacy Regulation (ePR).

The ePrivacy Regulation will be a law that will govern all electronic communications within the EU. It is part of the EU's "Single Digital Market Strategy," and its key points revolve around the following:

1. **Confidential Electronic Communications.** This will limit the eavesdropping on any and all electronic communications without user consent.
2. **SPAM and Marketing Communications consent.** This will require the explicit consent across all platforms (email, text, calls, etc.) and it will require that advertisers "reveal" their true identity (including real phone numbers) in all communications.
3. **Consent for Individual Metadata Processing.** This expands the confidentiality of electronic communications past the actual content to the metadata of the communication itself (e.g. number called, time, date, etc.)
4. **Behavioral Cross-Platform Confidentiality.** This will require the affirmative consent of a user, across any platform, for behavioral tracking, including website cookies.

As you can imagine, this is a fairly ambitious privacy legislation, which is why it has been stuck in debates for the better part of three years! It is a bold, "technology future proof" legislation, and as such, the obstacles to overcome are many. With the last version of the bill dead, a new approach will be needed to move it forward, and it rests in the hands of the new EU Croatian Presidency to deliver it. I am hopeful that within the next two to three years a reborn ePrivacy Regulation will be enacted, further strengthening data privacy in the EU and, by extension, around the world.

I hope you enjoyed our quick tour of Europe. Next up? We're traveling the Silk Road into Asia. Buckle up!

CHAPTER 7

Asia-Pacific Regulations

Privacy is the very essence of human existence. One wonders why the Indian Supreme Court took so long to reach that conclusion.

—Kalyan C. Kankanala,
Fun IP: Fundamentals of Intellectual Property

Asia, in its vastness and complexity, doesn't exactly lend itself to a continental overview the way that North America and Western Europe do. Luckily, we can start with the Asia-Pacific Economic Cooperation (APEC) member states and fill in the blanks as necessary. Even then, we will certainly not be able to cover every single country in Asia—that alone would take a few volumes. By necessity, then, we will only deal with the major economic powers in Asia and suggest resources for your deeper, country-specific investigations. My two top recommendations are to start with the IAPP at www.iapp .org and then look at the international law firm DLA Piper's compendium on "Data Protection Laws of the World" at dlapiperdataprotection.com. You will also find many additional resources listed in the Bibliography section of the book.

Let's begin with the APEC member countries. These are: Australia, Brunei Darussalam, Canada, Chile, China, Chinese Taipei, Hong Kong, Indonesia, Japan, Malaysia, Mexico, New Zealand, Papua New Guinea, Peru, the Philippines, Republic of Korea, Russia, Singapore, Thailand, the United States, and Vietnam.

APEC, as we discussed in Chapter 3, developed its voluntary privacy framework in 2004. In 2011 APEC introduced the Cross-Border Privacy Rules (CBPR), injecting a certification process into the mix. CBPR requires business to develop and maintain data privacy policies inline with the APEC Privacy Framework. Once those are in place, then they apply for certification via a local agency. The privacy policies are also required to be enforceable by local law.

APEC has been very careful not to step on the toes of any regional legal jurisdictions; the APEC Privacy Framework and CBPR defer to local law. Instead, they set up a baseline requirement that needs to be voluntarily met and locally certified. By having the certification requirement be enforceable by local law, they create a CBPR country certification component, on top of the business one. In essence, the CBPR creates an analogous system to the old US/EU Privacy Shield agreement, by creating a framework for cross-border privacy law enforcement.

What's the bottom line for your business? If you are doing business in any of the APEC member countries, then it is to your best interest to be CBPR-certified. Remember, though, that this will not be enough. You must dive deeper into each country's specific privacy laws and figure out exactly how they affect your business. Below, we'll examine the local legislation for the top three Asian economies (as ranked by purchasing power parity/gross domestic product): China, India, and Japan. We'll close out the chapter by looking into Australia's privacy regulations.

China

China passed the "Cybersecurity Law of the People's Republic of China" in late 2016. It was quickly followed by several guidelines, the three most prevalent of which are:

1. The Personal Information Security Specification from the National Information Security Standardization Technical Committee (TC260);
2. Guidelines on Personal Information Security Impact Assessment from the Draft National Standard of Information Security Technology; and the most recently
3. Guidelines on Internet Personal Information Security Protection.

The Cybersecurity Law was the first attempt to coalesce the hundreds of laws, rules, regulations, guidelines, and "strong suggestions" governing the protection of personal information in China. The Personal Information Security Specification is the closest thing to GDPR that China has so far, albeit with a somewhat unfortunate abbreviation, and without establishing a clear individual right to privacy. Below, you'll find relevant excerpts from both the law and the Personal Information Security Specification:

Jurisdiction

China, excluding Hong Kong, Macau, and Taiwan. Hong Kong had one of the earliest data privacy laws going back to 1996, now known as the PDPO. Macau has the Personal Data Protection Act of 2005, and Taiwan has their own Personal Data Protection Law since 2010.

Background

According to articles 1 and 2 of the Cybersecurity Law:

> **Article 1:** This Law is formulated in order to: ensure cybersecurity; safeguard cyberspace sovereignty and national security, and social and public interests; protect the lawful rights and interests of citizens, legal persons, and other organizations; and promote the healthy development of the informatization of the economy and society.
>
> **Article 2:** This Law is applicable to the construction, operation, maintenance, and use of networks, as well as to cybersecurity supervision and management within the mainland territory of the People's Republic of China.

Meanwhile, the corresponding introduction from the guidelines on Internet personal information security protection outlines its aim to protect data collected by "Personal Information Holders" defined as any entity that "controls and processes personal information." It is interesting to note that the guideline does not distinguish controller from processor, applying to both of them equally.

Introduction

In recent years, with the fast development of information technology and the popularization of internet, more and more entities collect and use personal information (PI) in bulk, bringing convenience to people's life but also producing problems such as illegal collection, abuse, and leakage of PI that seriously threaten PI security.

This Specification targets security challenges to PI and regulates related behaviors by PI controllers during information processing such as collection, retention, use, sharing, transfer, and public disclosure. It intends to restrain the chaos caused by issues like illegal collection, abuse, and leakage of PI, protecting individuals' lawful rights and interests and society's public interests to the greatest degree.

Intent and Major Provisions

The intent of the Cybersecurity Law is broad. Its essence, though, is captured by Article 16:

Article 16: The State Council and people's governments of provinces, autonomous regions, and directly-governed municipalities shall: do comprehensive planning; expand investment; support key cybersecurity technology industries and programs; support cybersecurity technology research and development, application, and popularization; promote secure and trustworthy network products and services; protect intellectual property rights for network technologies; and support research and development institutions, schools of higher learning, etc., to participate in State cybersecurity technology innovation programs.

On the other hand, the intent and provisions of the guidelines are more operationally focused—see, for example, the section below.

4. Basic Principles of Personal Information Security

PI controllers should follow the basic principles below when processing PI:

a. Commensurability of Powers and Responsibilities Principle: Bear responsibility for damage to the lawful rights and interests of the PI subject caused by PI processing.
b. Purpose Specification Principle: Process PI for legal, justified, necessary, and specific purposes.
c. Consent Principle: Obtain authorized consent from the PI subject after expressly providing the PI subject with the information including the purpose, method, scope, and rules of the processing.
d. Minimization Principle: Unless otherwise agreed by the PI subject, only process the minimum types and quantity of PI necessary for the purposes for which the authorized consent is obtained from the PI subject. After the purposes have been achieved, the PI should be deleted promptly according to the agreement.
e. Openness and Transparency Principle: The scope, purposes, and rules, etc., of PI processing should be open to public in an explicit, intelligible, and reasonable manner, and outside supervision should be accepted.
f. Ensuring Security Principle: Possess the appropriate security capacity taking into account the security risks [the controller] faces, and implement sufficient management and technical measures to safeguard the confidentiality, integrity, and availability of PI.
g. Subject Participation Principle—Provide the PI subject with means to access, correct, and delete the PI, to withdraw consent, and to close accounts.

The guidelines go into specific details for each one of the entries above, as exemplified by the PI collection requirements section:

5.3 Authorized Consent When Collecting Personal Information
Requirements for PI controllers include:

a. Prior to the collection of the PI, clearly provide the information subject with the following information and obtain the authorized

(continued)

(continued)

consent from the PI subject: the respective types of the PI collected by different operational functions of the products or services; the rules of collecting and using the PI (e.g., purpose of collection and use; manner and frequency of collection; storage location; storage period; [the controller's] data security capabilities; information related to sharing, transferring, and public disclosure; etc.).

b. When the PI is collected indirectly:

1. Require the provider of the PI to explain the information source and confirm the legitimacy thereof.

2. Understand the scope of the authorized consent obtained by the provider of the PI regarding the processing of that PI, including the purposes of use, authorized consent provided by the PI subject for transfer, sharing, and public disclosure, etc. If the organization needs to process PI for business needs beyond the scope of the authorized consent, it should obtain explicit consent from the PI subject within a reasonable period after obtaining the PI or prior to the processing of the PI.

The guidelines continue with substantive details on the use, processing, and retention of personal information, and there is also discussion of incident handling. But that is where the guidelines stop. There is no mention of penalties, of a specific regulatory authority that enforces the law, or any indication of an individual's right to action under either the law or the guidelines.

PII Definition

The guidelines distinguish between personal information (PI) and personal sensitive information (PSI) and define the terms as follows:

3.1 Personal Information (PI)

(is defined as) All kinds of information, recorded by electronic or other means, that can be used, alone or combined with other information, to identify a specific natural person or reflect activities of a specific natural person.

Note 1: PI includes names, dates of birth, identity card numbers, biometric information, addresses, telecommunication contact methods, communication records and contents, account passwords, property information, credit information, location data, accommodation information, health and physiological information, transaction data, etc.

3.2 Personal Sensitive Information

(is defined as) PI that, once leaked, illegally provided, or abused, can threaten personal and property security and/or easily cause personal reputational damage, physical and mental health damage, or discrimination.

Note 1: Personal sensitive information includes identity card numbers, biometric information, bank account numbers, communication records and contents, property information, credit information, location data, accommodation information, health and physiological information, transaction data, and the PI of children 14 years of age or under.

The Cybersecurity Law of the People's Republic of China also includes a definition of personal information, but almost as an afterthought, in a final section titled "Supplementary Provisions."

"Personal information" refers to all kinds of information, recorded electronically or through other means, that taken alone or together with other information, is sufficient to identify a natural person's identity, including but not limited to natural persons' full names, birth dates, national identification numbers, personal biometric information, addresses, telephone numbers, and so forth.

Inclusion Criteria

While no inclusion criterion is explicitly presented, both the law and the guidelines are clearly intended to cover all Chinese citizens.

Exclusions

There are no exclusions specified.

Enforcement Agency

There is no explicitly defined enforcement agency discussed by the Guidelines. The Cybersecurity Law makes reference to "competent departments" under the "legal responsibility" chapter, of which Article 59 is excerpted in the Penalties section below.

Penalties

The guidelines make no reference to penalties. The Cybersecurity Law, on the other hand, has a section on "Legal Responsibility," with a total of 16 articles. Article 59 is a typical example of the discussion.

Article 59: Where network operators do not perform cybersecurity protection duties provided for in Articles 21 and 25 of this Law, the competent departments will order corrections and give warnings; where corrections are refused or it leads to harm to cybersecurity or other such consequences, a fine of between RMB 10,000 and 100,000 shall be levied; and the directly responsible management personnel shall be fined between RMB 5,000 and 50,000.

Where critical information infrastructure operators do not perform cybersecurity protection duties as provided for in Articles 33, 34, 36, and 38 of this Law, the competent departments will order corrections and give warnings; where corrections are refused or it leads to harm to cybersecurity or other such consequences, a fine of between RMB 100,000 and 1,000,000 shall be levied; and the directly responsible management personnel shall be fined between RMB 10,000 and 100,000.

Complete Text

The complete (translated) text for the Cybersecurity Law of the People's Republic of China can be found at: https://www.newamerica.org/

cybersecurity-initiative/digichina/blog/translation-cybersecurity-law-peoples-republic-china/.

The corresponding translation for the Guidelines on Internet Personal Information Security Protection is at: https://www.newamerica.org/cyber security-initiative/digichina/blog/translation-chinas-personal-information-security-specification/.

Effect

Any business engaged in China is impacted by all these laws, regulations, and guidelines.

India

Privacy law in India is a very recent development. As of this writing, no law has yet been enacted, but one has been introduced in parliament, and its passage is expected sometime in 2020. The law is highly controversial because it has provisions that will grant the state power to violate its own rules.

India's journey in privacy started in 2017 when the Indian Supreme Court in a historic unanimous decision declared that "the right to privacy is protected as an intrinsic part of the right to life and personal liberty under Article 21 and as a part of the freedoms guaranteed by Part III of the Constitution."

The judgment, weighing in at 547 pages long, expanded on data privacy by stating:

> Informational privacy is a facet of the right to privacy. The dangers to privacy in an age of information can originate not only from the state but from non-state actors as well. We commend to the Union Government the need to examine and put into place a robust regime for data protection. The creation of such a regime requires a careful and sensitive balance between individual interests and legitimate concerns of the state like protecting national security, preventing and investigating crime, encouraging innovation and the spread of knowledge, and preventing the dissipation of social welfare benefits.

In our examination of India's privacy law, we will focus on the pending legislation titled "The Personal Data Protection Bill."

Jurisdiction

India.

Background

The stated intent of the Personal Data Protection Bill is:

> To provide for protection of the privacy of individuals relating to their personal data, specify the flow and usage of personal data, create a relationship of trust between persons and entities processing the personal data, protect the rights of individuals whose personal data are processed, to create a framework for organisational and technical measures in processing of data, laying down norms for social media intermediary, cross-border transfer, accountability of entities processing personal data, remedies for unauthorised and harmful processing, and to establish a Data Protection Authority of India for the said purposes and for matters connected therewith or incidental thereto.

Intent and Major Provisions

The intent of the bill is to create a GDPR-like law and corresponding agencies in India. As such it contains much of what you would expect from a GDPR-inspired legislation, including provisions for the obligations of the data fiduciary with entries spelling out the prohibitions for processing of personal data, limitation on purpose, limitations on collection, requirement of notice, quality of personal data processed, restrictions on retention of personal data, the accountability of data fiduciary, and the consent necessary for processing PII.

Of particular interest to us are the rights of the data principal (i.e., the individual). Chapter V of the bill spells those out as the rights to confirmation and access, rights to correction and erasure, rights to data portability, and the right to be forgotten. Sound familiar? It should, if you paid attention to the

GDPR entry (I warned you that there would be a quiz!). A few key excerpts from this section of the bill are below (edited and condensed for clarity):

Article 17.

1. The data principal shall have the right to obtain from the data fiduciary—
   a. confirmation whether the data fiduciary is processing or has processed personal data of the data principal;
   b. the personal data of the data principal being processed or that has been processed by the data fiduciary, or any summary thereof;
   c. a brief summary of processing activities undertaken by the data fiduciary with respect to the personal data of the data principal, including any information provided in the notice under section 7in relation to such processing.
2. The data fiduciary shall provide the information under sub-section (1) to the data principal in a clear and concise manner that is easily comprehensible to a reasonable person.
3. The data principal shall have the right to access in one place the identities of the data fiduciaries with whom his personal data has been shared by any data fiduciary together with the categories of personal data shared with them, in such manner as may be specified by regulations.

Article 18.

1. The data principal shall where necessary, having regard to the purposes for which personal data is being processed, subject to such conditions and in such manner as may be specified by regulations, have the right to—
   a. the correction of inaccurate or misleading personal data;
   b. the completion of incomplete personal data;
   c. the updating of personal data that is out-of-date; and

(continued)

(continued)

    d. the erasure of personal data which is no longer necessary for the purpose for which it was processed.

Article 19.

1. Where the processing has been carried out through automated means, the data principal shall have the right to—
   a. receive the following personal data in a structured, commonly used and machine-readable format—
      i. the personal data provided to the data fiduciary;
      ii. the data which has been generated in the course of provision of services or use of goods by the data fiduciary; or
      iii. the data which forms part of any profile on the data principal, or which the data fiduciary has otherwise obtained; and
   b. have the personal data referred to in clause (a) transferred to any other data fiduciary in the format referred to in that clause.

Article 20.

1. The data principal shall have the right to restrict or prevent the continuing disclosure of his personal data by a data fiduciary where such disclosure—
   a. has served the purpose for which it was collected or is no longer necessary for the purpose;
   b. was made with the consent of the data principal under section 11 and such consent has since been withdrawn; or
   c. was made contrary to the provisions of this Act or any other law for the time being in force.

The highly controversial provision of this bill is found under "Exemptions." In essence, it spells out a broad "get of jail card free" for the government.

Article 35.

Where the Central Government is satisfied that it is necessary or expedient—

i. in the interest of sovereignty and integrity of India, the security of the State, friendly relations with foreign States, public order; or

ii. for preventing incitement to the commission of any cognizable offence relating to sovereignty and integrity of India, the security of the State, friendly relations with foreign States, public order, it may, by order, for reasons to be recorded in writing, direct that all or any of the provisions of this Act shall not apply to any agency of the Government in respect of processing of such personal data, as may be specified in the order subject to such procedure, safeguards and oversight mechanism to be followed by the agency, as may be prescribed.

As you can imagine, this took off like a lead balloon for privacy advocates all over the world. Whether it survives committee review or not remains to be seen.

PII Definition

The proposed law distinguishes between personal data and sensitive data, defining them as follows:

"Personal Data" means data about or relating to a natural person who is directly or indirectly identifiable, having regard to any characteristic, trait, attribute or any other feature of the identity of such natural person, whether online or offline, or any combination of such features with any other information, and shall include any inference drawn from such data for the purpose of profiling;

(continued)

(continued)

"Sensitive Personal Data" means such personal data, which may, reveal, be related to, or constitute—

   i. financial data;
  ii. health data;
 iii. official identifier;
 iv. sex life;
  v. sexual orientation;
 vi. biometric data;
 vii. genetic data;
viii. transgender status;
 ix. intersex status;
  x. caste or tribe;
 xi. religious or political belief or affiliation; or
xii. any other data categorised as sensitive personal data under section 15.

Inclusion Criteria

As per the proposed law:

The provisions of this Act,—

A. shall apply to—

   a. the processing of personal data where such data has been collected, disclosed, shared or otherwise processed within the territory of India;

   b. the processing of personal data by the State, any Indian company, any citizen of India or any person or body of persons incorporated or created under Indian law;

   c. the processing of personal data by data fiduciaries or data processors not present within the territory of India, if such processing is—

i. in connection with any business carried on in India, or any systematic activity of offering goods or services to data principals within the territory of India; or

ii. in connection with any activity which involves profiling of data principals within the territory of India.

B. shall not apply to the processing of anonymized data, other than the anonymized data referred to in section 91.

Exclusions

The only exclusion is the ability of the state to essentially break the law on-demand.

Enforcement Agency

The enforcement agency is the proposed Data Protection Authority of India.

Penalties

The law incorporates stiff, GDPR-like penalties: For audit failures the proposed penalty is 2 percent of the company's annual turnover or 50,000,000 rupees, and for data protection failures, the proposed fine is 150,000,000 rupees, or 4 percent of the company's annual turnover.

Complete Text

The complete text for the proposed law can be found at the National Informatics Centre web server at: http://164.100.47.4/BillsTexts/LSBillTexts/Asintroduced/373_2019_LS_Eng.pdf.

Effect

Any business engaged in India will be affected by the law.

Japan

Japan's privacy law, the Act of the Protection of Personal Information (APPI) was enacted in 2003. Following a series of public data breaches the law was amended in 2015, and the new version took effect in 2017.

Jurisdiction

Japan; the so-called Amended APPI came into force in May 2017.

Background

The purpose of the bill is articulated in its first article:

> **Article 1** This Act aims to protect an individual's rights and interests while considering the utility of personal information including that the proper and effective application of personal information contributes to the creation of new industries and the realization of a vibrant economic society and an enriched quality of life for the people of Japan; by setting forth the overall vision for the proper handling of personal information, creating a governmental basic policy with regard to this, and establishing other matters to serve as a basis for measures to protect personal information, as well as by clarifying the responsibilities etc. of the central and local governments and establishing obligations etc. that a personal information handling business operator shall fulfill, in light of the significantly expanded utilization of personal information as our advanced information- and communication-based society evolves.

Intent and Major Provisions

The law, much like most of the modern privacy laws, has what you would expect in terms of requiring the business operators to specify a data utilization purpose and to not deviate from it, to follow proper data acquisition procedures, to notify the data subject of the data acquiring purpose, to ensure data accuracy and provide for data security, restrict third-party access to the data, and disclose to the public ways that the public can interact with the business with regards to their data.

It is through this obligation of the business operators that the public is granted the various privacy rights, such as correction or deletion of their data, but those rights are limited in scope. For example, the data subject can only request correction or deletion if the data has been used outside of the approved and stated scope or the data was obtained fraudulently.

The law does provide for a right of private action against the business operators, if they fail to comply within two weeks from the initial request for correction, deletion, and so forth.

PII Definition

APPI is fairly explicit in its definitions of personal and sensitive data.

Article 2

1. "Personal information" in this Act means that information relating to a living individual which falls under any of each following item:
   i. those containing a name, date of birth, or other descriptions etc. (meaning any and all matters (excluding an individual identification code) stated, recorded or otherwise expressed using voice, movement or other methods in a document, drawing or electromagnetic record (meaning a record kept in an electromagnetic form (meaning an electronic, magnetic or other forms that cannot be recognized through the human senses; the same shall apply in the succeeding paragraph, item (ii)); the same shall apply in Article 18, paragraph (2)); hereinafter the same) whereby a specific individual can be identified (including those which can be readily collated with other information and thereby identify a specific individual)
   ii. those containing an individual identification code
2. An "individual identification code" in this Act means those prescribed by cabinet order which are any character, letter, number, symbol or other codes falling under any of each following item.
   i. those able to identify a specific individual that are a character, letter, number, symbol or other codes into which a bodily partial feature of the specific individual has been converted in order to be provided for use by computers
   ii. those character, letter, number, symbol or other codes which are assigned in regard to the use of services provided to an individual or to the purchase of goods sold to an individual, or which are

(continued)

(continued)

> stated or electromagnetically recorded in a card or other docu-
> ment issued to an individual so as to be able to identify a specific
> user or purchaser, or recipient of issuance by having made the
> said codes differently assigned or, stated or recoded for the said
> user or purchaser, or recipient of issuance
>
> 3. "Special care-required personal information" in this Act means per-
> sonal information comprising a principal's race, creed, social status,
> medical history, criminal record, fact of having suffered damage
> by a crime, or other descriptions etc. prescribed by cabinet order
> as those of which the handling requires special care so as not to
> cause unfair discrimination, prejudice or other disadvantages to the
> principal.

Inclusion Criteria

The law applies to all Japanese citizens, as well as worldwide businesses that deal with their data.

Exclusions

The central government along with the local governments, and various administrative agencies are excluded from the law.

Enforcement Agency

The law is enforced through the Japanese Personal Information Protection Commission.

Penalties

The approach to penalties in Japan is very different than those in GDPR and other countries. They are softer, with a staged approach in the interaction between the Personal Information Protection Commission (PIPC) and the business.

First, the PIPC will contact the business directly to discuss the violation and only if the business does not comply, the PIPC will follow up with (in order) an administrative order to submit a report, followed by an administrative advice, followed by an administrative recommendation, and finally ending with an administrative order. If the administrative order is ignored by the business, then they can be fined up to 500,000 yen (about $4,500) and/or up to one-year imprisonment.

Complete Text

An English-language version of the law can be found at: https://www.ppc.go.jp/files/pdf/Act_on_the_Protection_of_Personal_Information.pdf.

Effect

Any businesses, irrespective of location, doing business in Japan and dealing with personal data.

Australia

Australia bears some resemblance to the United States in that its privacy legislation is a mix of multiple state and territory laws, but quite unlike the US, Australia has had a federal privacy law in the books since 1988. The Federal Privacy Act and the corresponding Australian Privacy Principles apply to businesses that have a minimum revenue threshold of 3,000,000 Australian dollars.

Jurisdiction

Australia; originally passed in 1988, amended in December 2019.

Background

The objectives of the legislation as stated are:

> a. to promote the protection of the privacy of individuals; and
> b. to recognise that the protection of the privacy of individuals is balanced with the interests of entities in carrying out their functions or activities; and
>
> *(continued)*

(continued)

c. to provide the basis for nationally consistent regulation of privacy and the handling of personal information; and

d. to promote responsible and transparent handling of personal information by entities; and

e. to facilitate an efficient credit reporting system while ensuring that the privacy of individuals is respected; and

f. to facilitate the free flow of information across national borders while ensuring that the privacy of individuals is respected; and

g. to provide a means for individuals to complain about an alleged interference with their privacy; and

h. to implement Australia's international obligation in relation to privacy.

Intent and Major Provisions

The pillars of the legislation are the 13 Australian Privacy Principles (APP):

APP 1—Open and transparent management of personal information

Ensures that APP entities manage personal information in an open and transparent way. This includes having a clearly expressed and up to date APP privacy policy.

APP 2—Anonymity and pseudonymity

Requires APP entities to give individuals the option of not identifying themselves, or of using a pseudonym. Limited exceptions apply.

APP 3—Collection of solicited personal information

Outlines when an APP entity can collect personal information that is solicited. It applies higher standards to the collection of 'sensitive' information.

APP 4—Dealing with unsolicited personal information

Outlines how APP entities must deal with unsolicited personal information.

APP 5—Notification of the collection of personal information

Outlines when and in what circumstances an APP entity that collects personal information must notify an individual of certain matters.

APP 6—Use or disclosure of personal information

Outlines the circumstances in which an APP entity may use or disclose personal information that it holds.

APP 7—Direct marketing

An organisation may only use or disclose personal information for direct marketing purposes if certain conditions are met.

APP 8—Cross-border disclosure of personal information

Outlines the steps an APP entity must take to protect personal information before it is disclosed overseas.

APP 9—Adoption, use or disclosure of government related identifiers

Outlines the limited circumstances when an organisation may adopt a government related identifier of an individual as its own identifier, or use or disclose a government related identifier of an individual.

APP 10—Quality of personal information

An APP entity must take reasonable steps to ensure the personal information it collects is accurate, up to date and complete. An entity must also take reasonable steps to ensure the personal information it uses or discloses is accurate, up to date, complete and relevant, having regard to the purpose of the use or disclosure.

(continued)

(continued)

APP 11—Security of personal information

An APP entity must take reasonable steps to protect personal information it holds from misuse, interference and loss, and from unauthorised access, modification or disclosure. An entity has obligations to destroy or de-identify personal information in certain circumstances.

APP 12—Access to personal information

Outlines an APP entity's obligations when an individual requests to be given access to personal information held about them by the entity. This includes a requirement to provide access unless a specific exception applies.

APP 13—Correction of personal information

Outlines an APP entity's obligations in relation to correcting the personal information it holds about individuals.

The Privacy Act provides for certain explicit rights to Australian citizens, including the right to know how their personal information is being collected, how it will be used, and who it will be disclosed to, provide options for anonymity, grant the right to request your own data, grant the right to opt-out from marketing communications, correct any personal information that is wrong, and file a complaint against a company or agency that they believe have violated the Privacy Act.

PII Definition

The Privacy Act defines personal and sensitive data as follows:

personal information means information or an opinion about an identified individual, or an individual who is reasonably identifiable:

a. whether the information or opinion is true or not; and

b. whether the information or opinion is recorded in a material form or not.

   sensitive information means:

a. information or an opinion about an individual's:
   i. racial or ethnic origin; or
   ii. political opinions; or
   iii. membership of a political association; or
   iv. religious beliefs or affiliations; or
   v. philosophical beliefs; or
   vi. membership of a professional or trade association; or
   vii. membership of a trade union; or
   viii. sexual orientation or practices; or
   ix. criminal record; that is also personal information; or

b. health information about an individual; or
c. genetic information about an individual that is not otherwise health information; or
d. biometric information that is to be used for the purpose of automated biometric verification or biometric identification; or
e. biometric templates.

Inclusion Criteria

Any business with annual turnover (aka revenue) of 3,000,000 Australian dollars (roughly US$2 million); also applies to Australian government agencies.

Exclusions

The Privacy Act does not cover:

a. state or territory government agencies, including a state and territory public hospital or health care facility (which is covered under state and territory legislation) except:

(continued)

(continued)

    i. certain acts and practices related to My Health Records and individual healthcare identifiers

    ii. an entity prescribed by the Privacy Regulation 2013

    iii. an individual acting in their own capacity, including your neighbours

    iv. a university, other than a private university and the Australian National University

    v. a public school

b. in some situations, the handling of employee records by an organisation in relation to current and former employment relationships

c. a small business operator, unless an exception applies (see above)

d. a media organisation acting in the course of journalism if the organisation is publicly committed to observing published privacy standards

e. registered political parties and political representatives

Enforcement Agency

The Australian Privacy Commissioner, along with several other agencies is responsible for the enforcement of the act.

Penalties

Following an investigation by the Australian Privacy Commissioner, and assuming that the offender is determined to have violated the law, the Commissioner may impose penalties ranging from rectification of damages and losses suffered by the consumer to fines of up to 420,000 Australian dollars for an individual and up to 2,100,000 Australian dollars for corporations (roughly, US$275,000 and US$1,380,000, respectively).

Complete Text

The complete text for the Australian Privacy Act can be found at: https://www.legislation.gov.au/Details/C2020C00025.

Effect

The effect of the law is worldwide, for any businesses dealing with data of Australian citizens.

***

We're done with the Asia-Pacific region. Time to cross the ocean and take a look at the magnificent African continent!

CHAPTER 8

African Regulations

You have little power over what's not yours.
—Zimbabwean proverb

Over the past twenty years, privacy legislation in Africa has been gaining momentum, with half the countries in the continent now having some form of data protection laws either already on the books or about to be enacted. Additionally, the three main regional organizations—the African Union, the Economic Community of West African States (ECOWAS), and the Southern African Development Community (SADC)—have all published or adopted privacy and cybersecurity acts. They are strongly influenced by—you guessed it—the European General Data Protection Regulation.

As with other regions that we examined, so with Africa we will look at the top three African economies by GDP: Nigeria, South Africa, and Egypt. We will also look at the Economic Community of West African States (ECOWAS) privacy framework, since its member states combined are responsible for over $668 billion in GDP.

Economic Community of West African States

The Economic Community of West African States (ECOWAS) has 15 member states: Benin, Burkina Faso, Cabo Verde, Cote d'Ivoire, Gambia, Ghana, Guinea, Guinea-Bissau, Liberia, Mali, Niger, Nigeria, Senegal, Sierra Leone, and Togo. In 2010 ECOWAS passed the Supplementary Act A/SA.1/01/10 on Personal Data Protection.

Jurisdiction

ECOWAS member countries.

Background

The preamble to the act reads:

> The high contracting parties,
>   CONSIDERING the important progress made in the area of Information and Communication Technologies (ICT) as well as the Internet which increasingly raises the problem of personal data protection;
>   CONSCIOUS that a technology such as the Internet, with its facilities of profiling and tracing of individuals, constitutes a favourable vector for gathering and processing personal data;
>   CONSCIOUS also that the increasing use of Information and Communication Technology (ICT) may be prejudicial to the private and professional life of the users;
>   NOTING that, notwithstanding the existence of the national legislations relating to the protection of privacy of the citizens in their private and professional life and relating to the guarantee of the free movement of information, it becomes a matter of urgency to fill the legal vacuum generated by the use of internet which is a new instrument of communication.

Intent and Major Provisions

The main intent of the Act is:

> Each Member State shall establish a legal framework of protection for privacy of data relating to the collection, processing, transmission, storage, and use of personal data without prejudice to the general interest of the State.

Moreover, the act calls for the establishment of a data protection authority:

1. Within the ECOWAS space, each Member State shall establish Its own data protection Authority. Any State that does not have shall be encouraged to establish one.
2. The data protection Authority shall be an independent administrative Authority responsible for ensuring that personal data is processed in compliance with the provisions of this Supplementary Act.

The act sets forth several principles guiding the processing of personal data, including the Principle of Consent and Legitimacy, the Principle of Legality and Fairness, the Principle of Purpose, Relevance, and Preservation, the Principle of Accuracy, the Principle of Transparency, the Principle of Confidentiality and Security, and the Principle of Choice of Data Processor.

Of particular interest is Article 34: Prohibition of Direct Prospecting. It reads:

Within the ECOWAS space, direct prospecting by whatever means of communication, usIng personal data in any form of an individual who has not stated his prior consent to receiving such prospecting shall be prohibited.

As you can imagine, this places quite a constraint on the poor users that the infamous "Nigerian Prince" can email within ECOWAS, so—no wonder—he has been targeting the American consumers!

In terms of individual rights, the act spells out the following: right to information, right to access, right to object, and the individual's right to rectification and destruction.

PII Definition

The act differentiates between personal and sensitive data as follows:

> **Personal data** means any information relating to an identified individual or who may be directly or indirectly identifiable by reference to an identification number or one or several elements related to their physical, physiological, genetic, psychological, cultural, social, or economic identity;
>
> **Sensitive data** means personal data relating to an individual's religious, philosophical, political, trade union opinions or activities, to his sexual life, racial origin or health, relating to social measures, proceedings, and criminal or administrative sanctions.

Inclusion Criteria

Everyone in ECOWAS jurisdictions is covered by the Act.

Exclusions

The Act excludes:

> 1. processing of personal data relating to data manifestly made public by the data subject;
> 2. the data subject has given his written consent, on whatever medium, to such processing, and in line with texts in force;
> 3. processing of personal data is necessary to protect the vital interests of the data subject or another person where the data subject is physically or legally incapable of giving consent;
> 4. processing, in particular of genetic data, is necessary for establishing, exercising or defending a legal right;
> 5. where legal proceedings or a criminal investigation is underway;
> 6. processing of personal data is necessary for reasons of public interest, in particular for historical, statistical or scientific purposes;

7. for the performance of a contract to which the data subject is a party or for the application of pre-contractual measures adopted at the request of the data subject prior to entering into a contract;
8. the processing is necessary for compliance with any legal or regulatory obligation to which the data controller is subject;
9. the processing is necessary for the implementation of a public interest mission or is carried out by a public authority or is assigned by a public authority to the data controller or to a third party to whom the data is disclosed;
10. the processing is carried out in the course of its legitimate activities by a foundation, an association or any other non-profit making body that exists for political, philosophical, religious, mutual benefit or trade union purposes.

Enforcement Agency

The local (ECOWAS member) Data Protection Authorities.

Penalties

There are no explicit penalties mentioned in the act. However, under "sanctions," the act mentions that the Data Protection Authority may provisionally or definitively withdraw the authorization of a data processor to operate, and it may issue a fine.

Complete Text

The complete text for the Act can be found at: http://www.tit.comm.ecowas .int/wp-content/uploads/2015/11/SIGNED-Data-Protection-Act.pdf.

Effect

The effect of the act is regional to the West African states, and global for any businesses operating in an ECOWAS member state that has adopted the act by creating their own state-specific privacy laws.

Nigeria

Nigeria has the greatest number of Internet users in Africa: two and a half times the number of the next closest country (Egypt) and almost four times as much as South Africa. Despite this, it has struggled with passage of a data protection law for almost ten years until 2019, when Nigeria's National Information Technology Development Agency issued the 2019 Nigeria Data Protection Regulation.

Jurisdiction

Nigeria, both citizens and residents.

Background

The Nigerian Constitution guarantees the right to privacy in Chapter 4, Article 37, which says: "The privacy of citizens, their homes, correspondence, telephone conversations and telegraphic communications is hereby guaranteed and protected." This protection, from a legislative perspective, is supported by several laws, the most prominent of which were the National Health Act, the National Identity Management Commission Act, the Credit Reporting Act, the Children's Right Act, and the Cybercrime Act of 2015.

Starting in 2007, the National Information Technology Development Agency (NITDA) was mandated to essentially develop data protection regulations, the result of which is the 2019 Nigeria Data Protection Regulation (NDPR).

Intent and Major Provisions

The NDPR draws heavily from the European Data Protection Regulation. It establishes data processing principles revolving around explicit consent, contractual or legal need, public interest, or critical need.

It also establishes several individual rights including the right to opt-out, the right to access their own data, the right of data transportability among controllers, the right to know how the data is used, the right of data correction and deletion, and the right to file a complaint with NITDA.

The law also requires the establishment of a Data Protection Officer who will be responsible for the data controller's compliance with NDPR.

PII Definition

The NDPR defines personal data as follows:

> **"Personal Data"** means any information relating to an identified or identifiable natural person ('data subject'); an identifiable natural person is one who can be identified, directly or indirectly, in particular by reference to an identifier such as a name, an identification number, location data, an online identifier or to one or more factors specific to the physical, physiological, genetic, mental, economic, cultural or social identity of that natural person; It can be anything from a name, address, a photo, an email address, bank details, posts on social networking websites, medical information, and other unique identifier such as but not limited to MAC address, IP address, IMEI number, IMSI number, SIM and others.

Note that the definition makes explicit reference to both location data and IP address.

Inclusion Criteria

Anyone dealing with the personal data of Nigerian citizens or residents, even if the citizens in question may not be current Nigeria residents.

Exclusions

There are no exclusions to the law.

Enforcement Agency

National Information Technology Development Agency (NITDA).

Penalties

The law imposes significant penalties (in addition to criminal liabilities) to violators. Specifically:

Any person subject to this Regulation who is found to be in breach of the data privacy rights of any Data Subject shall be liable in addition to any other criminal liability, the following:

a. in the case of a Data Controller dealing with more than 10,000 Data Subjects, payment of the fine of 2% of Annual Gross Revenue of the preceding year or payment of the sum of 10 million naira whichever is greater;

b. in the case of a Data Controller dealing with less than 10,000 Data Subjects, payment of the fine of 1% of the Annual Gross Revenue of the preceding year or payment of the sum of 2 million naira whichever is greater.

Complete Text

The link to the complete text for NDPR can be found at: https://nitda.gov.ng/wp-content/uploads/2019/01/Nigeria%20Data%20Protection%20Regulation.pdf.

Effect

The effect of the law is worldwide since it impacts not only businesses doing work in Nigeria and Nigeran citizens and residents but also Nigerian citizens that reside outside of Nigeria.

South Africa

Privacy legislation in South Africa is relatively recent. The Protection of Personal Information Act (PoPIA or PoPI) was passed in 2013, although it took years for it to come into effect (see below).

Jurisdiction

South Africa; all provisions expected to take full effect in 2020.

Background

The South African constitution enshrines privacy as a fundamental right in Article 14:

> Everyone has the right to privacy, which includes the right not to have—
>
> a. their person or home searched;
> b. their property searched;
> c. their possessions seized; or
> d. the privacy of their communications infringed.

The Protection of Personal Information Act, with all of its 156 pages, was created to further promote the protection of personal information, to establish processing standards, to establish the office of the Information Regulator, to provide data governance direction, and to regulate the cross-border flow of data.

Intent and Major Provisions

The intent of the act is spelled out in Article 2:

> The purpose of this Act is to—
>
> a. give effect to the constitutional right to privacy, by safeguarding personal information when processed by a responsible party, subject to justifiable limitations that are aimed at—
>   i. balancing the right to privacy against other rights, particularly the right of access to information; and
>
> *(continued)*

(continued)

    ii. protecting important interests, including the free flow of information within the Republic and across international borders;

b. regulate the manner in which personal information may be processed, by establishing conditions, in harmony with international standards, that prescribe the minimum threshold requirements for the lawful processing of personal information;

c. provide persons with rights and remedies to protect their personal information from processing that is not in accordance with this Act; and

d. establish voluntary and compulsory measures, including the establishment of an Information Regulator, to ensure respect for and to promote, enforce and fulfil the rights protected by this Act.

Like most mature privacy laws, PoPI sets conditions for the lawful processing of personal information including accountability, suitability, scope, transparency, and safety. It also outlines in detail the rights of data subjects, listed below (edited for length):

Rights of data subjects

A data subject has the right to have his, her or its personal information processed in accordance with the conditions for the lawful processing of personal information ... including the right—

a. to be notified that—
    i. personal information about him, her or it is being collected ...
    ii. his, her or its personal information has been accessed or acquired by an unauthorised person ...

b. to establish whether a responsible party holds personal information of that data subject and to request access to his, her or its personal information ...

c. to request, where necessary, the correction, destruction or deletion of his, her or its personal information ...

d. to object, on reasonable grounds relating to his, her or its particular situation to the processing of his, her or its personal information ...

e. to object to the processing of his, her or its personal information ... at any time for purposes of direct marketing ...

f. not to have his, her or its personal information processed for purposes of direct marketing by means of unsolicited electronic communications ...

g. not to be subject, under certain circumstances, to a decision which is based solely on the basis of the automated processing of his, her or its personal information intended to provide a profile of such person ...

h. to submit a complaint to the Regulator regarding the alleged interference with the protection of the personal information of any data subject ...

i. to institute civil proceedings regarding the alleged interference with the protection of his, her or its personal information.

PII Definition

PoPI defines personal information as follows:

"personal information" means information relating to an identifiable, living, natural person, and where it is applicable, an identifiable, existing juristic person, including, but not limited to—

a. information relating to the race, gender, sex, pregnancy, marital status, national, ethnic or social origin, colour, sexual orientation, age, physical or mental health, well-being, disability, religion, conscience, belief, culture, language and birth of the person;

(continued)

(continued)

b. information relating to the education or the medical, financial, criminal or employment history of the person;

c. any identifying number, symbol, e-mail address, physical address, telephone number, location information, online identifier or other particular assignment to the person;

d. the biometric information of the person;

e. the personal opinions, views or preferences of the person;

f. correspondence sent by the person that is implicitly or explicitly of a private or confidential nature or further correspondence that would reveal the contents of the original correspondence;

g. the views or opinions of another individual about the person; and

h. the name of the person if it appears with other personal information relating to the person or if the disclosure of the name itself would reveal information about the person.

Inclusion Criteria

The act explicitly includes both natural and legal persons in South Africa.

Exclusions

The Protection of Personal Information Act has a long list of exclusions, including instances of purely personal activities, de-identified data, national security reasons, anti-terrorism activities, and valid journalistic, literary, or artistic expression.

Enforcement Agency

The Protection of Personal Information Act is enforced by the South African Information Regulator.

Penalties

Violating the Act can result to imprisonment of up to ten years, and fines ranging between 1,000,000 and 10,000,000 Rand (approximately $66,000–$667,000).

Complete Text

The full text for PoPI can be found at: https://www.justice.gov.za/inforeg/docs/InfoRegSA-POPIA-act2013-004.pdf.

Effect

The effect of PoPI is limited to South Africa and businesses dealing with South African citizens' personal data.

Egypt

Egypt did not have a privacy law until 2017, when the first drafts of the Data Protection (draft) Law were circulated. As of June 2019, following the approval of the Egyptian Cabinet of Ministers, the Egyptian Parliament has passed the law.

Jurisdiction

Egypt.

Background

The Egyptian Data Protection Law is based heavily on the European General Data Protection Regulation, with some notable differences discussed below.

Intent and Major Provisions

Much as in the GDPR, the Egyptian law lists several data protection principles, including data collection principles for specific and legitimate uses, secure data processing, and destruction of the data following its intended use.

The law spells out several individual rights, including the right to be informed, the right to obtain an copy of your data, the right to correct the data, and the right to determine the extent of your data's use by the data controller. An individual has the right to file a complaint with the Personal Data Protection Center. Finally, much like with the GDPR, the law requires the appointment of a Data Protection Officer to ensure compliance with the law.

PII Definition

The law defines personal data almost exactly the same way as the GDPR as:

> any data relating to an identifiable natural person, or is one who can be identified, directly or indirectly, in particular by reference to an identifier such as a name, voice, picture, an identification number, an online identifier or to one or more factors specific to the physical, mental, economic, cultural or social identity of that natural person.

Similarly, the special data category is defined much in the same way:

> data which reveals the mental health, physical health, genetic health, biometric data, financial data, religious beliefs, political opinions, security status relating to the natural person. In all cases, data relating to children are considered sensitive personal data.

Inclusion Criteria

Egyptian citizens and Egyptian residents.

Exclusions

Excluded from the law are data held by individuals for private use, data used in official statistics and legal proceedings, and data in the possession of the government.

Enforcement Agency

The law will be enforced by the newly created Personal Data Protection Center.

Penalties

The fines under the law are less than those imposed by the GDPR but are still significant. They range from imprisonment and fines up to two million Egyptian pounds (about $125,000).

Complete Text

As of this writing there is no online resource that makes the complete text available.

Effect

The effect of the law is regional, limited to Egypt and businesses processing data of Egyptian citizens or Egyptian residents.

CHAPTER 9
South American Regulations

All human beings have three lives: public, private, and secret.
—Gabriel García Márquez, *Gabriel García Márquez: A Life*

Privacy legislation in South American countries goes back to the predecessor of the GDPR, the European Data Protection Directive of 1995. It was at that time that several countries passed privacy legislation aligning themselves with the EU directive. Since that time, and following the introduction of the GDPR, most South American countries have followed suit in updating their own privacy laws to align with the GDPR.

Leading the effort was Brazil with the passage of the *Lei Geral de Proteção de Dados* (LGPD), legislation based on the GDPR. It reflected the government's desire to closely align with the European Union and facilitate cross-border transfers between the block and Brazil.

We will examine the three largest economies in South America: Brazil, Argentina, and Colombia.

Brazil

Prior to Brazil's introduction in 2018 of their version of the GDPR, the *Lei Geral de Proteção de Dados* (LGPD), privacy in Brazil was regulated via 40 or more, and often at odds, laws. The LGDP, taking effect on August 15, 2020, unifies all these laws and aligns the country's privacy legislation with the GDPR.

Jurisdiction

Brazil.

Background

The main drivers behind Brazil's LGDP were the consolidation of the diverse and confusing privacy legislation already in effect and the strong desire for Brazil to ensure free and open cross-border transfers to the European Union.

Intent and Major Provisions

As per Article 1 of the legislation:

> This Law provides for the processing of personal data, including by digital means, by a natural person or a legal entity of public or private law, with the purpose of protecting the fundamental rights of freedom and privacy and the free development of the personality of the natural person.

The law mirrors the data-processing principles of GDPR in requiring that all processing is done "in good faith, with a specific legitimate purpose, within agreed scope, only as needed, and guaranteeing the data subject's free access to the data, ensuring the quality and security of the data, and handling the data in a transparent, non-discriminatory, and accountable way."

In terms of the individual's rights under the law, LGDP is fairly clear in Articles 17 and 18:

> **Article 17.** All natural persons (are) assured ownership of (their) personal data, with the fundamental rights of freedom, intimacy and privacy being guaranteed, under the terms of this Law.
>
> **Article 18.** The personal data subject has the right to obtain the following from the controller, regarding the data subject's data being processed by the controller, at any time and by means of request:
>
> I. – confirmation of the existence of the processing;
> II. – access to the data;

III. – correction of incomplete, inaccurate or out-of-date data;

IV. – anonymization, blocking or deletion of unnecessary or excessive data or data processed in noncompliance with the provisions of this Law;

V. – portability of the data to another service or product provider, by means of an express request and subject to commercial and industrial secrecy, pursuant to the regulation of the controlling agency;

VI. – deletion of personal data processed with the consent of the data subject, except in the situations provided in Art. 16 of this Law;

VII. – information about public and private entities with which the controller has shared data;

VIII. – information about the possibility of denying consent and the consequences of such denial;

IX. – revocation of consent

Finally, as you would expect, the law requires the appointment of a Data Protection Officer to ensure the company's compliance with the law.

PII Definition

Article 5 of the law defines the following classes of data:

For purposes of this Law, the following definitions apply:

I. – personal data: information regarding an identified or identifiable natural person;

II. – sensitive personal data: personal data concerning racial or ethnic origin, religious belief, political opinion, trade union or religious, philosophical or political organization membership, data concerning health or sex life, genetic or biometric data, when related to a natural person;

III. – anonymized data: data related to a data subject who cannot be identified, considering the use of reasonable and available technical means at the time of the processing.

Inclusion Criteria

The LGDP applies to any business that processes data of Brazilian residents, irrespective of whether they operate inside Brazil or are simply providing goods or services to Brazilian residents. More specifically, as per LGDP's Article 3:

> This Law applies to any processing operation carried out by a natural person or a legal entity of public or private law, irrespective of the mean, the country in which its headquarter is located or the country where the data are located, provided that:
>
> I. – the processing operation is carried out in the national territory;
> II. – the purpose of the processing activity is to offer or provide goods or services or the processing of data of individuals located in the national territory; or
> III. – the personal data being processed were collected in the national territory.
> §1 Data collected in the national territory are considered to be those whose data subject is in the national territory at the time of collection.
> §2 Data processing as provided in Item IV of the lead sentence of Art. 4 of this Law is exempted from the provisions of Item I of this article.

Exclusions

Article 4 of the LGDP includes a long list of exclusions, shown (edited) below:

> This Law does not apply to the processing of personal data that:
>
> I. – is done by a natural person exclusively for private and non-economic purposes;
> II. – is done exclusively:

a. for journalistic and artistic purposes; or

b. academic purposes ...

III. – is done exclusively for purposes of:

a. public safety;

b. national defense;

c. state security; or

d. activities of investigation and prosecution of criminal offenses; or

IV. – have their origin outside the national territory and are not the object of communication.

Enforcement Agency

Originally, the LGDP called for the creation of the Brazilian National Data Protection Authority (*Autoridade Nacional de Proteção de Dados* [ANPD]) and the creation of a National Council for the Protection of Personal Data (*Conselho Nacional de Proteção de Dados Pessoais e da Privacidade*) as independent agencies responsible for the enforcement of the LGDP, policy creation, and research.

The new president of Brazil vetoed this provision, and a few others, and instead established the new ANPD as a Brazilian Federal Government agency, reporting to the president. Its powers are essentially the same as originally proposed, and it remains the main enforcement agency for the regulation. ANPD will subsequently propose guidelines for the creation of the National Council for the Protection of Personal Data.

Penalties

The penalties for violating the LGDP are significant and in alignment with the severity of fines imposed by the GDPR. Penalties can be up to 2% of total revenue (in Brazil) or up to 50,000,000 Brazilian Reals (about $11,000,000).

Complete Text

You can find the complete text in Portuguese here: http://www.planalto .gov.br/ccivil_03/_Ato2015-2018/2018/Lei/L13709.htm and translated in

English here: https://iapp.org/media/pdf/resource_center/Brazilian_General_Data_Protection_Law.pdf.

Effect

The effect of the law is certainly regional, but its implementation has a global effect because of the expected effect in South America's stance on privacy and the alignment between Brazilian privacy law and that of the European Union.

Argentina

As of this writing, Argentina is in the process of reviewing a proposed bill (MEN-2018-147-APN-PTE) that would replace the outdated privacy legislation in place since 2000. The proposed legislation was proposed in 2017, and when enacted, it will create an Argentinian version of the European GDPR.

Reviewed, briefly, below is the existing legislation that is currently in effect.

Jurisdiction

Argentina.

Background

Privacy and protection of personal data was incorporated into the Argentinian constitution in 1994. In 2000, the Personal Data Protection Act (25,326) was enacted to regulate the principles outlined in the constitution under Section 43. The law, along with the associated decrees and regulations is known as the PDPA or DPA.

Intent and Major Provisions

Given its age, the PDPA is an excellent attempt to protect individual data, making Argentina one of the first countries in South America to implement such legislation. Under the law, the data subject must be provided by the data processor clear notifications explaining the purpose for the data collection, who will process the data and where, what are the options for refusing such processing, who will have access to the data, as well as clear guidelines on ways for the data subject to access, suppress or correct the data. There are additional restrictions on how the data may be used and where it can be disclosed, including a requirement for data destruction once the purpose for data use has been satisfied.

The law also requires that appropriate data security and confidentiality measures are in place, although it does not require the appointment of a data protection officer.

PII Definition

The PDPA defines personal data as "information of any kind referring to certain or ascertainable physical persons or legal entities."

Inclusion Criteria

Any business that processes an Argentinian's personal data is impacted by the law.

Exclusions

There are no exclusions in the current PDPA.

Enforcement Agency

The agency responsible for enforcement is the "Agency for Access to Public Information."

Penalties

The Agency for Access to Public Information can impose a variety of penalties, proportional to the violation. Monetary penalties can range up to 5,000,000 Argentinian pesos (about $81,000).

Complete Text

The English version of the regulation can be found at: http://www.jus.gob.ar/datos-personales/english-version/regulation.aspx.

Effect

The effect of the law is limited to Argentina.

Colombia

Colombia has a mature and sophisticated legislative privacy framework, in place since 2012. This framework, which aligns with the European GDPR in many areas, continues to be updated frequently, most recently with pending legislation that will introduce privacy-by-design and industry-specific privacy legislation. A brief overview of the applicable laws follows below.

Jurisdiction

Colombia.

Background

The Colombian constitution has an explicit right to privacy in Article 15:

> All individuals have the right to personal and family privacy and to their good reputation, and the State has to respect them and to make others respect them. Similarly, individuals have the right to know, update, and rectify information collected about them in data banks and in the records of public and private entities.
>
> Freedom and the other guarantees approved in the Constitution shall be respected in the collection, processing, and circulation of data.
>
> Correspondence and other forms of private communication may not be violated. They may only be intercepted or recorded on the basis of a court order in cases and following the formalities established by statute.
>
> For tax or legal purposes and for cases of inspection, the oversight and intervention of the State may demand making available accounting records and other private documents within the limits provided by statute.

In support of the constitutional right to privacy, Colombia, in 1973, enacted the Regulation of Data Protection Act (Decree 1377), which supplemented the original Data Protection Act of 2012 (Law 1581).

Intent and Major Provisions

Looking at the framework as a whole, the intent is to protect personal data processing and grant certain rights to individuals with regard to both consent and access to their data. Specifically, the laws prescribe the need for explicit notice on purpose, use, the owner's privacy rights, and explicit pathway for the data owner's access to their own data. Additionally, there are specific consent requirements, including the need for preservation of the consent while processing private data. The laws provide for the right of consent revocation at any time, with the obvious exceptions of legal or contractual obligations.

The laws also limit the time that data can be held for processing. There is also a requirement that data only be processed for a specific, intended purpose, following which, the data is to be suppressed or deleted.

PII Definition

The different laws and decrees vary in their definition of personal data. The most pertinent one is the definition of sensitive personal data under the original Data Protection Act of 2012 (Law 1581), which defines sensitive personal data as any data that can affect the owner's intimacy or that, if improperly used, can result in discrimination. It included data that reveals ethnic or racial origin, political affiliation, religious affiliation, membership data, health and sexual orientation data, and the recently added biometrics data.

Inclusion Criteria

Anyone who processes personal data in Colombia is affected by the law.

Exclusions

The current legislation excludes personal data collected by individuals for personal use, as well as personal data gathered by the government for national defense. Data used for security, intelligence, and counterterrorism purposes plus valid use of personal data used by journalists are also excluded.

Enforcement Agency

The enforcement agency is the Superintendence of Industry and Commerce (SIC). For financial institutions, the enforcement agency is the Superintendence of Finance (SOF).

Penalties

The penalties for violating the Colombian privacy law can be severe, including suspension and termination of business activities and fines up to $500,000.

Complete Text

You can find the original text (in Spanish) at https://www.sisben.gov.co/Documents/Informaci%C3%B3n/Leyes/LEY%20TRATAMIENTO%20DE%20DATOS%20-%20LEY%201581%20DE%202012.pdf and http://www.lasallecucuta.edu.co/infopdf/decreto1377.pdf.

Effect

The impact of the law is regional, focused on Colombia and businesses that process data there.

PART THREE
Privacy and Cybersecurity

Data is the pollution problem of the information age, and protecting privacy is the environmental challenge.

—Bruce Schneier, *Data and Goliath: The Hidden Battles to Collect Your Data and Control Your World*

CHAPTER 10

Introduction to Cybersecurity

Passwords are like underwear: make them personal, make them exotic, and change them on a regular basis.
—Overheard at SecureWorld Atlanta

Passwords like underwear? Were it only that simple!

If that advice were all we needed, there'd be no need for trillions of dollars in cybersecurity spending, there'd be no ongoing threats, miscry, and sleepless nights fighting hackers—there'd be no need for a book like this at all!

And yet here we are.

Still, it's not that passwords are not important—they are. What's also important is that we start this section with a smile. After all, you just went through a lot. You plowed through privacy, learned more than you probably wanted to learn, and then—then, you had to be dragged through the regulations section. Talk about adding insult to injury.

But you made it, and you're ready to start integrating all the things you learned in the previous two sections and apply them to a privacy and cybersecurity program. (Who's better than you? Nobody, that's who.)

To help lay down our program's groundwork, we will divide the topics into two sections. First, we'll address cybersecurity, pure and proper. Then, we'll layer in privacy.

So how are we going to go about this, you ask? Very carefully! Privacy and cybersecurity program development is not for the faint of heart. I should know, I wrote the book on it: *Cybersecurity Program Development for Business:*

The Essential Planning Guide was published by the nice folks at Wiley in 2018. And, like the title suggests, it will be our essential planning guide for our work here, and I'll be quoting from my earlier work extensively.

The difference between the two books is that the first one was a business-first cybersecurity program development guide, versus this one, which is a privacy-first cybersecurity program development guide. Yes, we will use the first book extensively—at the end of the day, cybersecurity program development's core is the same: Assets are assets, controls are controls, threats are threats, incidents are incidents, and so on—but with a significant twist: Privacy. Its effect, as you will see, will be mostly felt during asset discovery.

As with anything worth building, we'll start with a foundation. Our foundation will be the establishment of a common language, terminology, definitions, even a sprinkle of history. We have done so with privacy in the first part of the book. In this part, we'll need to do the same with information technology and cybersecurity terms. We need to create a "tech" primer, the go-to reference as we take the next steps of building our program together.

First, a question? How well do you speak "Tech"? (With an accent? That's okay, you should hear mine!) Still, we'll need to master a few key phrases so we can converse.

How much do you need to know for us to have an intelligent conversation about privacy? How much do you need to know about regulations affecting your business before you run screaming to your lawyer? The first two sections took care of these two questions.

In the following excerpt from my first book, we'll ask the same question about tech.

Everything You Always Wanted to Know About Tech (But Were Afraid to Ask Your Kids)

How much do you need to know about information technology (IT) and cybersecurity so that we can have an intelligent conversation about your tech environment, your business data, your personal information, potential threats, and your options to address those threats?

The answer is surprisingly fluid, as it is with any fast-changing field: How much do you need to know about medicine to have a meaningful conversation with your doctor about your health? How much do you need to know about law to understand and engage with your attorney? How much do you need to know about cars to talk to your mechanic?

It's a tricky question with no easy answers, and to some degree, it involves lots of individual choice. Some people dive deep into research before consulting with a medical expert (such as "Google Medical School graduates"). Others shy away from it entirely, depending on the expert advice of professionals. But no matter where on the spectrum you find yourself, at least everyone around the table should speak a common language. For example, you may not know precisely how your engine works, but you know what an engine is.

Not so much with technology. The minute we start talking tech, eyes glaze over, mouths yawn, and palms sweat. For some reason, we forget we share a common language—and we need to fix that.

Of course, that is more easily said than done, especially when it comes to computers. Still, the success of this book's message rests in its ability to reach you, be understandable, and actionable. We definitely need to be able to communicate at some level. To do this, I have chosen to abuse metaphors, go back to basics as needed, keep everything as simple as possible, use short case studies to illustrate examples, and live by Mark Twain's adage, *Humor is the good-natured side of a truth*.

Our goal is a simple one: When done with this section, I'd like you to have the same tech facility you have when talking about your car. I am not expecting you to be a mechanic, but I am hoping that you'll get to know a bit about its history, the location of the engine, what the steering wheel does, how to start it, and how to change the occasional flat tire.

It will also be good if you get to learn to drive the thing without killing anyone!

In the Beginning[1]...

There was darkness. And void. It was probably pretty cold, too. Then, the lights came on, rocks started spinning in the heavens, and before you know it, fish were walking on land, and all creatures big and small were living in glorious, albeit analog, bliss.

Shortly thereafter, an English mathematician by the name of Charles Babbage came up with something he called the Difference Engine, now credited as the first computer. Three years later, it was hacked by Ada Lovelace

---

[1]An extraordinarily brief history of computers, networks, the Internet, and everything, creatively pilfered from *The Internet: A Historical Encyclopedia—Chronology* by Chris Moschovitis, Hilary Poole, Erica Pearson, Tami Schuler, and Theresa Senft. ABC-CLIO, 2005.

when in 1843 she published "Sketch of the Analytical Engine," officially firing the starting gun and setting the world racing down the information highway.

Moving right along, past the invention of the telegraph, the telephone, and the radio, almost a hundred years after Ms. Lovelace, Alan Turing, another Brit, published a paper titled "On Computable Numbers," detailing the design of a digital computer.

It didn't take long for the rest of the world to get into the game. In 1938, Konrad Zuse built the first electromechanical binary computers, the Z1 and—of course—the Z2. A year later, John Atanasoff completed the first entirely electronic binary computer. World War II drove the development of electronic deciphering devices of which the German Enigma and the British Colossus are the best known.

The public didn't get to see a computer until 1944, when IBM constructed a room-sized machine, the sexily named Automatic Sequence Controlled Calculator, at Harvard University (it was nicknamed Mark I by Harvard engineers). Not to be left behind, in 1946 the University of Pennsylvania inaugurated ENIAC, which weighed over 30 tons with its 17,000-plus vacuum tubes.

Things were going splendidly up until 1947, when a dead moth was found short-circuiting the vacuum tubes of a Mark II computer, giving rise to the term bug, usually preceded by several expletives.

The same year, John Bardeen, Walter Brattain, and William Shockley, working at Bell Labs, invented the first transistor. The rest, as they say, is history: In the blink of an eye, we went from massive mainframe computers to personal computers, tablets, smart phones, wearables, and even quantum computers. As of this writing, there is even experimental work of storing terabytes' worth of data in biocomputers that use the DNA helix for memory. So much for digital devices!

Paralleling the development of all these computers is the development of the networks that connected them. It started when the United States, quite annoyed by the incessant blip-blip-blip of Sputnik, formed the Advance Research Projects Agency (ARPA) in 1958. ARPA's head of its command-and-control division, J.C.R. Licklider, sent a memo to his colleagues boldly asserting that the time was right for a network of interconnected computers. He was right!

Several geniuses later (Leonard Kleinrock, Robert Taylor, Paul Baran, Ted Nelson, and more) and ARPANET was born. From then on, everything is a blur. Between 1969 and 1990, we had NET-mania: ARPANET, ALOHANET, TELENET, USENET, and—yes—FIDONET, to name a few. At some point, all these NETS were talking to one another, and everyone agreed to call the collection of all these connected networks, computers, and devices INTERNET and get it over with.

In between all that, Ray Tomlinson invented email, and soon he received one from a Nigerian prince asking for money. Skipping past some incredible advances in computer science with even more funky acronyms (UNIX, ETHERNET, TCP/IP, RSA, DNS, PING, and so, so, much more), we finally arrive on the glorious year of 1990, when Tim Berners-Lee and Robert Cailliau first use the phrase "World Wide Web" as the name of a hypertext system that they had just developed, filling the world with links, most of which you should avoid clicking on.

And here we are!

Key Definitions

We have a big advantage in our vocabulary-building exercise in that, unless you've been living under a rock, you already know most of the terms you need. This, therefore, should help clarify the terms as opposed to introduce them.

- **Hardware:** Any physical device that can store, process, or transmit data in digital form. Examples include everything from supercomputers to personal computers, laptops, tablets, cellphones, wearables, switches, routers, and digital appliances of every imaginable (and some unimaginable!) kind. Going forward, and as a matter of convenience, I will be using the term digital device as synonymous with hardware.

- **Software:** In its broadest definition, software is a set of instructions that guide hardware in performing a task. Nothing happens without software. Think car and driver. You may be familiar with the distinction between the operating system (OS) of a computer or phone and its applications (or apps), but while they are indeed different, both are software; they just do different things. The OS is the software that controls the use of the actual hardware, while the applications make requests of the operating system to have the hardware perform specific tasks.

- **Network:** In this context, a network is a collection of connected (again, most often digital) devices. You can have a network of computers—such as the one in your office that enables you to send a document to your office printer—and you can also have a network of networks—such as your point-of-sale terminal network that connects to a credit-card authorization network. Whatever its size, the point of a network is to enable communications. Networked devices can share data and software, leveraging their connection to increase processing power. The Internet is a network of networks. In fact, it is the network of networks—you might think of the Internet as one giant ocean, but in fact it's more like a huge number of interconnected streams, rivers, and lakes. And like Tolkien's "one ring," the Internet is there connecting them all!

- **Digital Services:** Simply put, a service delivers value to a customer through action (a human doing a task for the customer) as opposed to manufacturing (producing a product). Similarly, for digital services: A collection of hardware and software, networked or not, combines to deliver value. For example, a digital service can be something as simple as digital storage. Other digital services include access to processing power or to a particular application.

- **Hosting:** Be it a business (such as hosting a website) or a service (hosting storage), the term hosting means the capacity to deliver digital services located off-premises (remote) to the consumer. There are many nuances to the term (for example, near hosting, far hosting, distributed hosting), but the easiest way to think of it is that the computers are located in someone else's office—that office hosts the computers on your and others' behalf. That other firm runs and maintains them, pays the electric bills, and so on—while you get to use the computers by accessing them remotely.

- **Cloud:** Or cloud computing, is the delivery of hosted digital services, on demand, over a network, and commonly over the Internet. If these services are being delivered through private and proprietary means, then the term used is private cloud. If the network is the Internet, then it's called public cloud. If we combine them, we refer to it as a hybrid cloud. Terms like "Software as a Service" (SaaS) and "Infrastructure as a Service" (IaaS) are now used to differentiate between cloud-delivered application services and hardware services.

The "as a service" tag is getting appended to more and more digital services these days, for example, Architecture as a Service (AaaS), Platform as a Service (PaaS), and Everything as a Service (XaaS). The main advantage of cloud computing is its scalability, redundancy, reliability, pricing, and on-demand availability. The main disadvantages are that all of these "as a service" are nothing more than "hosted subscriptions," rather than items you own. "As a service" is kind of like renting an apartment in a location you can't always control, with co-tenancy issues (you moved from your apartment to one with roommates), conflicts of interest (the renter has different priorities from the landlord), and potential problems with accessibility (no Internet access means no cloud access).

- **Digital Ecosystem, Digital Realm, Digital World, Cyberworld, and the like:** The collection of all of these definitions (hardware, software, networks, services, etc.) also sounds really smart and cool when you use it in a bar.

That's it. That's more than enough for a technology primer. Next up: A cybersecurity primer.

CHAPTER 11

A Cybersecurity Primer

It takes 20 years to build a reputation and a few minutes of cyber-incident to ruin it.

—Stéphane Nappo, global chief information security officer, Société Générale International Banking

This chapter will be our core resource for cybersecurity program development. Remember, we'll layer privacy in later. You need to know the cybersecurity fundamentals first.

The material below, which is adapted from my first book, is stripped down to the essentials, the "need to know" stuff. You can refer to it again and again to refresh your understanding, look up a term, and review essential principles.

Think of this chapter as the essential ingredient for what will eventually become our privacy and cybersecurity program. In Part 1, you got intimate with the first ingredient: privacy! This, here and now, is the cybersecurity ingredient.

Cybersecurity Defined

This is my definition of cybersecurity; it is the same one I used in the first book, and it remains unchanged:

> Cybersecurity is the ongoing application of best practices intended to ensure and preserve confidentiality, integrity, and availability of digital information as well as the safety of people and environments.

There are other definitions out there, most with more complexity. But I—and I'd hazard most businesspeople—needed something different: a simple, meaningful definition we can pin to our monitors, consult frequently, and easily understand.

This definition includes the dynamic nature of the field (it's ongoing) and the four best-practice pillars: confidentiality, integrity, availability, and safety.

The pillars of cybersecurity used to be a triad: confidentiality, integrity, and availability. Safety is the newest member of the roster, making it a lovely quartet, and introduced to address everyday-life threats posed by the Internet of Things (IoT).

The Meaning of Security

The word security is at the heart of cybersecurity, so let's take a moment to break it down. Security is a practice dealing with all aspects of prevention, protection, and remediation from any type of harm to an asset. The bulletproof glass in front of the Mona Lisa is security.

Information security is also a practice, one that aims to protect any type of information assets. The fireproof safe where you keep your will is a form of information security.

Now, cybersecurity is a subset of information security, focusing specifically on protecting digital information assets in their ecosystem.

Confidentiality

We addressed confidentiality early in Part 1, on privacy. There, for our purposes, we equated confidentiality with secrecy and examined the question of who, exactly, gets to define what is secret (aka confidential), and arrived at a confidentiality scale that we will use in our work:

Top Secret:	Board of directors' eyes only
Secret:	Board and executive committee's eyes only
Confidential:	Board, executives, and management team's eyes only
Public:	Everyone, and the horse they rode in on

Table 11.1 Privacy vs. Confidentiality

Privacy is...	Confidentiality is...
a right of people	a property of data, any data, not just PII
a right to control access across a person's physical, decisional, informational, and dispositional dimensions	an agreement on the rating of data
a right protected by law around the world	an attribute of data that can be regulated

Feel free to go back and review the "Confidentiality vs. Privacy" discussion in Chapter 2 again, but for our purposes here, we need only remember the "Privacy is ... " vs. "Confidentiality is ... " as outlined in Table 11.1.

Integrity

Integrity, our next term, is an easier topic to get your head around than confidentiality.

If you ask an accountant to define integrity, she may refer you to the American Institute of Certified Public Accountants 2013 publication titled "Information Integrity," which sports the following definition:

> Information integrity is defined as the representational faithfulness of the information to the underlying subject of that information and the fitness of the information for its intended use.

This is painstakingly accurate and also why I don't ask my favorite accountants to define things for me. I have synthesized instead the following definition of integrity in the cybersecurity context:

> Integrity is the set of practices and tools (controls) designed to protect, maintain, and ensure both the accuracy and completeness of data over its entire life cycle.

In short, you want to have a way to make sure that the numbers in your Excel spreadsheet don't change on their own. If you are wiring $5,000, you don't want it to morph into $50,000 without your approval. You want to be assured that the payroll is correct, and that your love letter addressed to Mary doesn't suddenly start with "Dear Maria." That would be a serious integrity problem. Trust me. I know what I am talking about!

How do you achieve integrity? You do it by implementing digital signatures, write-once-read-many logging mechanisms, and hashing. These conversations tend to be a bit too technical, so suffice to say that you need to know about them enough to understand your cybersecurity expert's explanation and recommendation for your specific requirements.

Availability

Availability, pillar number 3, is the set of practices and tools designed to ensure timely access to data. If your computer is down, availability is compromised. If your Internet connection is moving at a snail's pace, availability is compromised.

How do you ensure availability? In one word? Backup. In two words? Redundancy and backup.

Safety

Finally, term number 4: safety. It is the newest pillar in cybersecurity but one whose impact is potentially the most critical. This is where cybersecurity incidents could result in injuries, environmental disasters, and even loss of life.

You may be a user of a connected medical device, potentially putting you at mortal risk if that device is hacked. Or you may be in a connected car, plane, or train. Or you may be in charge of a business that is responsible for water purification for thousands of people or of a utility that millions of people rely on for life-sustaining services such as electricity.

The concept of safety steers the cybersecurity conversation away from the purely technical to more of a people-centric approach. Therefore, as you approach your own cybersecurity program development, keep this last pillar at the forefront of your thinking. Ask yourself how your cybersecurity decisions go beyond information security and potentially involve the prevention of physical harm to human beings or the environment.

Measuring Cybersecurity's Success

Here's a key question: How do you measure cybersecurity's success?

Ask yourself: How do you measure *any* security effort's success? By the absence of impact.

If you have a house that keeps getting broken into and you install an alarm system and the break-ins stop, ta-da! Success. No more break-ins.

If you're riding in your bulletproof limo and you're peppered by bullets? No problem! You keep on trekking. (I might advise that you reconsider your life choices, but that's a different matter.)

Success in cybersecurity, therefore, will be the absence of problems on confidentiality, integrity, and availability of digital information no matter where it is (stationary/stored, traveling/transmitted, or processed).

What about safety, you ask? Same metric. We want to look at the absence of problems on the safety of any assets governed or affected by digital information. This is, by the way, one of the arguments used against including safety as a fourth cybersecurity pillar: ensuring zero effect on confidentiality. Integrity and availability imply—some argue—that you already have safety. I do see their point. Personally? I feel safer in the redundancy of including it!

It's important to note that absence of problems does not mean that the effect of your cybersecurity efforts can't be quantified. There are tools that will quantify the number of attacks your business systems are currently enduring, likely many without your knowledge. That's right, you may already be experiencing digital break-ins even if you are not aware of them. Establishing these baselines will be a key step, and we will discuss cybersecurity success metrics in more detail later.

Ensuring and Preserving

Remember our definition? Cybersecurity is the ongoing application of best practices intended to ensure and preserve confidentiality, integrity, and availability of digital information as well as the safety of people and environments.

Let's focus on ensure and preserve for a moment. How does one go about it, exactly? This question has engaged scholars, scientists, legislators, and citizens the world over for many years. The results of their hard work are expressed in the form of standards.

In the most abstract sense, a standard is a set of properties that something must meet to be considered appropriate to its function. This something can be a product or a service or even a material. For example, people know that 24-karat gold is 100 percent pure because they have accepted that standard of purity. Similarly, people may be familiar with the International Standards Organization (ISO) 9001 quality management standard, the Institute of Electrical and Electronics Engineers (IEE) 802.3 Ethernet standard, or the ever so popular American National Standards Institute (ANSI) Z315.1-2012 Tricycle Safety Requirements standard.

Now, get ready for another dizzying assault of acronyms that you must memorize fully. There will be a quiz!

When it comes to cybersecurity the main standards that apply are (alphabetically):

1. The European Telecommunications Standards Institute (ETSI) TR 103 family of standards;
2. The IASME standards for small and medium-sized enterprises (IASME stands for Information Assurance for Small and Medium-sized Enterprises);
3. The Information Security Forum (ISF) Standard of Good Practice (SoGP);
4. The International Society for Automation (ISA) ISA62443 standards for industrial automation and control systems;
5. The Internet Engineering Task Force (IETF) via their Request for Comments (RFC) 2196 memorandum;
6. The Information Systems Audit and Control Association, now known only as ISACA, through their COBIT framework and Cybersecurity Nexus (CSX) resources;
7. The Institute for Security and Open Methodologies (ISECOM) with their Open Source Security Testing Methodology Manual (OSSTMM) and the Open Source Cybersecurity Playbook;
8. The ISO 27000 family of standards (ISO 27000–ISO27999);
9. The National Institute of Standards and Technology (NIST) Cybersecurity Framework (CSF); and
10. The North American Electric Reliability Corporation (NERC), which via its Critical Infrastructure Protection (CIP) family of standards addresses electric systems and network security.

Believe it or not, this list is far from complete, and I will bet you several copies of this book that there are at least a dozen more international standards organizations that are going to send me nasty letters for my obvious and glaring omission herein for which I sincerely apologize. My bad!

Now, please don't get me wrong. This whole book lives and dies on the work of the thousands of dedicated experts who've toiled in endless committee meetings and real-life environments to produce this extensive body of knowledge.

I cannot be clearer on this: Without their continuing and never-ending dedication, skills, expertise, and hard work, we would all be in the dark, not even knowing where to start addressing privacy or cybersecurity. I am eternally grateful to their work and will acknowledge them in every opportunity I get. They are the true visionaries in cybersecurity, the ones we all learn from and are guided by, including the advice in this book.

To give you a sense of the knowledge scope involved in cybersecurity alone and the corresponding depth of expertise required, consider the complex domain map created by Mr. Henry Jiang (Figure 11.1), and then layer the concept of privacy on top of that. Enough said!

Why is all this important? Because meaningful advice must be grounded on solid research and hard science. Because no one person can possibly master a subject as deep and complex as cybersecurity, let alone information security and privacy. And because we must check our own interpretation of what's right and filter our own opinions and experiences through the lens of proven, peer-reviewed work.

This book draws from all these standards. It is my interpretation and translation of their advice into what I consider appropriate for the current business climate and threat landscape.

My personal favorite, and most prominently influencing this book, is number 9 in my alphabetical list: the NIST CSF. I feel that NIST, despite being US-based, has truly managed to incorporate a universal approach to their framework. They make this available to everyone for free on their website https://www.nist.gov/cyberframework. Moreover, I believe that the NIST CSF is truly extensible, adaptable, and easily mapped with many governance frameworks, an excellent example of which is the ISACA COBIT to NIST mapping (a must-read for all you framework buffs!).

But wait. There's more!

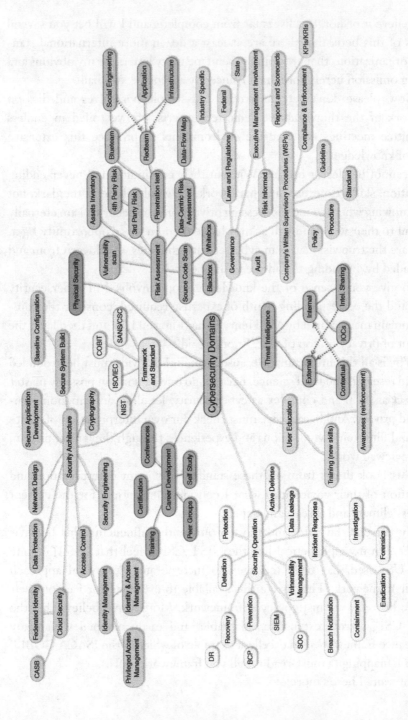

Figure 11.1 Cybersecurity Domain Map
(Source: Henry Jiang, The Map of Cybersecurity Domains. LinkedIn © 2017, Henry Jiang.)

In January 2020, NIST published version one of the NIST Privacy Framework. (What could possibly be better? Not much!) As the name suggests, this document integrates, and is a natural extension of, the NIST Cybersecurity Framework. It can be found, always for free, at: https://www.nist.gov/privacy-framework/privacy-framework. Needless to say: yes, you should read it cover-to-cover! We'll be referring to it extensively in this book.

Acronyms aside, what do all these standards tell us about ensuring and preserving confidentiality, integrity, and availability of digital information as well as the safety of people and environments?

Each standard has its own spin on this. My favorite, NIST CSF, does so by recommending five key functions: identify, protect, detect, respond, and recover. I trust you'll immediately notice something missing?

Think about it while we review the five functions:

1. The **identify** function is where you develop an understanding of what your risks are, what your assets are, and what your capabilities are.
2. **Protect** is your set of plans and actions that put in place the right controls (remember: controls do stuff) to protect the assets.
3. **Detect** is the set of plans and actions that you will use to identify, classify, and so on, an attack against your assets.
4. **Respond** is the set of activities that you engage in response to an attack.
5. Finally, **recover** refers to whatever plans or protocols you have in place to bring things back to normal after an attack.

Before going on to discuss these functions a bit more, and since we're dealing with NIST as it is, I thought I'd give you a quick glimpse of how the NIST Privacy Framework views the corresponding functions.

In NIST PF, we have:

1. **Identify—P:** Like in NIST CSF, this is where you develop the organizational know-how to manage privacy risk that comes from data processing. You'll look at how and where the data processing takes place, you'll need to understand the privacy impact of the individual's whose data you process, and you'll perform privacy risk assessments to gauge and prioritize privacy risk.
2. **Govern—P:** This is where you put in place the governing structure that will help you manage privacy risk on an ongoing basis.

3. **Control—P:** Is where you create and put in place the appropriate privacy controls (and just like in NIST CSF: Controls must "do stuff"!) that will allow for data processing to go on while managing privacy risks.
4. **Communicate—P:** This is where you establish the right communications protocols across the company that allow for everyone in the organization to know how data is being processed and how to manage the associated risk properly.
5. **Protect—P:** This is where you integrate data processing and cybersecurity. You want to make sure that wherever data processing is taking place the necessary cybersecurity safeguards are in place.

We'll be discussing these at length in the chapters that follow; for now, consider this a sneak preview! Now, back to our original programing: The NIST CSF functions.

Each one of these CSF core functions needs to be looked at, and each one will be different from individual to individual and business to business. Believe it or not, experts agree a good cybersecurity program should have tremendous freedom and latitude in approach. You have to do what is right in your world without imposing some monolithic, one-size-fits-all solution.

Now, did you notice anything missing from the five functions: identify, protect, detect, respond, and recover?

The term *retaliate* (or, as per my vindictive editor: *revenge!*) might come to mind. It's a thought. It's also a highly illegal, so we'll just leave it at that and move on.

What about *prevent*? Isn't that something you would hope is a function of a good cybersecurity program?

It depends. First of all, there are those who would argue that prevention is a fool's errand. How do you prevent a nation-state from launching a cyberattack? How do you prevent a cybercriminal from targeting a financial institution or you, personally?

In essence, how do you prevent crime? Okay, if prevent is unattainable, how about deter?

These are questions that criminologists have studied for more than a hundred years. The answers are complex and vary by region and culture and even by circumstance. How do we even begin to incorporate prevention or deterrence in the new cyber front? Some wonder if it is best to focus on what we *can* do, rather than waste time on prevention.

I disagree with this view. I believe that there are meaningful steps that we can take to both prevent and deter cybercrime.

In early 2017, I wrote an editorial titled "Clear and Present Danger." It presented my thinking on prevention at the nation-state level. Its main point was:

> We need a concentrated effort in this new front for the survival of humanity. We need our leaders to be educated and alert of the danger this poses. We need our people to be sensitized to the danger of cyberattacks, think "duck and cover" for the cyber age. We need our allies to reinvigorate their frameworks for resolving conflicts peacefully to include cyberwarfare. A cyberattack to one country should be considered an attack to us all, with the commensurate and immediate response. And we need our international organizations to recognize the danger of cyber actor proliferation and take immediate and decisive action.

My argument should be obvious: Just as alliances and treaties help prevent war, there should be new alliances and new treaties to prevent a cyberwar.

These are steps that we can take to prevent cyberwarfare. Certainly that's true at the nation-state level. But what about closer to home? Can we prevent or deter cyberattacks against businesses or individuals? I believe we can.

The right legal and technical frameworks can deter cybercriminals from attempting an attack. They attack us because that's where our money is. Make it hard enough to get at the money and some attacks can be deterred before they even occur.

How do you do this? You start by deploying the best preventative control ever devised: education! Endless studies prove that cybersecurity awareness training is the most effective preventative control deployed in any organization. Certain industries that follow a rigorous, engaging, and interactive cybersecurity awareness training program have reported attack reductions in excess of 40 percent. If that's not deterrence, I don't know what is.

Thus, we should add deter in front of identify, protect, detect, respond, and recover. Deterrence is a critical function of any cybersecurity program and an integral part of our responsibility to any organization we're charged to protect. It also serves as a constant reminder that cybersecurity is people-centric, not technology-centric. It is people who make a cybersecurity program a success, and it is the same people who, left in the dark, can be the weakest security link.

Deterrence is not a question of education alone. It is also built on reducing what's called your attack surface. As part of the deter function you need to take a close look at your business. What you do, who are your partners, what are the threats, and how have they changed over time? There may be things that you can do to further deter cybercriminals from targeting your organization by changing certain things about the business itself. A slight change in workflow may make it not worth the trouble for someone trying to breach your data.

For example, a client of mine who is an immigration attorney used to accept scans of sensitive documents by email and, worse, upload the documents to his website unencrypted. A simple change—moving this workflow to a secure, encrypted provider—reduced his attack threat significantly. Now, instead of having to hack a simple website, the potential attacker would have to breach a Fort Knox–like level of security made affordable through cloud services. The same type of simple solution may work for your company. Just shifting from an unsecured handshake with a partner to a secure one is not only prudent, but it may prove to be a significant deterrent to an attacker.

Establishing a cybersecurity culture across the company has multiple deterrence benefits. Not only does the ongoing awareness make for better and safer employees, but the same employees can contribute their thoughts and ideas on how to reduce your attack surface and, most importantly, they are sensitized to both external and internal threats. Now, they know that if an employee is snooping around the network and copying files onto USB drives, they may constitute a real cybersecurity threat to the business, and they can raise the alarm accordingly. This, in itself, is a deterrent to a potential insider threat from manifesting itself. In short, a cyber-aware employee can be your best cybersecurity control yet!

Speaking of which, it is time that we take a deeper dive into what these controls are all about.

Cybersecurity Controls and Defense in Depth

Now that we have our six functions—deter, identify, protect, detect, respond, and recover—the next obvious question is, where do we go from here?

First you develop a strategy that's right for you. What does this look like? It depends on your business. As you would expect, cybersecurity strategy will vary greatly from business to business, just as marketing strategies or daily operations vary from firm to firm. No two companies are exactly alike, even within the same industry. What is right for one law firm may be too much for another. One may be dealing with intellectual property (IP), trademarks, and patent law, versus another that may focus on criminal law, and a third on tax and estate law. All want to be secure, of course, but the priorities and data life cycles can be very different.

You'll recall that controls are actions that mitigate risk. They, generally speaking, will prevent, detect, correct, or compensate against risk. More specifically:

- **Preventative controls** are designed to prevent the attack from reaching the asset in the first place. A nondigital preventive control might be a pair of big burly guys, armed to the teeth, who physically guard your assets. Digital preventive controls include, as we already discussed, cybersecurity awareness training as well as more technical controls such as firewalls and intrusion prevention systems (IPS, designed to both detect and thwart an attack).
- **Detective controls** are designed to identify that an attack is occurring, including what kind of an attack, where it came from, what it used, and, if you're lucky, who may be behind it. For example, motion detectors that set off sirens waking up the aforementioned big burly guys and send them to go chase the intruder are detective controls. These days, these motion detectors can take the form of sophisticated cameras, detecting motion plus capturing images and sounds. Digital detective controls include antivirus and antimalware systems, as well as intrusion detection systems (IDS, designed to detect abnormal patterns in networks or systems and raise the alarm).
- **Corrective controls** are designed to minimize the damage from an attack. Examples include restoring from backup, patching the systems

with the latest security fixes, upgrading to the latest version of applications and operating systems, and the like.

- **Compensating controls** are designed to compensate for the failure or absence of other controls and mitigate the damage from an attack. Examples include having a hot failover site (a geographically separate site that mirrors your environment, available the instant you need it), isolating critical systems from the Internet (aka air-gapping), and, in general, backup and disaster recovery plans that can keep the lights on while everyone else is in the dark.

Now we can talk strategy!

Defense in Depth

The best way to use all these controls is by layering them across systems in a way that achieves what is called defense in depth. This has the effect of putting multiple and diverse barriers (controls) between the attacker and the asset.

This strategy looks different from case to case but has proven to be the best way to protect yourself and your assets. Think moats, slippery walls, hot boiling oil, tar, arrows, secret tunnels, and all the fun, creative ways people used to protect their castles and their lives. Now translate those to the electronic realm, and you've got the defense-in-depth concept down pat.

We'll spend more time with defense in depth in subsequent chapters. For now, you understand the key concept behind it, as well as its main goal:

Protect the organization from cyber risk.

The Threats

Just because you're paranoid doesn't mean they aren't after you.
—Joseph Heller, *Catch-22*

We have just done a high-level walkthrough of the building blocks of a cybersecurity program. All of this, of course, exists in a broader context, usually referred to as the threat context or threat landscape.

Who is out there? What harm are they attempting to cause you and why? As you would expect, threats vary business to business: The threat context for a restaurant is going to be quite different from that of a brokerage firm or a utility company.

It's important to distinguish between a threat (the impending prospect of something bad happening) from an attack (the realization of a threat). Keep in mind that cyberattacks are not accidental—they don't just happen: they are planned. Cyberattacks involve organized efforts by someone(s) to accomplish something particularly wicked with regard to your digital assets. Attackers will be stealthy, they will be persistent, and they will not stop unless they are either successful or busted.

The people behind such cyberattacks are called a lot of things, but this is a family book, so we'll stick to threat agents.

Threat Agents

The European Union Agency for Network and Information Security (ENISA) produces the annual "ENISA Threat Landscape Report." The 2016 report (published in January of 2017 as "ENISA Threat Landscape Report 2016—15 Top Cyber-Threats and Trends") lists the following threat agents. For a good measure, I have added a motive summary (i.e., likely reasons for why are they doing what they're doing). You will want to take a look at this list to see which threat agents are most likely to apply to your business context.

1. **Cybercriminals**
   Motives: "show me the money," plain and simple.
2. **Insiders** (e.g., employees)
   Motives: money and revenge, not necessarily in that order.
3. **Nation-States**
   Motives: cyberwarfare or intellectual property theft, competitive intelligence gathering, and so forth.
4. **Corporations**
   Motives: cyber corporate warfare or intellectual property theft, competitive intelligence gathering, and so forth.
5. **Hacktivists**
   Motives: activism of one sort or another, often but not always altruistically motivated (freedom of speech, fight against injustice, etc.).

6. **Cyber Fighters**
   Motives: nationally motivated "patriots" such as the Yemen and Iranian Cyber Army.
7. **Cyberterrorists**
   Motives: to create fear, chaos. Terrorist by any other name.
8. **Script Kiddies**
   Motives: young people "hacking for the fun of it" and causing havoc, be it intentional or not.

Key Trends Influencing Threat Agents

The preceding threat agents flourish in today's technology environment thanks to a variety of accelerating trends. ENISA has noted these four key trends that influence the activities of threat agents, which still hold true today:

1. **Consumerization of cybercrime:** Just as Lowe's and Home Depot made home renovations more available to the masses, new tools are making cybercrime broadly accessible. There are many do-it-yourself hacking kits available for purchase or even free download. It is also fairly easy to hire a hacker to attack a target. Worse: There are both franchising opportunities and affiliate programs for cybercriminals as well as exciting new commercial avenues such as ransomware-as-a-service whereby you can get your own custom ransomware kit for little money up-front for a percentage of the extorted profits. A financial win-win for everyone involved, unless, of course, you're one of the victims. All this leads to:
2. **Low barriers to entry for technical novices:** If you're motivated, you can start your career as a cybercriminal easily. There are hacker universities in which you can get training, and when you purchase some of the ready-made hacking kits, you can even get expert tech support!
3. **Dark net mystique:** The dark net is now similar to how the Internet was in the 1990s. It is perceived as being used only by dangerous geeks, and normal users are discouraged from peeking in. For that matter, one has to jump through a whole set of technical hoops to gain access, further making the dark net an excellent hideout for cybercriminals.

4. **Low rates of attributions:** It remains practically impossible to arrest cybercriminals. Even after major cyber-events, commercial or espionage related, no meaningful attributions were made and practically no arrests. This makes being a cybercriminal a low-risk/high-reward line of work.

Threats, threat agents, and trends. How do we go from that to hackers? Are hackers the threat agents? And are hackers cybercriminals? Nothing could be further from the truth.

The Nature of Hackers

Back when the Internet was a cyber Wild West, the term *hacker* was no insult—quite the opposite, it was a term of respect. The Internet as we know it was created by people who proudly called themselves hackers because a hacker was anyone skilled at building, exploring, and expanding the capabilities of all sorts of systems.

Nefarious, bad-guy hackers should really be referred to as thieves, vandals, criminals, really-really-really-bad people, and so forth. Unfortunately, the distinction between good hackers and bad hackers never caught on, and these days the term hacker is usually not meant as a compliment. But not all hackers are alike: The differences between them can be night and day, black and white, Jedi versusSith, or your choice of fundamental opposing forces.

Historically speaking, all hackers do have one thing in common: high levels of technical skill. Hackers explore the details of programmable systems and figure out how to stretch their capabilities. This is very important because the skills involved are far from inconsequential. It requires a combination of inborn talent and endless study, competition, and practice. All great hackers, irrespective of which side they are on—night or day, good or evil, black hat or white hat—share these hard-won attributes. You might not be surprised to learn then that many old-school hackers have been recruited (or volunteered) to solve some of the world's most intractable problems such as curing diseases, distributing vaccines, or developing next-generation safe nuclear reactors.

Hackers also, it should be said, tend to have very healthy egos and are usually not above showing off their skills. Knowing a bit about the hacker personality helps set the context for your cybersecurity program and—importantly—how you communicate about it.

For example, it is one thing to consider oneself fit because you go to the gym every day and quite another to consider yourself an Olympic-level athlete. Similarly, it is one thing to work toward protecting your assets from cyberattacks and quite another to try to bait a hacker by boasting of your unbreakable defenses. If you do, you do so at your own peril. Given the character of hackers, it is foolish to underestimate them and even more foolish to challenge them.

Attack Process

Having been introduced to the hacker mentality, we are now ready to discuss the actual process of a cyberattack. How does it unfold, what does it entail, and what can you do about it?

Remember, at its core, a cyberattack represents actions taken by threat agents against your assets. All cyberattacks have certain attributes and will typically follow a general process, a cyberbattle plan of their own.

A cyberattack unfolds through an attack vector. That is the path that the attacker takes to compromise your asset. Although most attack vectors are pointing inward (ingress) toward systems and assets, there are attacks that point outward (egress). Those outward attacks focus on ways to extract data and assets as opposed to gaining access and potentially damaging data.

On the attack vector rides the attack payload. Think of this as a container (e.g., the outside of a bomb) that delivers the exploit (the explosives) that take advantage of one or more vulnerabilities exposing the target to the attacker. There are many types of payloads, all of which are essentially sections of malicious programming code most often wrapped in a layer of innocuous programming code designed to fool your defenses. There is a whole scientific discipline dedicated to analyzing and studying payloads, something far beyond the scope of this book for our purposes, but suffice it to say that payloads can be very complex and very elegant at the same time.

Types of Attacks

There are myriad classifications for cyberattacks. Here are some major vocabulary terms, the ones most commonly used and the ones you'll be hearing in cybersecurity discussions.

- **Advanced persistent threat (APT):** An APT says what it does and does what it says—it's a coordinated, persistent, resilient, adaptive attack against a target. APTs are primarily used to steal data. They can take a long time to research, plan, coordinate, and execute, but when they succeed, they are frequently devastating. You definitely do not want to be on the receiving end of one, and if you are, you had best have a very strong incident response plan in place.

- **Brute force attack:** If there is any elegance in hacking a system, then this method lacks it. A brute force attack, much like a brute, doesn't use any brains, only force—in this case, computing force. So, if I wanted to guess your password with a brute force attack, I would use a very fast computer to try every single combination possible of the number—a task that can take a large amount of time or a startlingly brief amount, depending on the complexity of the password. For example, a 4-digit numerical PIN takes only a few hours to crack by brute force. (If you would like to test your own password or PIN to determine how long it would take for a brute force attack to crack it, go to http://passfault .com, an open web application security project [OWASP] site, and give it a try.)

- **Denial of Service (DoS) attack:** DoS attacks come in two flavors: single-source and distributed. A single-source DoS attack occurs when one computer is used to drown another computer with so many requests that the targeted one can't function, while a distributed DoS (DDoS) attack achieves the same result through many (meaning thousands or millions) of computers. In DDoS attacks, the computers are usually under the coordinated control of a botnet (see "A Brief Cyberglossary of Terms" in the next section), working together to overwhelm a target with requests, rendering the target computer inoperable. Of late, this type of attack has gotten more and more press because instead of using compromised computers as part of the botnet, the hackers have been using any digital device (for example, nanny cameras, thermostats, etc.) that is connected to the Internet. Most of these devices lack even the most rudimentary security, and too many users don't bother changing the default password, further contributing to the ease of compromising these devices and using them as bots.

- **Man-in-the-Middle attack:** In this type of an attack, the hacker intercepts the communication between two systems, replacing it with his own, eventually leading to his gaining control of both systems. For example, a man-in-the-middle attack can be used to gain access to credentials and to then fake normal operations while the attacker compromises the target.
- **Phishing attack:** Phishing and spear phishing are attacks that use social engineering methods. Social engineering in this context is just a fancy word for lying. Hackers convince a victim that the attacker is a trusted entity (friend, established business, institution, or government agency) and trick the victim into giving up their data willingly. The goal of these attacks is to gain your trust so that you divulge sensitive information to the attacker. The degree of sophistication of such attacks vary, from the now-famous Nigerian prince, to emails that appear to be from a bank or the Internal Revenue Service, to extremely sophisticated cons that can trick even the best-prepared and skeptical victim.

A Brief Cyberglossary

This brief cyberglossary includes most major terms in the cybersecurity parlance. This jargon gets hurled about in both the media and inside businesses. Some of the terms overlap. Therefore, it's handy to have a glossary to refer back to. Some terms you've heard about, some you've seen hanging in the post office, and some are likely new and exciting, like rootkit. Keep in mind that this is only a partial list:

- **Adware:** Those can be innocuous and very, annoying at the same time. They are nasty little programs that once on your computer they … show you ads! That is if you're lucky. Because these days adware has been replaced with much nastier wares.
- **Botnet:** A composite name made up from roBOT and NETwork. It is used to describe both the tool (software) and the collection of connected compromised computers that can be used to launch a large-scale cyberattack, typically in the form of denial of service attacks, which we'll explore more further on.
- **Industrial control systems (ICS):** These are the small computers that run inside of large machines. Think of a fan in a factory that will

turn on and off based on something such as temperature. ICSs are often a key vulnerability because they are often based on older technology and may not be easily updated with patches that protect them against attacks. Other terms in this category include SCADA systems (supervisory control and data acquisition distributed control systems) and PLCs (programmable logic controllers). ICSs are typically found in industries such as electric, water and wastewater, oil and natural gas, transportation, chemical, pharmaceutical, pulp and paper, food and beverage, and discrete manufacturing (e.g., automotive, aerospace, and durable goods). SCADA systems are generally used to control far-flung assets using centralized data acquisition and supervisory control. PLCs provide regulatory control.

- **Internet of Things (IoT):** IoT refers to yet another network, this one made up of physical devices that aren't usually thought of as computers—for example, thermostats, appliances, cars, even wearables (devices that you wear as part of your clothing or accessories). These devices' main function is to sense and communicate to a controller that then takes action based on the sensor readings. IoT devices are often vulnerable to attacks because they use simple circuits that are not well defended or secured.
- **Key loggers:** These are a subset of a larger class called spyware that can record everything as you type it and send it off. As you might imagine, they can be quite devastating since you type your passwords, secret documents, and even that secret recipe for grandma's meatloaf. Key loggers continue to evolve, and modern key loggers can trap keystrokes, mouse movement, and screen content. Nasty little bugs.
- **Malware:** This is the general category for software designed to do bad things. A key logger is malware. So is adware. It doesn't sound good to call them badware, so malware it is. You get the picture, and yes, it seems these days there is more malware than goodware.
- **Operational Technology (OT):** OT is synonymous with industrial control systems (ICS), discussed earlier, but is used more narrowly for businesses as opposed to massive infrastructure.
- **Ransomware:** A ransomware attack happens when a hacker locks your computer (typically by encrypting data) and extorts you for money to unlock it. The dark beauty of ransomware is that you can go big (as when hackers took over the computer system of a hospital

in California and demanded thousands of dollars in ransom), or
you can go small and hit thousands of computers asking for a few
hundred bucks from each user. With so many options and so many
vulnerable systems, ransomware has become a big and profitable
business. So much so that on the dark web you can buy a "build your
own ransomware kit" and deploy it to the target of your choice.

- **Rootkit:** A rootkit is a collection of software that, once installed, mod-
ifies the operating system to hide itself and other nasty little bugs that
are within it or will soon be forthcoming. A rootkit is the endgame, the
goal of any sophisticated attack. Once a rootkit is installed, the intruders are set. They can stay as long as they want undetected, compromise
additional systems, exfiltrate or corrupt data, and in general have their
wicked way with your assets.

- **SCADA:** Stands for "supervisory control and data acquisition." Do
you remember an incident in 2010 when the Iranian centrifuges at
their super-secret plant went all crazy and spun themselves to obliv-
ion? That's because a SCADA controller was hacked. So the best way
to understand a SCADA device is by thinking about any of those fancy
industrial controllers that monitor and direct industrial devices, such
as centrifuges, refrigeration systems, or power generators. They monitor them, they process data from them, and directly interact with these
devices to effect a result (such as the opening or closing of a valve, spinning up or down a centrifuge, or cooling or heating a reactor). SCADA
systems are often vulnerable because they generally run on older technologies that are difficult to patch and upgrade.

- **Spyware:** This is the general name of a class of software designed
to—you guessed it!—spy on you. Key loggers, already discussed, are
part of this ever-growing family tree. There are "legal" spywares that
an employer or a parent can deploy on a computer to monitor usage.
I put "legal" in quotes because although you can purchase, install, and
deploy these tools, their use is frequently challenged. For example, if
a company has a bring-your-own-device (BYOD) policy to work, are
they within legal bounds to install spyware on it?

- **Trojan:** This term refers to the infamous Trojan horse that the Greeks
used to take Troy. In case you're not up to speed with your Homer,
after a futile ten-year siege against the city of Troy, the Greek army

pretended to leave, built a huge statue of a wooden horse, hid a team of commandos in its belly, and when the Trojans (thinking the war was over) wheeled the horse in, the Greeks got out of the horse, opened the gates for the waiting army, and burned the place to the ground. Similarly, this class of malware disguises itself as a legitimate application, gains entry, and the rest is history.

- **Viruses:** Viruses are a type of malware that your run-of-the-mill antivirus programs are supposed to catch before they do damage. They mimic biological viruses (hence the name), requiring a host and a trigger (don't click that link!). The problem with computer viruses is much the same as in the biological world: To inoculate against a virus, you must first kill it, rendering it harmless, and then inoculate the host to build antibodies against it. That's why the flu inoculations don't always work: You're being inoculated with last year's virus signature. If this season's virus is similar, you're in luck, but if not, you're in bed wheezing and sneezing. The same goes with your computer. If there is a signature for the incoming virus, then your antivirus application should catch it and stop it. If not, or if you haven't gotten the update, then get yourself a good backup!

- **Vulnerability:** Vulnerabilities are a weakness in an information system, system security procedures, internal controls, or implementation that could be exploited or triggered by a threat source. There are millions of them in hardware, operating systems, and software ready to be exploited by adversaries. What's sad is that a vast number of technical vulnerabilities are known, and technical fixes (patches) exist for them. Unfortunately, in many cases these patches have not been applied, rendering systems open to attack.

- **Worm:** This is a type of computer virus (defined earlier) that is designed to spread over computer networks by making copies of itself without any intervention by its maker.

- **Zero Day:** Zero-day exploits are vulnerabilities in existing systems that are known only to the hacker. For example, let's say there is an undiscovered vulnerability in the new release of your favorite word processor; it's utterly unknown to the product developers and to the users, but it's lurking there nonetheless. This would be called a zero-day vulnerability because it is completely unknown to the world at large;

therefore, it has been exposed for zero days. Once the vulnerability is discovered, the race begins to fix (or patch) it before a hacker can use the vulnerability to damage the system in some way.

And how are zero-day exploits found? Hackers on the prowl for such vulnerabilities discover them and put them up for sale on the dark web. Depending on how serious the vulnerability is, this information can fetch significant amounts. Countries, other hackers, and of course the manufacturers are willing to pay top dollar to be the ones to have the secret. It is a "use once" vulnerability, though. Once revealed, it will be patched by the manufacturer or mitigated with some control or another, and the advantage will be lost.

That's it for our brief glossary of terms. For our purposes in this book, the preceding list should provide you with enough terminology to engage in and understand critical conversations around cybersecurity. There are, of course, many more terms, some quite technical in nature (e.g., buffer overflow, spoofing, cross-site scripting, and SQL injection) that require both security, IT, and development professionals to evaluate and address.

How much do you need to know about these extensive lists of threats and actors?

Remember, I trust you to be able to make the right judgment call on what your risk is. Only you know the specifics of your environment. For example, you are aware if your business is likely to trigger the interest of hacktivists, those actors who might want to harm your system because of their allegiance to a certain cause or ideology. You are best in a position to know if your business relies on machinery using automated controllers (such as ICSs, PLCs, and SCADA systems). You will be the one to evaluate whether your intellectual property is valuable enough to your competitors, such as foreign companies looking for a shortcut, to become the target of a hack.

Now, you're ready to take the next step, and look at a high-level overview of what will be your privacy-by-design cybersecurity program!

CHAPTER 12

Privacy-Centric Cybersecurity Program Overview

> There was this absolutely horrible moment where I realized
> there was absolutely nothing at all that I could do.
>
> —Amy Pascal, former CEO of Sony Pictures

When it comes to designing a cybersecurity program—privacy-first or otherwise—what is the most important thing to know before you take the first step? You need to know where you are right now.

The probability that you're designing a cybersecurity program from scratch should be low. I would certainly hope that you have *something* in place, ideally something robust enough that we can take and mold into a privacy-first cybersecurity program.

Be that as it may, hope alone will not suffice! We'll still need to "do the do" and look at the program (existing or not) anew.

We will start by answering a few rather existential questions:

What's the Point of It All?

For every business there is a vision, a mission, and one or more goals. This may seem trivial, but it is very important to put those down on paper. If it is your business, then you already know them. This will be our starting point.

Vision and Mission Statements

A mission statement is your company's raison d'être. It's as existential as it gets. It tells the world why you exist. A vision statement, on the other hand, is more directional than it is existential. One is who and why we are; the other is what we are.

The website TopNonProfits.com has collected the top vision and mission statements for several nonprofits. I have taken a few and paired them up to show the difference between mission (top) and vision (bottom) statements:

ASPCA

@ Mission: To provide effective means for the prevention of cruelty to animals throughout the United States.
@ Vision: That the United States is a humane community in which all animals are treated with respect and kindness.

Cleveland Clinic

@ Mission: To provide better care of the sick, investigation into their problems, and further education of those who serve.
@ Vision: Striving to be the world's leader in patient experience, clinical outcomes, research, and education.

Creative Commons

@ Mission: Creative Commons develops, supports, and stewards legal and technical infrastructure that maximizes digital creativity, sharing, and innovation.
@ Vision: Our vision is nothing less than realizing the full potential of the Internet—universal access to research and education, full participation in culture—to drive a new era of development, growth, and productivity.

Feeding America

@ Mission: To feed America's hungry through a nation-wide network of member food banks and engage our country in the fight to end hunger.
@ Vision: A hunger-free America.

Smithsonian

@ Mission: The increase and diffusion of knowledge.
@ Vision: Shaping the future by preserving our heritage, discovering new
knowledge, and sharing our resources with the world.

Now, there are those who will argue that mission and vision statements are a waste of time. There is one goal, and one goal only: make money. The end. After all, as one executive director of a national nonprofit told me, "No money? No mission." I agree. There is truth to the "make money" imperative. But is it your—or your company's—true mission? Does it reflect your company's real vision? If so, it is what it is, so write it down!

From our perspective, this is the starting point of establishing what's of value to you. This will be vital later, when we establish the right level of protection for it.

Culture and Strategy

With your mission and vision statements in hand, the next thing you need to understand is your company's culture. To clarify, we're talking about organizational, or corporate, culture. This is not about any ethnic or societal culture (although it may well be influenced by them). This is business. And as such, it has been studied within an inch of its life. I'll spare you the diatribe and focus on David Needle's definition from his *2004 Business in Context: An Introduction to Business and Its Environment*. He writes:

Organizational culture represents the collective values, beliefs, and principles of organizational members and is a product of such factors as history, product, market, technology, strategy, type of employees, management style, and national culture; culture includes the organization's vision, values, norms, systems, symbols, language, assumptions, beliefs, and habits.

What he didn't write—and actually no one did, despite misattribution to Drucker—is: *"Culture will eat strategy for lunch any day of the week,"* or some variant thereof. This statement appears in the literature in various guises (e.g., in Thomas W. Lloyd's 2000 monograph in the form of "Culture beats strategy") but although the source of the idea is mysterious, the wisdom is real.

The bottom line here is this: in a fight between culture and strategy, culture always wins. *Always*. That's why you need to spend some time understanding your corporate culture. Without that understanding, your cybersecurity and risk strategies will fail.

Are you in an entrepreneurial "damn the torpedoes" culture or more a risk-averse environment? Are you in a highly regulated industry? Are you in the armed forces? Whatever the case, you'll need to identify the culture and understand it. There are some things that your culture will allow that others will not. For example, if you try to institute strict authentication and access controls in an entrepreneurial, no-risk-is-too-big environment, you are guaranteed to fail. The staff will not follow suit, they will bypass the controls, and you'll have to deal with a staff revolution (and we know how those end... Chop! Chop!). On the other hand, if you are too lax in an environment that is expecting safety through rigorous controls, you'll be dismissed as irresponsible and too dangerous to work with.

How do you determine culture? Let's say you just walked through the door day one in your job at a new company, and you're somehow charged with reviewing cybersecurity risk and making a recommendation. You don't know anyone yet, and it will take some time for you to assimilate into your new company's culture. What can you do to determine the culture of your new home? Why, you ask, of course! It will take more than asking a couple of people by the water cooler, though. It will take a survey.

As luck would have it, Kim Cameron and Robert Quinn wrote *Diagnosing and Changing Organizational Culture* in 2005 (second edition in 2011), and in it you will find their "Organizational Culture Assessment Instrument"—a short but very useful survey that, when followed, will provide you with a cultural profile for your company. Their survey assesses a company across six dimensions:

1. Organizational dominant characteristics;
2. Organizational leadership;

3. Employee management;
4. Organizational glue;
5. Strategic emphases; and
6. Criteria of success.

Each one of these has four rankings in the spectrum of personal versus controlling, nurturing versus results-minded, teamwork versus conformity, trusting versus policing, humanistic versus efficiency-first, and people-centric versus company success.

Off to See the Wizard

Save your cultural survey results—you will be needing them later. Now you are ready to talk with the people in the IT department. Why the jump to technology first? To be sure, there are many departments, profit centers, and so forth, that you could focus on first, so why IT? Because cybersecurity and IT are inseparable. IT doesn't own cybersecurity (the organization does), but consider this: No information technology? No cybersecurity. It's simple. The word cyber by definition is about information technology. One cannot exist without the other. IT and cybersecurity are twins. Sometimes opposing twins, to be sure, but twins nonetheless.

What happens if there is no IT department in your company? Then you should talk with the vendor who's responsible for supporting IT. What happens if there is no such vendor? Well, figure out if there is anyone charged with IT in the company and ask her. What happens if she doesn't exist?

Let's cut to the chase: Companies come in all sorts of shapes and sizes. Some are totally virtual, whereas others are multinational behemoths. Even those we call virtual have tremendous variation in their use, adoption, and support of technology. You may be in a company in which all technology is provided as a service (remember infrastructure as a service, software as a service, etc.? If not, maybe zip back to the "cloud" definition in the Cybersecurity Primer). Alternatively, the company may be operating under a bring-your-own-device (BYOD) IT model, so you—the individual user—may be responsible for maintaining your own devices. On the opposite side of this spectrum are the IT stormtroopers: a humorless bunch walking about stomping on any electronic device they don't recognize.

The majority of companies are somewhere in between these extremes. They have one or more people in their IT department—whether employee or vendor provided—and they maintain a set of technologies that are hybrid (on premise, cloud, and a mix of company-provided and BYOD) and have some degree of control over what kind of software is running where and doing what. We'll talk about them, and we'll call them the IT department.

What happens with the fringe cases? You'll still need the information; it's just that the way you go about it will differ. In the virtual company case, you'll determine who the vendors are, what services they provide, and so on. Think of them as your virtual IT department. In the stormtroopers case, bring your papers and make an appointment. Besides, if the stormtroopers are in the building, I'd hazard a guess that the company has a formal risk and audit function, and they'll need to be included in all this as well.

No matter what, no matter who, this is an excellent opportunity for you to build a bridge with the IT department, irrespective of structure and delivery. In most cases, you'll be welcomed. It isn't often that non-IT professionals take an interest in what's behind the black door and all those blinking lights. Connect with the IT leadership and get a good understanding of the role of technology in your company.

What Does Organizational IT Typically Look Like?

To begin with, IT in organizations is manifested in more than one way. Many different analysts and research firms have given the phenomenon different names. For example, Gartner Research has coined the term *bimodal IT* to describe a basic, "keep the lights on and trains moving" version of IT that exists beside a "go wild, innovate, and experiment" version of IT.

Then there is *shadow IT*. That's the version of IT that springs up as a result of unanswered (or frustrated) user needs. For example, let's say corporate policy prohibits more than 5 MB email attachments, and to get to the company's file-sharing server, you have to jump through all sorts of hoops. The user, acting out of urgent need or defiance, opens up a Dropbox account and shares the credential with colleagues and clients.

Each one of these modes will have its own cybersecurity considerations, with shadow IT being particularly tricky to support and secure. For example, there are companies whose infrastructure (the stability part) is absolutely critical to operations. Think of a trading system. If the system goes down during trading hours, the company loses business, with potential losses in the millions. Alternatively, there are companies whose infrastructure is not as critical when compared with their ability to deliver an answer quickly. In this case, think software development. A firm could be running on a distributed infrastructure all over the world with little worry about any one component of it being unavailable, and yet it must be able to deliver a necessary fix to an application as fast as possible because, say, there may be lives depending on it, as in the case of a hospital management system.

Going back to your discovery needs, your IT team will be able to provide you with their specific assessment. They can identify their systems, the locations, what's critical, and what's not. They'll supply you with exciting documentation such as network diagrams, systems inventory, application inventory, licensing documentation, and they'll cap it off with the disaster recovery and business continuity plans. Depending on the size of your organization, these assessments will fit in a neat little binder, or the mailroom will drop off a pallet. Either way, you'll be good to go.

The IT department will also give you their views of what's at risk and when they do, take careful notes—especially on the intersection of technology and business operations. This will prove very useful as you move forward with asset valuation, business impact analysis, vulnerability, and risk assessments.

So far you have gathered the following pieces of information:

1. Mission and vision statements;
2. Cultural assessment findings; and
3. IT documentation and assessment.

Now you're ready to understand what's at risk.

What's at Risk?

This is the part where you get to walk around and pose this question: *"How much is this worth to you?"* Remember: We're not doing a privacy risk assessment (yet!).

The *"this"* in *"How much is this worth to you"* is the asset you're interested in protecting, and the only one who can determine its worth is the person who owns it.

Without getting overly complex here—after all, this is only the overview chapter!—the asset owner is the person who, one way or another, is responsible for the asset. For example, the CFO is responsible for the financial assets of the company. What are those? They can range from simple things such as Excel spreadsheets, access to the bank accounts, and the accounting system files all the way to a massive ERP (enterprise resource management) applications. The CFO is the one who is responsible for all of this, and she's the one who can tell you how much these assets are worth to her. By worth I don't really mean monetary value. I mean things such as: How long can she be without those assets, how much data can she afford to lose, and, in cases of loss, how quickly does she need to be back in business?

Where do you start this risk assessment? First, identify your business managers. Each one will typically be responsible for a line of business or a department. Sit down with each one and ask him or her to identify all the things that are absolutely necessary to do their jobs. The list is likely to include multiple assets, both hard (computers, facilities, etc.) and soft (software, workflows, etc.). You should work with each manager in ranking and prioritizing each asset. At the end of these meetings, you will have a very clear idea of each department's assets, and the corresponding effect of each asset's loss.

If you want to get formal about this, you can ask for a department-by-department business impact analysis, and from the results, you can derive both the assets and the business impact of their loss or disruption. But what fun is that? Make it personal and get in there! Roll up your sleeves and work with your colleagues in getting all this done. You'll certainly gain a better understanding of what's going on with the business and make a whole bunch of new friends. (Or enemies, if they don't want to be bothered … But hey! You're the one trying to cover their assets! They'll see the light eventually.)

Okay, you're almost done. You've made tremendous progress in gaining an understanding of your organization, more than most employees, or even some managers, ever do. You should celebrate! Go have a nice lunch. Nothing crazy, though: there is still work to be done. Skip the martinis.

Threat Assessment

So what's left? Well, the next step in the process should be a threat assessment. Now, that can be really intimidating, but it needn't be. Here's why:

Performing a threat assessment requires skill and expertise that you may not have readily available. It requires up-to-date threat intelligence access, and it requires understanding the threat behavior. As an example, consider a house on the top of a large hill. The owner has done all the work up to this point, recognizes the asset at risk (the house), and is getting ready to deploy controls to protect the asset. One of the controls he chooses is a sump pump. Now, sump pumps are wonderful and really, really useful if you're flooded, but the house is at the top of the hill. Is the threat of a flood realistic? Wouldn't it be better to invest in a lightning rod? Don't get me wrong, you may still want the sump pump in case one of the pipes burst, but what's the priority here?

That's exactly why you should not be intimidated by performing a threat assessment: You are armed with common sense, and you are ready to take this on! You also need to remember you're not alone in this. There is a whole community out there watching, analyzing, and sharing all sorts of threat intelligence and best practices. In the United States, the Department of Homeland Security is running the United States Computer Emergency Readiness Team (US-CERT), whose mission is to "strive for a safer, stronger Internet for all Americans by responding to major incidents, analyzing threats, and exchanging critical cybersecurity information with trusted partners around the world." You will find them at: https://www.us-cert.gov, and you'll get all the alerts and tips you need to get a very good feel of what's going out there in cyberspace.

According to a recent ISACA cybersecurity snapshot, the top three threats facing organizations are social engineering, insider threats, and advanced persistent threats. I'll go out on a limb here and predict that these rankings will stay around for a few more years. Could there be new, disruptive technologies that would alter these rankings? Certainly, but consider that both social engineering and insider threats are people-centric, not technology-centric. People will always be both the biggest asset and the biggest threat in cybersecurity.

Finally, of these threats, I would suggest that most organizations would need to seriously consider and address the first two: social engineering and insider threats. The third category, advanced persistent threats (APT), is particularly nasty and typically focuses on big multinationals, governments, physical infrastructure (think power grid, water supply, etc.), and the military. That's not to say that your firm should not consider APT. It always depends on who you are and what you do. Again, I trust that you know best.

Social engineering threats tend to be planned well ahead of time. The attacker harvests information about the target from publicly available sources (social networks, professional networks, corporate websites, public records, even data aggregators) and then uses that information to impersonate and compromise the target. How common are social engineering attacks and how likely are you to be targeted? Extremely and very. And the more public information you have openly available and accessible on the Internet, the easier it gets. If, for example, your corporate website has photos and bios of the executive team, then a hacker already knows who does what at the company, as well as some information about each person's background. If you happen to be working in finance, even better. And if your company is big, indicating a potentially large accounting department, even better yet! Any leftover blanks can easily be filled in with a quick visit to LinkedIn. From there, on to social networks, school alumni associations, and public records. In short order, a solid profile of an executive has been formed, and it can now be used to gain access to processes and workflows controlling money movement, intellectual property, deal secrets, and so forth. In extreme cases, the profile could even turn into personal extortion, turning the executive into an insider threat.

Speaking of which, insider threats are your basic good-people-doing-bad-things threat. Yes, there are bad people doing bad things, too—but hopefully you minimized that risk (remember "deterring"?) by doing your pre-employment due diligence, including a thorough background check.

For our purposes, an insider threat is any employee who attempts to use his or her position of privilege to commit illegal acts. The reasons vary: family emergencies, divorce, unexpected medical bills (the good-people-doing-bad-things part), or thrills, espionage, and kleptomania (the bad-people-doing-bad-things part). These reasons top my list. Bottom line, and whatever their excuse may be, the result is the same: data exfiltration.

Perhaps a fake vendor is created, and invoices are sent to the employee who approves them, or expense reports are fraudulently submitted, or something similar with one goal: money! If it is corporate espionage, then the employee steals data, which she either sells to a competitor or gives away in hopes of a procuring a better position with the competitor. (Obviously, if the employee is not working for a corporation but for a government, we go from corporate espionage to Bond. James Bond. You know the rest.)

Advanced persistent threats are the stuff of migraines. The no-lights, no-sound, pray-for-quick-and-painless-death kind of migraines. The "advanced" part speaks to the incredible sophistication and technical skill involved, from crafting payloads to delivering them, and from finding zero-day vulnerabilities to exploiting them. The "persistent" part speaks to the I-will-not-stop-until-I-succeed commitment of the attacker against the target.

Any which way you look at APTs, they are nasty, painful, and expensive. If you have serious reason to believe that you may be the target of an APT, take this book and walk over to your cybersecurity department and ask them what are they doing about it. If you don't have a cybersecurity department, walk over to the CEO's office and, kindly yet firmly, suggest to her that you need to create one. Yesterday is good.

Have we exhausted the possible threats? Not by a long stretch! There are zero-day threats, end-point threats (computers, tablets, phones being compromised), and Internet of Things (IoT) threats (such as your car deciding to turn off when you're driving at 75 mph). There are operational technology (OT) threats (hacking industrial control systems), threats of new forms of fraud (crowdfrauding, rent-a-hacker, hacktivists, cryptojacking), denial of service threats, and all the other fun stuff we defined in Chapter 11.

As we move forward with our cybersecurity program development, we may need to drill deeper and consider the threat landscape in more detail. But for now, we're ready to continue framing our overview.

At the Club House Turn!

At this point, you have nothing on privacy but plenty on cybersecurity:

1. Mission and vision statements;
2. Cultural assessment findings;
3. IT assessments;
4. Asset valuations;
5. Business impact analyses; and
6. Threat assessments.

Now you need to think about your vulnerabilities, the kind of controls you need to put in place to plug them, your processes, and your people.

Let's start with the vulnerabilities. Every system has them. Every single one. If someone tells you otherwise, he is lying. The goal here is to identify them and apply controls to protect them. Some vulnerabilities you may be able to eliminate altogether. Others, you may have to live with. Those are the ones you need to worry about. And finally, there are the vulnerabilities you don't even know about. Those will keep you up at night, but even for those, there's usually something you can do.

Step one: discovery! We have to uncover those vulnerabilities. There are several ways of doing this, starting with vulnerability and penetration tests. Testing will identify most vulnerabilities and dictate necessary steps to eliminate or remediate them. We'll discuss all this in detail in the chapters that follow, but suffice it to say that when we're done, we'll need to apply a whole set of controls.

At this point in the game, though, having finished with asset valuation, business impact analysis, and threat and vulnerability assessment, you're ready to bring everything together. You are ready to conduct your risk assessment.

A risk assessment is always company-specific; there is no standard risk assessment or template. You have to create it for your own specific environment. Now, I recognize that this assessment soup can get confusing. We have threat assessments, vulnerability assessments, business impacts, risk analysis, risk evaluation, risk registers, and finally, risk assessments!

That's a lot of assessing! What's what here?

Let's recap and make it personal:

- **Threat assessment:** Who's out to get you? Why? How likely is an attack? How bad can it get?
- **Vulnerability assessment:** How easy is it to get you? What's stopping people from doing it? What tools might they use?
- **Risk analysis:** Combine equal parts of threat assessment and vulnerability assessment. Mix, cook, and serve in the form of risk probability over time and potential business impact.
- **Risk register:** A go-to menu of your risks, listing as much information as possible, including risk type (e.g., what, who, why), evaluation date, description, probability, impact, classification (e.g., low, medium, high), response (e.g., accept, insure, run for the hills), and risk owner (who's on the hook for it?). It's fine to go all in when creating your risk

register, but keep in mind that throwing everything and the kitchen sink in a risk register will make it difficult to maintain and update. Think comprehensive, but not overwhelming.

- **Risk evaluation:** Compare your risk analysis to business-specific reality. Deal only with pragmatic, real, and present risk. Avoid paranoid thinking and rabbit holes. To wit: Accept meteor strike as "risk I won't worry about," and sleep easier.
- **Risk assessment:** Using all of the preceding, identify the issues, rank them, and answer what happens if you stick your head in the sand and ignore them. I like my risk assessments to be short and sweet. For each identified risk, think name, rank, and serial number. Rank, of course, is the key here. Other than that, that's it. If I want the details, I can always refer back to the source documents.

Now that we have all this information, clear and prioritized, we can now start thinking about what controls to place where.

Mitigating Risk

Controls, as we discussed earlier, do stuff. You know the drill by now. They are preventative (think STOP signs), detective (think cameras), corrective (think backup), and compensating (think failover sites). Now that you understand both your assets and the threat landscape, you can start making intelligent choices about which controls to apply to protect yourself. The goal to remember is defense in depth. You want your controls laid out in layers. You want the ability to thwart an attacker at all the different stages of an attack, across various systems, and you need controls to mitigate all the vulnerabilities you discovered.

The last factors to consider in developing your cybersecurity program are processes and—again—people. In a sense, we've come full circle: we started with people, and we are ending with people, only this time we're adding a crucial link. Processes. They are absolutely critical in your program's success. Processes are the essence of how business is done. They link assets, connect people, and create value. Some processes cannot be disturbed and must be protected as is. Others have more flexibility and can bend to accommodate controls.

To find out which is which, you'll have to map all key processes in the company. This may not be fun, but it is essential that it be done and done correctly. Your work in this may brush up against bigger issues such as overall information security, not just our favorite subset of cybersecurity. For example, consider a credit card processing workflow. It's not only the systems that need protecting. The whole process—from the moment your client gives you his or her credit card number to the moment that the transaction is complete and filed—must be carefully thought out and appropriately protected. You may discover that you may need a different set of controls, which are not necessarily cybersecurity controls, to protect these mission-critical processes and people.

People, of course, are what this is all about.

People are the ultimate value creators, the true engine of creativity, innovation, and the spirit of your company. They are your biggest asset, and as such your top priority in ensuring their protection.

People can also be your largest liability. They can be a liability if they are not aware of the threats, if they are ill-prepared to deal with the environment, or worse yet, if among them there is a "bad apple" who is intent on compromising everyone else's hard work.

You can apply controls to protect assets and systems, but you cannot control people. That should not be confused. Ever. Interestingly enough, well-trained, sensitized, cybersecurity-aware people are the best way for the company to survive and thrive. That makes them one of your most effective controls, since through their training and awareness they actually do stuff to protect the assets! We will review how to develop the right cybersecurity awareness program in the chapters that follow.

Incident Response Planning

We're almost here! We have managed to get:

1. Mission and vision statements;
2. Cultural assessment findings;
3. IT assessments;
4. Asset valuations;
5. Business impact analyses;
6. Threat assessments;

7. Vulnerability assessments;
8. Risk assessments;
9. Process and workflow maps;
10. Control and defense-in-depth deployments; and
11. Cybersecurity awareness programs.

Other than the corresponding privacy entries, of course, what else is missing?

There used to be a saying that there are two certainties in life: death and taxes. This book is not about either. It's about the third certainty: a cybersecurity incident. What's missing, therefore, is our incident response plan.

Based on your work so far, you have created the necessary foundation on which to build an incident response plan. You have put in place the processes and controls to deter, identify, protect, detect, and recover. You've got one more step to go: respond.

No two incident response plans are alike—The variables alone are overwhelming. For one, you can't define beforehand what type of incident you'll be dealing with. Second, no two businesses are alike, no two systems are alike, and no two workflows are the same. We do payroll one way; you do it another way. We use LINUX; you use Windows. And so on. So how can you create an incident response plan? By preparing for surgery!

Like cybersecurity incidents, no two surgeries are alike. But all surgeries have a checklist to be followed, such as: premedicating the patient against infection (preventative control), having enough blood in place (corrective control), and having imaging and diagnostic equipment ready (detective controls). It's the same with cybersecurity incident response.

You should develop a checklist that you practice, refine, drill, refine some more, test, tweak, and so on. Depending on the size of your company, you may create a red team and a blue team and practice simulated cyberwarfare in which one team attacks while the other defends and recovers. You will develop an arsenal of tools to use throughout the operation—from forensic capabilities to data recovery. You develop communication plans for the company, its clients, the press, vendors, and even the authorities. All of these become part of your incident response plan, a living document that should be constantly reviewed and adjusted as circumstances change.

Now you're done!

You have your response. The board has reviewed your program and approved it. Everything is in place. You can sleep more easily ... until tomorrow, when you have to review the whole thing all over again, making sure that your program remains current and reflects your changing business and the changing world. Cybersecurity program development is not a once-and-done. It's not a date; it's a marriage. And you'll need the commitment and effort to keep it thriving.

For now, let's take stock of where we are and what we have after this whirlwind of a chapter:

1. Mission and vision statements;
2. Cultural assessment findings;
3. IT assessments;
4. Asset valuations;
5. Business impact analyses;
6. Threat assessments;
7. Vulnerability assessments;
8. Risk assessments;
9. Process and workflow maps;
10. Controls and defense-in-depth deployments;
11. Cybersecurity awareness programs; and
12. Incident response plans.

That's a lot of work! For me, it feels like we've been riding a bullet train. Have you ever stared out the window of one of those speeding trains? In the far distance, you can see the countryside, but up close? Everything is a blur. That's pretty much the speed we traveled in this cybersecurity program overview chapter. You should have been left with a sense of landscape, lots of blurry details, and sense of existential emptiness for not having touched on privacy risk at all! Not to worry. It's coming!

We'll get to the details one step at a time, integrate it with our privacy program, and when we're done, we'll discuss the last item, item 13: Privacy and Cybersecurity Program Management.

CHAPTER 13

Privacy by Design Overview

> Freedom and self-determination in the digital world are crucially dependent on keeping sovereignty over our personal information.
>
> —Heiko Maas
> German Minister for Foreign Affairs, 2015

The phrase *privacy by design* means different things to different people. It is essentially a framework to proactively ("by design") integrate privacy principles into the design of software, hardware, networks, and business practices. Yet... questions abound! What does it really mean? Where do we apply it? How do we apply it? For some, privacy by design (PbD) is essentially a religion. For others, it's little more than a bunch of vague suggestions. Yet, all agree that we all need to implement some version of privacy by design everywhere we can, right here, right now.

If privacy by design is a "religion," then it must have a God. By all accounts, that would be Dr. Ann Cavoukian, and her origin story is amazing.

Dr. Cavoukian, an Egyptian-born of Armenian descent, immigrated to Canada in 1958. There, she studied at York University and the University of Toronto, where she received her PhD in psychology. Her stellar career included heading the Research Services Branch for Ontario's Attorney General, serving as the first director of compliance at the Ontario Office of the Information Privacy Commissioner, and ultimately becoming the assistant commissioner in 1990. In 1997 she was appointed as the first woman to be privacy commissioner of Ontario, a position she was reappointed to for an unprecedented three terms, all the way through to 2014.

It was during her tenure there that she created her now-famous "Privacy by Design Framework." In 2010, the framework was unanimously adopted by the International Assembly of Privacy Commissioners and Data Protection Authorities as *the* International Framework for Privacy and Data Protection and translated into no less than 38 languages.

As of 2017, Dr. Cavoukian is the Distinguished Expert in Residence, Privacy by Design Centre of Excellence at Ryerson University, sits on numerous boards, and continues her thought leadership and tireless advocacy on privacy. Also, in 2017 Dr. Cavoukian was retained by Sidewalk Labs (an Alphabet subsidiary, best known for one of their other tiny holdings: Google) to be an advisor to the smart city WATERFRONT Toronto project. But when Sidewalk Labs walked away from their earlier promises with regard to privacy protections, Cavoukian resigned. In her resignation letter she noted, "I imagined us creating a smart city of privacy, as opposed to a smart city of surveillance."

Dr. Cavoukian's seven foundational principles of PbD expand and build on the Fair Information Principles—also known as the FIPs, which we touched upon in our regulation section. As originally presented by her, these principles are:

1. **Proactive not Reactive; Preventative not Remedial**
   The Privacy by Design approach is characterized by proactive rather than reactive measures. It anticipates and prevents privacy invasive events before they happen. PbD does not wait for privacy risks to materialize, nor does it offer remedies for resolving privacy infractions once they have occurred—it aims to prevent them from occurring. In short, Privacy by Design comes before-the-fact, not after.

2. **Privacy as the Default**
   We can all be certain of one thing—the default rules! Privacy by Design seeks to deliver the maximum degree of privacy by ensuring that personal data are automatically protected in any given IT system or business practice. If an individual does nothing, their privacy still remains intact. No action is required on the part of the

individual to protect their privacy—it is built into the system, by default.

3. **Privacy Embedded into Design**

    Privacy by Design is embedded into the design and architecture of IT systems and business practices. It is not bolted on as an add-on, after the fact. The result is that privacy becomes an essential component of the core functionality being delivered. Privacy is integral to the system, without diminishing functionality.

4. **Full Functionality—Positive-Sum, not Zero-Sum**

    Privacy by Design seeks to accommodate all legitimate interests and objectives in a positive-sum "win-win" manner, not through a dated, zero-sum approach, where unnecessary trade-offs are made. Privacy by Design avoids the pretence of false dichotomies, such as privacy vs. security, demonstrating that it is possible, and far more desirable, to have both.

5. **End-to-End Security—Lifecycle Protection**

    Privacy by Design, having been embedded into the system prior to the first element of information being collected, extends securely throughout the entire lifecycle of the data involved—strong security measures are essential to privacy, from start to finish. This ensures that all data are securely retained, and then securely destroyed at the end of the process, in a timely fashion. Thus, Privacy by Design ensures cradle to grave, secure lifecycle management of information, end-to-end.

6. **Visibility and Transparency**

    Privacy by Design seeks to assure all stakeholders that whatever the business practice or technology involved, it is in fact, operating according to the stated promises and objectives, subject to independent verification. Its component parts and operations remain visible and transparent, to both users and providers alike. Remember, trust but verify!

7. **Respect for User Privacy**

    Above all, Privacy by Design requires architects and operators to keep the interests of the individual uppermost by offering such measures as strong privacy defaults, appropriate notice, and empowering user-friendly options. Keep it user-centric!

The criticism around these guidelines centers on the argument that they are vague and cannot easily be applied to systems design. In other words, how can a poor developer ever be expected to understand such complex abstract topics as these privacy principles? It would be so much better if there was a checklist, something that an engineer can follow and be guaranteed that PbD will be in place!

Right! The "We. Are. Engineers. And. We. Need. Checklists!" argument.

I will not dwell on this, other than to note that these principles have been substantively integrated into GDPR, have been recognized as a fundamental and recommended practice by the US Federal Trade Commission, were included in the Privacy, Trust, and Innovation report by Canada's Privacy Commissioner, and were part of the 2014 Mauritius Declaration on the Internet of Things. Clearly, one person's "too vague" is another person's gold standard!

Most recently, in 2018 the European Data Protection Supervisor (EDPS) issued their "Preliminary Opinion on Privacy by Design" in hopes of:

> ... contributing to the successful impact of the new obligation of "data protection by design and by default" as set forth by Article 25 of the General Data Protection Regulation by raising awareness, promoting relevant debate and proposing possible lines for action.

In this opinion, the EDPS made a set of specific recommendations to the European Union institutions, and set forth its own position on privacy by design:

> With this Opinion, the EDPS makes a number of recommendations to EU institutions:
>
> - to ensure strong privacy protection, including privacy by design, in the ePrivacy Regulation.
> - to support privacy in all legal frameworks which influence the design of technology, increasing incentives and substantiating obligations, including appropriate liability rules,

- to foster the roll-out and adoption of privacy by design approaches and PETs in the EU and at the Member States' level through appropriate implementing measures and policy initiatives,
- to ensure competence and resources for research and analysis on privacy engineering and privacy enhancing technologies at EU level, by ENISA or other entities,
- to support the development of new practices and business models through the research and technology development instruments of the EU,
- to support EU and national public administrations to integrate appropriate privacy by design requirements in public procurement,
- to support an inventory and observatory of the "state of the art" of privacy engineering and PETs and their advancement.

The EDPS will:

- continue to promote privacy by design, where appropriate in cooperation with other data protection authorities in the European Data Protection Board (EDPB),
- support coordinated and effective enforcement of Article 25 of the GDPR and related provisions,
- provide guidance to controllers on the appropriate implementation of the principle laid down in the legal base, and
- together with the DPAs of Austria, Ireland and Schleswig-Holstein, award privacy friendly apps in the mobile health domain.

So why do we care? This may all sound like a lot of mumbo-jumbo that systems engineers need to figure out when they develop the latest and greatest applications. We'd be inclined to say, "Not our circus, not our monkey" and move on. I am saving that line for later, though!

But the fact is that the seven privacy principles are not simply intended for systems design. As Dr. Cavoukian wrote:

Privacy by Design advances the view that the future of privacy cannot be assured solely by compliance with regulatory frameworks; rather, privacy assurance must ideally become an organization's default mode of operation.

Initially, deploying Privacy-Enhancing Technologies (PETs) was seen as the solution. Today, we realize that a more substantial approach is required—extending the use of PETs to PETS Plus—taking a positive-sum (full functionality) approach, not zero-sum. That's the "Plus" in PETS Plus: positive-sum, not the either/or of zero-sum (a false dichotomy).

Privacy by Design extends to a "Trilogy" of encompassing applications: 1) IT systems; 2) accountable business practices; and 3) physical design and networked infrastructure.

She also wrote:

There is a growing understanding that innovation, creativity and competitiveness must be approached from a "design-thinking" perspective—namely, a way of viewing the world and overcoming constraints that is at once holistic, interdisciplinary, integrative, innovative, and inspiring.

Privacy, too, must be approached from the same design-thinking perspective. Privacy must be incorporated into networked data systems and technologies, **by default**. Privacy must become integral to organizational priorities, project objectives, design processes, and planning operations. Privacy must be embedded into every standard, protocol and process that touches our lives.

Dr. Cavoukian is right: PbD principles apply to every aspect of a business, be it information systems, applications, networks, or business practices. The whole business ecosystem needs to be rethought, with privacy by design as its foundation.

In our narrow sliver of this business ecosystem, the cybersecurity sliver, we must take our mission of value preservation to a new level: value preservation through a PbD lens. That is now the enhanced role of cybersecurity, just as much as it is the new responsibility of information technologies, human resources, and business strategy. Both value creation (IT et al.) and value preservation (cybersecurity et al.) must be reborn with PbD as an essential element of their DNA.

In my book on cybersecurity program design, I wrote about how the success of a cybersecurity program depends on buy-in from the highest levels of an organization. Without that top-level support, a cybersecurity program is bound to fail. And that was before Privacy (capital "P") was the main consideration! Back in those heady days, we were "just" trying to protect our corporate assets.

We are still going to do "just" that, but we're going to do it by looking at how we protect the privacy dimensions of our assets first and then at how we protect the asset itself. What's the difference? In the past, cybersecurity was only concerned in mitigating information technology risk to the business. You do this by first understanding what your assets are and what they are worth and then by designing and deploying a defense-in-depth strategy to protect them.

Now, at every stage of our cybersecurity program, we prioritize the privacy dimension first. We will classify the assets across various privacy metadata, as well as all the other "standard" asset classification metadata, and then we will rank them by privacy first. We are enforcing a privacy-centric view across all our assets, and as a consequence, we are taking the position that the privacy dimension of the asset is by far the most important one, while other dimensions, critical as they may be, may come in second.

To be successful in this, we will need a mental shift regarding the traditional cybersecurity views on what asset, threat, control, and risk classifications are. We will also need a cultural shift of the whole business, and the only way we can accomplish that is if everyone—from the board on down, is on the same page in ranking Privacy (again with a capital "P") as the most important asset of the company. Anything less will not do.

Make no mistake about this: Unless everyone, from the board, to the executive team, management team, and each individual contributor is committed to this view, the privacy and cybersecurity programs will fail. You cannot pay lip service to Privacy or to cybersecurity. You're either all in, or you're out.

Now that you're all in, how do you actually implement a Privacy and cybersecurity program?

Surprise—you can't! Thank you for buying the book and reading this far, but that's about it!

No single individual can develop and maintain both a Privacy and a cybersecurity program. Can't happen! Why?

Because, as you know by now, Privacy is an entire discipline dealing with people's rights and the effect of those rights on how an organization processes, stores, and disseminates this person's data. Moreover, privacy programs must deal with a whole slew of regulatory and governance implications that are constantly changing and affecting the business workflow. Depending on the size and scope of the organization, this will require anywhere from a few dedicated resources to an entire Privacy army, headed by a general herself supported by the necessary structure. Legal, HR, product development, operations, marketing, sales, and all sorts of other departments will be required to maintain privacy garrisons of their own and coordinate upstream.

Bottom line? Just as you "can't just walk into Mordor," you can't just show up alone and develop a privacy program!

Then, what are we to do?

We need boundaries! We need to focus on exactly what are we here to do:

We are here to develop a privacy-centric cybersecurity program! And, if we already have a cybersecurity program, we will modify it into a privacy-centric one! Period.

Can we do that? Oh, yes. Yes, we can! How?

Well … where there is a will, there is a way, and the way is called a framework! A privacy framework that you'll need to use alongside your cybersecurity framework.

Phew! That was close.

The Case for Frameworks

What is a framework? According to our friends at Merriam-Webster, it is a basic conceptual structure (of ideas). I like to think of frameworks as playbooks. Take football, for example. You have the rules of the game, and each team has a playbook, which is the specific team's framework for winning. Not all playbooks work well for all teams, yet all teams must obey the same rules of the game. This is an important distinction, and it applies equally well in business.

In management science as a whole—and in technology and risk management in particular—there are several excellent, at times competing, at times complementing, frameworks. Note that a framework is different from a standard, which is itself different from a methodology (e.g., Six Sigma, plan-do-check-act, kaizen). A standard, as per ISO, "is a document that provides requirements, specifications, guidelines, or characteristics that can be used consistently to ensure that materials, products, processes, and services are fit for their purpose." You either meet or do not meet a standard. For example, you are either PCI DSS compliant or you are not.

Frameworks are different and a bit looser. You can claim, and you would be right in doing so, that your technology follows the COBIT framework even though you are using only parts of it—the parts that apply to your organization.

This is exactly why you should consider adopting a framework as a guide in managing your technology, privacy, and cybersecurity. A good framework should be comprehensive, flexible, adaptable, and straightforward to implement. Over the years there have been many frameworks that have seen the light of day. Who can forget:

- **COSO** (Committee of Sponsoring Organizations of the Treadway Commission);
- **CMMI** (ISACA's Capability Maturity Model Integration);
- **COBIT** (ISACA's Control Objectives for Information and Related Technology);
- **ISO/IEC 27001** (the International Organization for Standardization Security and International Electrotechnical Commission on Information Security);
- **ISO/IEC 27701:2019** (the International Organization for Standardization Security and International Electrotechnical Commission extension to ISO/IEC 27001 and ISO/IEC 27002 for privacy information management);
- **ITIL** (Information Technology Infrastructure Library);
- **BiSL** (Business Information Service Management Library);
- **NIST CSF** (National Institute of Standards and Technology Cybersecurity Framework);
- **NIST PF** (National Institute of Standards and Technology Privacy Framework);
- **TOGAF** (The Open Group Architecture Framework); and
- **PMBOK** (Project Management Body of Knowledge).

I have a few personal favorites: CMMI, which was developed by Carnegie Mellon (now part of ISACA) and used as a process improvement and appraisal framework, COBIT, also by ISACA, and the two NIST frameworks: CSF and PF. If you'd indulge me, I'd like to briefly introduce you to them all.

CCMI

CMMI is all about process and assessing your process maturity. What is a process? It can be anything from software development to service delivery and everything in between. CMMI breaks down the maturity of a process into five levels: In Level 1, processes are unpredictable, ad hoc, and frequently changing in reaction to events. Level 2 processes are repeatable, and if you're lucky, they have repeatable results. Level 3 processes are defined, they are documented, and are subject to review and improvement. Level 4 processes are managed using a variety of reliable metrics. Level 5 processes are optimized with a focus on continual improvement.

I am willing to bet you that you instinctively placed your organization in one of these levels. You know what CMMI level you are at. If you think you are at CMMI level 3, you would be in good company, and in a decent rank! It turns out that CMMI level 3 is the threshold you need to be at to implement a variety of other frameworks such as the balanced scorecard (another personal favorite) for aligning performance, goals, strategy, and management.

COBIT

COBIT is the 800-pound gorilla of frameworks for the management and governance of IT. The one ring to rule them all. The unified theory of everything. The answer to the ultimate question about life, the universe, and everything. That's COBIT! Get to know it, get to like it, and you'll be a much happier person—trust me!

COBIT is based on five principles:

- Principle 1: Meet stakeholder needs. An excellent principle, really, leading to the goals cascade:
    - Stakeholder drivers influence their needs;
    - Then, stakeholder needs translate to enterprise goals;
    - Those cascade to IT goals; and
    - IT goals cascade to enabler goals.
- Principle 2: Cover the enterprise end to end. Nothing left out, everybody in the pool.

- Principle 3: Apply a single integrated framework.
- Principle 4: Enable a holistic approach.
- Principle 5: Separate governance from management.

Okay, so it's a bit heavier than CMMI, but it's all muscle. Not a gram of fat.

That said, I suspect you got a bit overwhelmed by the principles. It makes sense that you would: Framework-talk can be overwhelming and intimidating. That's okay! Don't worry! If you are interested in implementing COBIT, then start by visiting the ISACA website, download the framework, and explore the many publications that support its implementation. Once you have read over the material, you can make more informed choices about how, how much, and when to implement COBIT.

The important thing to remember is that COBIT, CMMI, and the rest of these frameworks exist, and they evolve with the times. Brilliant people all over the world have dedicated their lives to building and refining these notions—not because everyone must implement them but because everyone should know that there is a source of guidance, a place to get help, a resource with trusted, verified, scientific answers to problems.

NIST Frameworks

NIST's Cybersecurity Framework (CSF) is extremely popular in the United States and for good reason. It is easy to understand, extremely well documented, and with the right investment of skill and resources can be implemented across all size companies and industries. It was born out of Executive Order 13636, "Improving Critical Infrastructure Security," which reads in part:

"It is the policy of the United States to enhance the security and resilience of the Nation's critical infrastructure and to maintain a cyber environment that encourages efficiency, innovation, and economic prosperity while promoting safety, security, business confidentiality, privacy, and civil liberties."

The functions discussed in E.O. 13636 have become cybersecurity mantra: *identify, protect, detect, defend, respond,* and *recover.* What's not to love?

NIST upped their game by releasing their Privacy Framework (PF), described as "a voluntary tool developed in collaboration with stakeholders intended to help organizations identify and manage privacy risk to build innovative products and services while protecting individuals' privacy." Again, if you're not in love by now, I don't know what it will take! NIST has given you everything (for free, I might add), and you're still hedging? Shame!

Remember, we have the five NIST CSF functions:

1. Identify
2. Protect
3. Detect
4. Respond
   and
5. Recover

We also have the five NIST PF functions, conveniently identified with – P:

1. Identify – P
2. Govern – P
3. Control – P
4. Communicate – P
   and
5. Protect – P

What do these look like next to each other? Funny you should ask! NIST itself has provided us with this amazing graphic (see Figure 13.1):

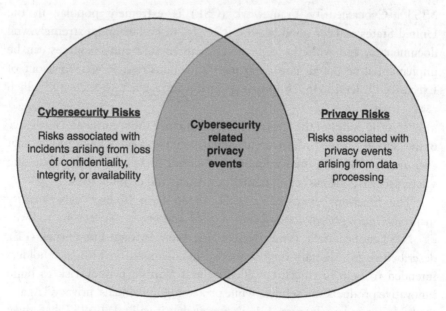

Cybersecurity Risks

Risks associated with incidents arising from loss of confidentiality, integrity, or availability

Cybersecurity related privacy events

Privacy Risks

Risks associated with privacy events arising from data processing

Figure 13.1   Cybersecurity and Privacy Risk Relationships

How does this map to the corresponding functions? NIST has you covered (see Figure 13.2):

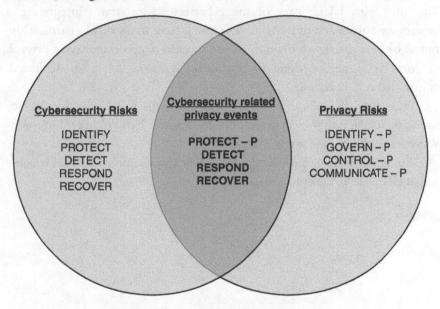

Figure 13.2   Cybersecurity and Privacy Functions Mapping

So how does this help us in staying focused? How does this create the necessary boundaries between a Privacy program and a cybersecurity program? This is how (see Figure 13.3):

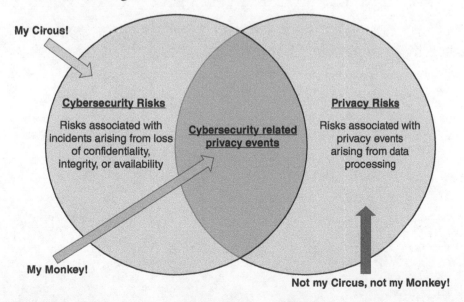

Figure 13.3   Cybersecurity and Privacy Program Boundaries

There you have it!

Leave the Privacy program management to your privacy counterparts. You stick with taking care of the cybersecurity program, integrating a privacy-first approach to it. Mind you, you'll have to do this in partnership, but as we have discussed, the only way to succeed in cybersecurity or Privacy, or for that matter anything of real value, is through honest, dedicated, committed collaboration.

How does this look in practice? In practice you will be doing a privacy metadata intake into your cybersecurity framework. Now, if that is not a conversation ender, I don't know what is.

But not to worry! We will take it a step at a time, and things will become much clearer in the chapters ahead.

CHAPTER 14

Cover Your Assets!

Eventually all things are known. And few matter.
—Gore Vidal
Burr (1973)

So it begins the actual work of creating a privacy-centric cybersecurity program. It was a long path that got us here, but you made it! We will divide the work into several phases:

1. **Assets:** What are we protecting and why?
2. **Threats:** Who's out there to get us?
3. **Vulnerabilities:** What are our weak points?
4. **Environments:** What is our operating environment?
5. **Controls:** How are we protecting ourselves?
6. **Incident Response Planning:** When all else fails, what's our plan?

We will deal with each phase separately, breaking down the various steps needed to build your cybersecurity program. Step one is a review of your assets. In my view this is the most critical phase of the program, because without proper asset identification and valuation, you will have no idea of what, or how, to protect it.

As discussed, a prerequisite for all our privacy-focused cybersecurity work will be input from your counterpart who's running the privacy program. She will have gone through the hard work of implementing one of the privacy frameworks, and we'll be the beneficiaries! That's the "privacy metadata intake" we referenced earlier. For our purposes, we'll assume that your counterpart is wicked smart and has implemented the NIST Privacy Framework—that way we can use the NIST terminology throughout our discussions.

You'll recall that we defined assets as anything of value. So what exactly are these things of value in your world? Always remember the basic rule: if it is of value to you, it is of value to someone else, and it will need appropriate care and protection.

Of course, all things in context, and our context is privacy-centric cybersecurity. It may well be true that your most valuable asset is a physical product—always worth considering and protecting! But in our case, we need to look at that physical asset from a privacy and cybersecurity perspective.

Even if your most important asset is a physical thing of great value, the questions to ask are the same, and they always start with: Does this asset carry any privacy risk?

You would think that there would be many more questions to ask surrounding the asset. That's true. There are. But if the answer to the privacy risk question is no, then any cybersecurity risk associated with the asset is far more straightforward.

Think of it as a two-step exercise:

1. Step 1: Does the asset carry any privacy risk? Remember, this would be risk to privacy as a result of data processing.
2. Step 2: Does the asset carry any cybersecurity risk? This is the usual risk associated with the triad (confidentiality, integrity, availability) plus one more (security).

We'll walk through the details of each of these steps below in detail, but the point is that you can have two equally valued assets in an organization, and one carries privacy and cybersecurity risk, while the other carries only a cyber-security risk. Let's think about a hospital as an example: A patient records system has both privacy and cybersecurity risk, while the medical-supply inventory system carries only cybersecurity risk.

For a different example, let's consider a company that produces high-end analog watches, which cost $150,000 each. The company lives or dies based on the sales of this very expensive analog item, so in that sense the watch is the firm's most important asset. From a cybersecurity perspective, however, it is not the watch itself that is the asset, but rather, all the data relating to the watch, such as its design, manufacturing plans, marketing strategy, and so on. If the design is stolen, then someone can replicate the exact watch and flood the market with knockoffs, causing enormous damage to the company.

What of the privacy-first perspective? Does this physical asset carry any privacy risk? Well, the watch itself does not store, process, or disseminate any personal identifiable information. It is just an (expensive) analog watch. It doesn't know your name, your ID, your blood type, your age. It doesn't know anything except the time. But that's not where the story ends.

We know that the watch is the end product of a long and complex manufacturing process, the result of years of intellectual labor, and sold to a discriminating clientele secured through intricate marketing and proprietary lead lists, forged into extremely valuable relationships for the firm. Do you think that there is a privacy risk associated with any of this? You bet!

So what are your assets of value? The category must include your company's personally identifiable information (PII) data and any protected health information (PHI) data, along with all the supporting (curating and controlling) systems, processes, workflows, and people. There is no distinction on whose data that may be—in other words, employee PII must be treated with the same reverence as customer PII. Other examples of assets of value include all intellectual property (designs, product information, research, etc.), strategic plans, financial plans, merger and acquisition plans, and tactics. If in doubt whether a cyber asset is of value, ask a few simple questions:

- What happens if the associated asset PII is exposed, corrupted, or exfiltrated?
- What happens if this asset is destroyed or corrupted?
- What happens if it becomes public? Or falls into the wrong hands?

If the answer is "nothing," scratch your head as to why are you maintaining worthless assets, and move on. Those assets are not worthy of protection, much less your attention! If, on the other hand, you discover that all sorts of things happen if the assets are exposed, corrupted, become unavailable, or are destroyed, then start cataloging!

How exactly do you go about doing this? What are the questions you need to answer to have a complete picture of the value of these digital assets? You undergo an asset classification and valuation. This is a fairly existential exercise! You will need to understand and document the true essence of your company. Depending on size and product or service offerings, your work will range from interviewing the executive team and the board all the way to having an honest talk with just yourself if you're self-employed. This work may take you down a complex path. One interview may lead you to dig further and interview more people at different layers of the organization. But at the end of the day, you will have come up with a list of valuable assets for your company.

Asset Classification

A good first step will be to get a grip on the total universe of our assets. What is included in our definition? Assets would typically fall into one of the following categories: data, hardware, software, systems, processes, and workflows.

Data

It is important to differentiate between information and data. Frequently, people use the terms interchangeably, and that's okay for everyday use, but we should be clear on the distinction because the implications can be significant.

Data is information that has been captured, stored, and represented in some medium. Data is often an expression of information, but that doesn't mean that data is a complete representation of that piece of information.

Consider a pot of boiling water. I have a sensor in the pot that measures the temperature of the water and transmits this datum, which is stored in my system in a field called "water temperature." That's data! But there's a lot beyond that number that we could notice about the actual physical event of boiling water: the magic of phase transition from liquid to gas; the beauty of the rising bubbles; the mathematics of turbulence of the water's surface, and so on. That's all *information* about the boiling water, but it's not data.

Personally identifiable information and the corresponding privacy metadata lives and dies in this gray world between information and data. It is our job to understand it and capture it because it is the most critical asset in our valuation. It is also the primary determinant of the asset's value.

Information Security versus Cybersecurity

Before we go further down the information-versus-data rabbit hole, let's stop and discuss why the difference matters in cybersecurity.

You'll remember that cybersecurity is part of information security. Information security does indeed care about all kinds of information (e.g., events) and all forms of data, not just digital. But the scope of this book is more limited, to privacy-first cybersecurity only. As such, we need to stay focused on digital data, with a specific focus on privacy implications.

To that end, we need to know how data is stored, processed, and transmitted. This is necessary for us in order to understand the privacy risk as a result of data processing. We then take that knowledge and integrate it with our three-plus-one pillars: *confidentiality*, *integrity*, *availability*, and *safety*.

I need to emphasize boundaries! When it comes to cybersecurity and information security, you need to let someone else worry about posting guards on the entrances, motion sensors, and keyless access. If that someone exists in your organization, then you'll need to get to know her, become fast friends with her, and integrate security systems accordingly. But otherwise, stay focused on the cyber side of security. You'll have more than enough to do!

That said, I cannot emphasize enough the importance of overall information security and its direct effect on the success of a cybersecurity program. As an example, consider the potential PII data loss from printouts left unattended on a printer in an unsecure area—while that data loss is not in digital form (and consequently is outside the purview of this book), it still matters and should definitely matter to you!

Cybersecurity should never be treated in isolation. It should always be addressed in the context of people and the environment, especially in the age of the Internet of Things and the Internet of Everything. After all, one unsecured wearable device brought into a secure network is all a hacker needs to gain access.

Hardware

Hardware is all the electronic equipment that stores, processes, or transmits data. It's also the stuff that controls other stuff, such as thermostats, and all the fun gizmos that make the Internet of Things possible. Why did I limit myself to "electronic" just now? Okay, you got me! Computer hardware can also be mechanical or even quantum. But unless you're Charles Babbage building the Difference Engine out of wood, or you work at an advanced computing facility, electronic hardware is the only kind you need to worry about.

Software

Software is the applications—from operating systems to apps—that use hardware to get things done. This includes, of course, software that runs in the IoT.

Systems

A system is a collection of hardware, software, and networks that processes data. Systems can be internal or external, and they are frequently a combination of both.

Processes and Workflows

These are the sequence of steps involved in the creation, transformation, processing, storing, and transmitting of data across systems. The definitions for process and workflows can be confusing, but as far as we are concerned, processes and workflows are assets that contribute value to the company, and as such, are worthy of careful consideration and protection.

How exactly do you protect processes and workflows? It depends. The first step, no matter what, is knowing about them—that is, documenting and cataloging them. This step will reveal any dependencies on systems that these processes and workflows may have. Your thinking about protection starts there, and it cuts both ways: How does the process affect the system and how does the system affect the process? We'll look at this closer when we discuss controls. For now, keep this in the back of your mind and think about concepts like business continuity and disaster recovery.

Asset Metadata

It's a party now! We hit the most critical piece of data that we need to collect for our program: metadata. Once we've listed your universe of assets, what do we need to know about them?

When I do an asset classification and valuation, I insist on knowing at least the following pieces of information. These are my "dirty dozen" critical asset metadata:

1. **Owner:** Who is the owner of the asset? If we're talking about a root-level digital asset, such as a finalized product (e.g., a product design,

a filing for litigation, financial statements), then the owner is the enterprise. If, on the other hand, we're discussing a value-generating system such as an e-commerce website, a medical records system, or a content management system, then the owner may be a business unit. More on this when we discuss business impact analysis further on.

2. **Custodian:** Who is the custodian of the asset? That cannot be "the enterprise" in general. That is always an identifiable person, department, business unit, or vendor. You need to be able to say, "Fatima is the custodian. Go get her!"

3. **Location:** Where is the asset geographically located? This is key, especially if the asset ends up living in the cloud. Again, be specific.

4. **PII Classification:** Rate the asset 1 through 4: anonymized, pseudonymized, explicit, or sensitive.

5. **PII Life Stage:** Identify the stage of the asset in the PII life cycle: collection, processing, storage, transfer, use, maintenance, or destruction.

6. **Confidentiality Classification:** Rate the asset 1 through 4: public, confidential, secret, or top secret.

7. **Criticality Classification:** Rate the asset 1 through 4: nice-to-have, optional, essential, or mission critical.

8. **Impact Classification:** This is a pain measurement: if the asset is suddenly unavailable, corrupted, or destroyed, how damaging would that be? A rating of 1 through 4 works here, too: would the pain be none, minor, moderate, or severe?

9. **Maximum Tolerable Downtime (MTD):** This is the point in time at which if the asset is not recovered, the impact becomes severe.

10. **Recovery Point Objective (RPO):** This is the particular point in time you'll need the asset to recover to.

11. **Recovery Time Objective (RTO):** How long you are willing to wait before getting the asset back into use?

12. **Resources:** Who will be needed to bring the asset back to life within the RTO and at RPO. Remember, be specific. Use names.

Before we go on, an important safety tip: when it comes to PII metadata, we've only scratched the surface. Our friends running the privacy program have tons more! For example, they capture PII consent state, PII consent date,

PII audit status, PII purpose, and PII use limitation. For our purposes, we only need to know that we're protecting PII. For their purposes, they need to know everything about the PII in question from type to stage and everything in between. Remember: boundaries!

Why do we only need to know PII classification and PII life stage? Because these two are enough to guide us in control selection, and at the end of the day, that's what we are here to do. Pick the right controls to protect these assets. All the other PII metadata are very important, of course—just not for our purposes. Stay focused and keep it simple! The goal for us is to intake from the privacy program the appropriate level of privacy metadata in order for us to do two things: first, complete the handshake with the privacy program by fulfilling our obligation to protect PII during data processing; and second, have enough data for us to fulfill our cybersecurity obligations to the business.

I am also going to let you in on a little secret! Those are exactly the same questions that I want to know when I am doing a quick-and-dirty business impact analysis, business unit by business unit.

The difference?

When I am doing an asset classification and valuation, I am looking at "root" assets—assets of value at the enterprise level. When I am doing a business impact analysis, I am looking more at systems—specifically, systems that are critical for each business unit to contribute to the production of the root assets. Some might argue that the distinction is artificial, and they may be right. But I like to think of the whole exercise as a continuum. Asset classification and valuation feeds into business impact analysis, which feeds into business continuity and disaster recovery, all of which contribute to a solid privacy-first cybersecurity program.

This may become clearer with a couple of examples:

Let's start with the asset "network switch." Who owns this asset? The enterprise! (Did you say IT? Nope. IT doesn't "own" anything. IT is the custodian, though, of pretty much everything, and certainly of enterprise-level technology assets.)

Is the asset "network switch" PII encumbered? You bet! It may well traffic data that is PII. Therefore, if it does, it needs to be (a) known and (b) protected accordingly.

What about the PII life cycle stage? Do you care about that when it comes to this switch? Excellent questions! I am glad you've been paying attention.

When you're dealing with these kinds of devices, which are pass-through, you should assume that the PII going through it is at its most sensitive state. In other words, err on the side of caution, exactly because you have no idea what kind of traffic will go through this thing! So consider everything as "PII sensitive," and "PII stage: collection" (the most error-prone stage of PII life cycle). Protect accordingly! (Sneak preview: What's the right control for this device? All traffic through the switch is encrypted.)

Now, let's move to another example of an enterprise asset: "file storage."

Who's the owner? Overall, the enterprise is the owner, and IT is the custodian. Hmmm ... but what if there is "file storage" dedicated exclusively for the use of—say—the accounting department? Who's the owner?

The owner of "file storage" remains the enterprise, even though the items stored are available exclusively to the accounting department. Why? Because "file storage" is a root-level asset. Root-level assets belong to the enterprise.

Systems, though, are a whole other ball game! So in this example, although the "accounting share" of the "file storage" asset is enterprise-owned, the accounting system that is using that same storage is owned by the accounting department. It's a question of system vs root asset. To look at the system's PII metadata will require a business impact analysis (BIA), but we're getting ahead of ourselves here.

After you have collected all of the metadata for the root-level enterprise assets, you are ready to take the next step. Like peeling an onion, you need to perform the same exercise on a business-unit-by-business-unit level. This in turn may lead you down even more levels as you discover system and workflow dependencies.

Yes, I know this promises to be hours of uninterrupted fun! The sooner you start, the sooner you'll finish. You're welcome!

Notice that I have avoided mentioning any specific asset valuation at this point. So far what we have is a spreadsheet of valuable assets whose owner is the enterprise, and a few whose owner may be a business unit. We haven't assigned any dollar value; we have only accomplished a listing of important stuff that we'd be loath to lose. Before we start talking dollars and cents, we must perform the business impact analysis work, using the same metadata at the business unit level with a slightly different focus.

A Fleeting Glimpse into the Other Side

Before we jump to the next logical step in our process (business impact analysis), I thought it would be useful to take a quick peek into the work of the Privacy program professionals. I think it will serve you well to at least have some idea on what is entailed in setting one of those beasts up.

Unlike cybersecurity programs, which can be fairly black-and-white, privacy programs have a lot more nuance and complexity. Simplistically speaking, in cybersecurity program development we look at the assets, their value, threats against them, their environment, associated risk, and risk appetite. From there we decide on controls, layer them, and constantly monitor for breaches. Rinse-lather-repeat and pray that your controls are good enough to alert you on the inevitable breach coming your way.

Privacy program development, on the other hand, is a horse of a totally different color! Here, you are not only dealing with assets, but you're also dealing with the *how*: how these assets got to you, how are they stored, how are they processed, how are they used and re-used, and any third-party rights that may encumber their use. For that matter, you may not even "own" the assets that you are entrusted to protect.

Consider the hospital example. Does the hospital "own" the PII of their patients? The PII is certainly required to deliver hospital services, but is PII considered a hospital asset? If you answered no, consider that were the hospital to be breached and the PII exfiltrated and disseminated, then the hospital would face all sorts of liabilities. Why? Because the role of the hospital is that of custodian. They may not own the PII, but they are expected to take really good care of it.

It gets worse! Consider any of the myriad possible workflows between an individual and a business. Most transactions between the two will involve the exchange of PII. The transaction has a life cycle of its own, and so does the relationship between the individual and the business—that relationship exists apart from any single transaction. It is typical to have a long-established relationship with a client with whom you engaged in several transactions. The management of the customer's PII can get very complicated very quickly, especially when the client starts requesting that her PII be removed from certain transactions and not others. You can imagine that establishing workflows around such requests can be a nightmare.

But dealing with privacy nightmares is exactly what the privacy professionals do for a living. How do they do it? Very carefully!

For one, they typically track a slew of metadata associated with the specific PII that they are dealing with. At a very top level, those include the two we already know about, plus PII:

- age;
- audit status;
- authorized users;
- classification;
- consent status;
- life stage;
- location;
- owner;
- source;
- type; and
- use limitations.

Keep in mind that this is at a top level, and this list is by no means complete. This table is not only per PII record (bad enough) but per system, division, business unit, and so forth. Then, just for fun, a privacy professional must do conflict resolution across all these records. What does this mean?

Imagine that PII record "Chris Moschovitis" is present in system X since 2001, sourced directly from the consumer, with enumerated use limitations, in an "active" life stage. Now, the same record appears in system Y of a different business unit, purchased via a marketing list, with dubious consent history, and appears there since 2019. What is the legal requirement for the business that is storing those duplicate records? Yes, the most restrictive one wins, but it's not that simple! Marketing paid good money for this record, and now you're saying they can't use it because the consent in system X is restrictive to that transaction?

On top of all this conflict-resolution fun, a privacy professional must continuously adapt their lens to reflect the current regulatory environment in every country of operation. What's legal here is not legal there, and what's legal there, is half-legal someplace else! Still, it's the job of the privacy professional to coordinate legal resources, audit resources, operational resources, human resources, and technology and cybersecurity resources to all dance to the same tune, day after day after day. And when they are done, report back to the board so that they can accept any risk and give further guidance.

The fact that the privacy professionals do all this work makes them invaluable to your cybersecurity program's success. By intaking the results of their work, you are able to build a robust, privacy-centric cybersecurity program, and by staying in-tune with them, you'll be able to keep that program current and successful.

Knowing all this, my recommendation to you is to not only treat these professionals with the respect they are due but to also give them a wide berth when you pass them in the corridor! After all, they know where your PII lives! Just saying.

Business Impact Analysis

Having completed the enterprise-level asset discovery, we are ready to dive into business unit specifics. You could apply the same exact methodology we followed for the enterprise with each business unit, and you would be right. You'd also be tired. Very tired! That's because if you attack a business impact analysis (BIA) from the start by creating that unit's asset listings, you'll be spending endless hours cataloging and cross-referencing assets into systems and so on.

I recommend going at it from the top and digging down only to the point that is useful to your specific cybersecurity program. To do this, you'll need to look at the world from the point of view of systems, not assets.

Systems, in this context, will have several root-level assets. A system, in this case, is defined as the collection of hardware, software, processes, workflows, and people that act to create, preserve, modify, disseminate, and curate data throughout its life cycle *in a business unit*.

Say that three times fast, and notice: We included *people* in the business unit system. That is what is important in a business impact analysis, because when it comes to the resources you'll need to secure this system, you must consider all the people necessary for recovery and operations.

Now, let's take this definition, and on a business-unit-by-business-unit basis, identify our dirty dozen properties, expanded in more detail further for our BIA purposes:

The owner: We have moved past the enterprise as the owner. Now we're looking at humans. We need to find the one true subject-matter expert when it comes to a specific business unit, system, and assets. No one will know it better than the owner. She will know what it takes to run it, where the possible vulnerabilities are, what the impact of its loss may be to them, and by extension, to the company. This is why the owner must lead this identification and classification effort for the particular business unit, systems, and assets. They are also very invested in the longevity and health of their world, which makes them even more in tune with the threats against it.

The custodian: Just as the owner is critical in helping you understand all the nuances about the business unit and its systems, the custodian is critical to providing an ecosystem context. Think of a horse and a barn manager. The barn manager doesn't get to decide who rides the horse (that's the owner's job), but the barn manager is responsible for providing a safe environment, food, water, coordination with the vet, and so on. The custodian is important to you because she can provide information that's critical to understanding what it takes to keep the owner's business viable, which in turn will define all sorts of priorities and criticalities. (e.g., No hay? No horse! Or at least a very hungry, cranky horse! Don't ride that horse.)

Location: The location of a business might sound like a painfully obvious detail, but keep in mind that location is not just a real estate question anymore. Of course you need to know the physical location of the business unit, especially if there are multiple locations all over the planet. This information will also provide valuable context ("What do you mean you can't find the CFO in India?") and exposes all sorts of vulnerabilities that are specific to geography, time, and local regulations.

But beyond real estate, our particular interest are locations in the cloud. Forget the obvious (where is the cloud, exactly?), and start thinking about new and exciting terms like cotenancy (your data has roommates that you didn't know or approve), transborder data flow (your data lives on servers in multiple countries), regulatory and compliance issues (e.g., data in Europe is regulated differently from data in the United States), right-to-audit issues (the cloud provider must agree to your ability to audit), certifications, and so on.

Do remember, please, that if your data is in the cloud, then by definition you are a tenant. This matters because the landlord may have different priorities than you do. Let's take a real-world example. Imagine that there is a robbery in your building but not in your apartment; the landlord may or may not notify you. Now translate that into digital terms: If your cloud is breached, but your specific data is not affected, will you even find out the breach occurred? Wouldn't you want to know? Bottom line: If your data is in the cloud, you will need to do additional homework to make sure you're protected.

PII Classification: This is where we dive deeper with the specific business unit PII assets, and you will do this using the business unit's PII definition. Sure, there is the "master" definition of PII based on where you're doing business and so on, but the business unit has a specific view of PII.

Think of it this way. A hospital, as a whole, has a very accurate definition of PII. That's essentially imposed on that enterprise by the local regulators. But the hospital's radiology unit and the hospital's accounts receivable unit have very different views of PII. One is medical in nature. The other strictly financial. Radiology doesn't care if you paid your bills, and accounting doesn't care that your lungs are clear.

Likewise, your enterprise may have separate business units with different definitions of PII. With that in mind, you'll partner with your counterparts in the privacy program and, business unit by business unit, you will intake and rate the specific business unit's PII asset 1 through 4: anonymized, pseudonymized, explicit, or sensitive.

PII Life Stage: Partnering with the privacy program professionals and the business unit "owner," you will also record the stage of the business unit's asset in the PII life cycle: collection, processing, storage, transfer, use, maintenance, and destruction. You will create a numerical score (1: less critical, 4: most critical) for each one of the stages above, with a total possible maximum score of 28 and lowest possible score of 7.

Now, it is important to note that your organization may have different weights for each one of the stages, based on the type of business and systems used. Your privacy counterparts will be instrumental in providing you with guidance for your specific environment.

To illustrate how a business unit can use the PII life stage field, consider the following example:

A business unit decided on the following values for a specific application based on their specific environment:

Collection: Ranked as 4 for most critical. This is a stage where PII is coming into the organization. Be it an external feed, or raw data entry, this stage is vulnerable to mistakes and possible interception from external and internal agents.

Processing: Ranked as 2 for medium-low criticality. This is the stage that PII is being transformed via some process. The risk is that the process may be flawed and the PII intercepted there, but in this example, the process does not involve communications or enhancements, only data transformation; hence the lower rating.

Storage: Ranked as 3 for medium-high criticality. Static as the storage may be, it is exposed to exfiltration by external and internal agents.

Transfer: Ranked as 4 for high criticality. Communications, even between internal systems, are inherently vulnerable, so the ranking needs to reflect the increased risk associated with this transfer.

Use: Ranked as 3 for medium-high criticality. This is where PII is used in the course of doing business. In this example PII is essential in the value-delivery process, so it is ranked accordingly. Examples of this would be PII used in order fulfillment. Where this PII be patient data at a medical office, it would have been ranked as 4. If it were mailing-list data, it would have been ranked as 2.

Maintenance: Ranked as 3 for medium-high criticality. This is where PII is stored and curated over time. Maintenance is prone to errors and has the similar exposure to PII storage.

Destruction: Ranked as 2 for medium-low criticality. This is where PII goes to die! This final resting process is nonetheless very important, especially as it is where opt out and deletion requests must be processed and be compliant with the appropriate regulations. In this example, destruction is ranked as 2 because the data was associated only with order fulfillment processes. (Again, as an example, if the business unit was dealing with medical PII, it may well have ranked destruction as 4.)

Table 14.1 PII Life Stage Value (Sample)

PII Life Stage	PII Life Stage Value
Collection	4
Processing	2
Storage	3
Transfer	4
Use	3
Maintenance	3
Destruction	2

So for this system employed by this business unit the score will be 21.

Similarly, for a different system that only stores PII, the score would be a value from 1 to 4. What kind of system only stores PII but doesn't process? How about network file storage? Storing PII in a file on the network, unencrypted, is asking for trouble! I'd score that as 4.

For a system that collects, processes, and then transfers the PII, the score will be the sum of the corresponding entries as ranked from 1 through 4, and so on and so forth. The higher the total score per system, the higher the exposure.

Now, before we move on, we need to make something clear: just as business units may handle PII differently, so a specific system may itself have multiple components that deal with PII differently. For example, a marketing system may process multiple PII sets, each one with different PII classifications, and at different stages in the PII life cycle.

Yes, that is the definition of hell, but it is what it is. The question is: What do you do about it?

You must catalog this metadata across each subsystem and component as necessary. If your universe is small enough, you'll be able to do this with spreadsheets and good due diligence. You will manage this recursively, system by system, component by component. It all depends on the size of the business and the extent of PII in use, processing, storage, and so forth. The less PII, the easier it gets, obviously!

But if your universe is anything but small, you will need to depend heavily on the privacy program professionals and get access to their enterprise-PII management software. Otherwise you'll be in a world of hurt! Just think of the fun times ahead that the privacy professionals will have when a data subject decides to remove consent, and they have to wake up the data protection officer (DPO) and clue her in that she has to go and change half a dozen systems to reflect that. Fun, fun, fun! You, of course, will have a corresponding role to play, as this exercise continuously affects assets, their value, and the controls rolled out to protect them.

Simply identifying and deploying enterprise PII management software is an expensive, enterprise-level project involving multiple stakeholders, and multiple vendors across several time zones. (My specialty! What's not to love?)

Business Unit Data Protection Officer

You may be surprised to find this entry at the BIA level—after all, a DPO is an enterprise-level position. While this is true, many business units will appoint an "in-unit" DPO, specifically to manage and coordinate with the enterprise DPO. Remember, PII management takes a village. Most frequently, the business unit DPO role is filled by the business unit "owner."

Confidentiality Classification

Like before, I recommend that you use a scale from 1 to 4, with 1 assigned for "public," 2 being "confidential," 3 for "secret," and 4 for "top secret."

Two tips: First, avoid the trap of having more classifications than necessary. Keep it as simple as you can.

Second, use an even number of classifications to avoid giving anyone the option to pick the middle number as a safe bet. Since you're doing all of this work in partnership with the asset's owner, insist that both of you carefully think through this classification. You'll be surprised at the dividends down the line.

If in doubt, use scenarios. Ask what-if–type questions. What would happen if this data were leaked to the public? What is the impact of a payroll report mistakenly being circulated company-wide? Can you identify groups of users with clear delineations for information access? Who needs to know this data, and who should not know? Are there policies in place that delineate access rights to the data?

Criticality

Again, I recommend that you use a scale from 1 to 4, with 1 assigned for "nice-to-have," 2 being "optional," 3 for "essential," and 4 for "mission critical."

These are applicable across the spectrum, from business units to assets, and you need to be as objective as possible when assigning them. Not all assets are critical. They may all be *valuable*, but that doesn't make them critical. You may be able to operate okay for months without the employee lunch menu database but be forced to close your doors if accounting can't pay vendors or meet payroll.

Scenarios are very helpful in establishing criticality, especially when framed by a specific business unit function—that is, when limited in scope. If you start talking criticality at the enterprise level (as in, which business unit is more critical than another), then you had best do so only in the presence of the executive committee and the board. Otherwise all these friends you worked so hard for are going to be looking at you sideways. ("What do you mean, facilities management is not as critical as finance? Let me see you work with no heat!")

Impact

This is the measurement of pain on a scale from 1 to 4, from "none," to "minor," to "moderate," to "severe." How painful would an outage be in terms of business impact? Would you be out of business? If so, the impact is severe! Would fees associated with the outage be so high that the business will lose money for the year? I'd call that "severe," too. Just the quarter? Let's go with "moderate." You wouldn't even notice the charge in the P&L? I'd call that "minor." You should feel free to come up with your own terms, but my advice is keeping it down to no more than four.

An interesting side note: The business unit owner will make one determination of impact, but the executive team may take a different view. And since the board is the ultimate decision maker on all matters of risk, they may decide that even an impact classification of severe is not worthy of a set of controls, despite your advice to the contrary. Sounds crazy, I know, but these differing points of view are entirely appropriate.

There are times when yours is not to reason why.

Maximum Tolerable Downtime (MTD)

Let's assume the business unit is out of commission for some reason—cyberattack, power outage, whatever. Ask the question: "How long can the business unit owner tolerate the outage?" That's the amount of pain that the business owner is willing to accept before things turn ugly. What's ugly? Like the severity of impact, "ugly" is a continuum. One version of "ugly" would be going out of business—that's pretty ugly. Less ugly would be finding yourself unable to comply with a contract or regulation, while much uglier would be a loss of life because of the outage. You get the idea. The MTD provides a baseline for building disaster recovery and business continuity plans.

Recovery Point Objective (RPO)

The RPO tells you the "when" in time you need to be able to recover to. Let's say your accounting system shuts down. It's out. Gone. Nothing is running. Can't pay invoices, can't processes receivables, and can't run payroll. The IT department and the accounting vendor look at the situation and they tell you that the system will be back in two days' time, and the data will be restored from last week's backup.

Here's the question you should be able to answer *before* the failure: Is that okay? If so, it means that once you get the system back (in two days), you'll have to reenter all transactions that happened between the last good backup and the day you have the system back.

If you agree that this is okay, you have implicitly accepted two values. First, you have accepted an RPO of one week. The second is our next category.

Recovery Time Objective (RTO)

Your RTO is the maximum amount of time that you're willing to wait to be back in business. Or to put it in a more positive light, RTO is how fast you'd like to have the problem go away and be back in business! In the preceding example, you accepted an RTO of two days. This is different from your MTD, which you may have set as one month, because with no payroll for a month, you'll be left with no employees and no business. Hence, MTD is your maximum tolerable downtime.

Now, consider that instead of an accounting system going down, you're a brokerage firm, and your brokerage system crashes. No more trades. No more reconciliation. No more portfolio management. You have no idea where the orders that were in the pipeline are, what's executed and what hasn't, what the values are, and so on.

What's your RTO in this instance? If you said a few seconds, you would be right! Anything more could put you out of business. And your RPO? Right up to the last second before the outage. You can't afford to lose *any* transactions. (To say nothing about those "men in black" from the regulators, who will want to have a friendly chat with you about the outage.)

Resources

This is one of the most important pieces of information you'll collect. What are the resources necessary for recovery? (Remember to always think in terms of business unit needs and system-specific needs.) They need to be accurately identified and cataloged in an actionable, meaningful way. You'll need not only the "Who is doing what?" question answered but also how to get in touch with these resources, including backup plans if the resources are not available.

For example, if your can't-live-without-it custom application was written in Etruscan by Molly, who has since retired to Oahu, it is probably a good idea to: (a) have all of Molly's up-to-date contact information, (b) have identified the last few remaining Etruscan speakers, and (c) reflect on the lesson learned about keeping mission-critical systems up to date and not in dead-and-gone language.

Similarly, you need to keep in mind that resources will be placed in contention if more than one system goes south (a likely event in the case of a cyberattack).

Now, the good news: You will be pleasantly surprised at how easy it is to collect these pieces of information from a business unit owner. But you will be unpleasantly surprised at the difficulty of collecting the same if you have not found the right business owner! In other words, don't necessarily look at the organizational chart and expect that a department head is the right owner of a business unit. That person may be the administrative head, but the real owner is someone who not only takes action but has experience and expertise running the unit.

This is not as unusual as it may sound, nor is it necessarily a problem. There may well be cases, for example, that the vice president of finance is an excellent strategist and an invaluable member of the management team, but it is the controller who is the business unit owner because she knows everything there is to know about it. You need to engage the vice president, be deferential to her, and include her in the process, but roll up your sleeves with the controller by your side.

There are also software applications that you can use to help you with BIA, asset classification, and so on. Bring your wallet! These tend to be expensive and frequently are part of a bigger business continuity management solution. Don't get me wrong; some of them are excellent, and if the size of your company warrants an enterprise-grade solution, you should look at them. But as far as mid- and small-business markets are concerned, at the time of this writing, my recommendation is to stick with my one-spreadsheet-to-rule-them-all solution, which comes next.

One Spreadsheet to Rule Them All

Assuming you're operating in a small to mid-sized business and do not have asset management and PII management software, you're left with your trusted spreadsheet. The good news is that spreadsheets are vastly underrated! At this stage of their evolution they come with incredible features making them both easy to use and powerful as database systems.

The best way to manage this is by creating one spreadsheet per business unit. The name of the spreadsheet file itself is the name of the unit. All spreadsheets live in the same directory to make linking easy. Your spreadsheet should look something like Table 14.2.

Each row is taken up by a system owned by the business unit. Owner, custodian, location, business unit data protection officer, and resources can be initials or spelled out. PII classification, confidentiality, criticality, and impact are numbers 1 through 4. PII life stage is a value computed as we discussed above.

Table 14.2 Business Impact Analysis Table (Sample)

Asset/System	Owner	Custodian	Location	PII Classification	PII Life Stage	BU DPO	Confidentiality	Criticality	Impact	MTD	RPO	RTO	Resources

MTD, RPO, RTO are numbers in hours (or minutes, or seconds, depending on the situation; just make sure you're consistent across all spreadsheets).

Additionally, I recommend that you make system, owner, custodian, location, and resources links to other spreadsheets that contain more granular data, all the way to a single asset. Where do you stop? Wherever it is appropriate for your firm! Remember, no two companies are alike. For example, for one midsized company, you may have something that looks like Tables 14.3 through 14.7.

Important safety tip: What happens if the FINANCE SERVER is home to more than one application (as is frequently the case)? Then, the highest of the values prevail.

Which highest value? Excellent question!

You are right—there are a dozen fields here! Which highest value, from which field, would rule supreme?

If we were excluding privacy from the conversation, the dominant value would always be impact driven. The system whose impact is the highest wins.

Table 14.3 Business Impact Analysis Table for Finance (Sample)

Asset/System	Owner	Custodian	Location	PII Classification	PII Life Stage	BU DPO	Confidentiality	Criticality	Impact	MTD	RPO	RTO	Resources
SlowBooks	CM	IT	NY	1	16	CM	3	3	3	40	24	48	IT
Payroll	CM	IT	NY	4	22	CM	4	3	3	40	24	48	IT
TimeTracker	CM	IT	NY	1	12	CM	3	3	3	40	24	48	IT

Table 14.4 Business Impact Analysis Table for an Accounting Application (Sample) Spreadsheet name: SLOWBOOKS

Asset/System	Owner	Custodian	Location	PII Classification	PII Life Stage	BU DPO	Confidentiality	Criticality	Impact	MTD	RPO	RTO	Resources
FINANCE SERVER	ENT	IT	NY	1	16	CM	3	3	3	40	24	48	IT

Table 14.5 Business Impact Analysis Table for an Accounting Application (Sample)

Asset/System	Owner	Custodian	Location	PII Classification	PII Life Stage	BU DPO	Confidentiality	Criticality	Impact	MTD	RPO	RTO	Resources
FINANCE SERVER	ENT	IT	NY	4	22	CM	4	3	3	40	24	48	IT

Impact drives a lot of the other variables. You can't have a system whose impact is marked as 4 (severe) yet its criticality is 1 (nice to have)! Similarly, impact drives the recovery time objective, the recovery point objective, maximum tolerable downtime, and so forth. In short, absent of privacy considerations, impact wins!

Now, add privacy in the mix. Which highest value reigns supreme? Is it PII classification or PII life stage?

PII classification gives us an overview of the type of PII in use. Is it anonymized? Is it explicit? And so on. PII life stage, on the other hand, is a combination of values across seven dimensions: PII collection, processing, storage, transfer, use, maintenance, and destruction.

Clearly, even if the PII is anonymized yet the PII Life Stage value is high, this alone describes to us a system with a potentially significant privacy exposure. Therefore, the ruling variable for our purposes must always be PII life stage.

Let's look at our example:

Consider the case where the FINANCE SERVER is the home for all three of the applications above: SlowBooks, Payroll, and TimeTracker. What would the corresponding FINANCE SERVER entry look like?

You guessed it! It would have the "Payroll" entry values because they are the highest. It would look like this:

Why? Because out of all the entries, "Payroll" has a PII life stage value of 22, the highest among the other three: 16 for SlowBooks and 12 for Time-Tracker.

Now, let's go back to our regularly scheduled program:

Clicking on the second-level spreadsheet's system entries (FINANCE SERVER) would take you to another spreadsheet that contained the specific information about that system. This could be configuration information, vendor information, warranty information, and so forth, or contact and account information for the services in use.

When you are done, you can choose to combine these spreadsheets into an enterprise-wide one that lists business units instead of systems. Where do you get the classification, criticality, and impact numbers? That's a bit tricky. Yes, you could theoretically apply a formula based on the individual business units' impact assessments, but you would be off.

As I am sure you realize, a business unit may have one or more systems scoring high on classification, criticality, and impact, while the business unit overall may score low at an enterprise level. That is why assigning those numbers are best left to the executive management team and (if necessary) to the board. Your goal for that spreadsheet is to arrive at a prioritization for each business unit, for purposes of business continuity and disaster recovery. This prioritization will filter down to your cybersecurity program work, as you tackle the creation of an incident response plan in case of a cyberattack.

You can also separate out different components of these spreadsheets for easier review and presentation. You can even use these spreadsheets to create and inform your risk register, or, for example, you can separate out impact and criticality by creating an impact-specific spreadsheet per system. That table could look like Table 14.6.

Of course, as much as I wanted to list "CEO Blog" as a "Mission-Critical" system with "No Impact," I was advised against it and left the entry blank. After all, how many mission-critical systems do you know that have no impact? (The rest of the examples are also to be taken with a grain of salt. Or two. Used only for demonstration purposes. Please don't send hate mail. Thank you!)

Table 14.6 Impact/Criticality Systems Spreadsheet (Sample)

Impact/Criticality	Nice to Have	Optional	Essential	Mission-Critical
No Impact	Lunch ordering	Online 401K review	Building lease and drawings	
Minor Impact	Ad hoc reporting	Expense reports	Travel advance	Inventory control
Moderate Impact	Online ticketing	HR appraisals	HR hiring	Financial systems
Severe Impact	Policies and procedures	Fixed assets	Payroll	Fulfillment

Table 14.7 Systems/Criticality Spreadsheet (Sample)

System/Criticality	Nice to Have	Optional	Essential	Mission-Critical
System 1	X			
System 2		X		
System 3			X	
System 4				X
System 5			X	
System 6			X	

Another example of a table you can derive is shown in Table 14.7

You can derive any combination you need: criticality by location, impact by asset/system, resources by MTD. Each one can provide different insight on how to best manage the overall risk to the organization.

One of the most useful ones, though, is the privacy/systems spreadsheet. That is a simple "sort descending" view by PII life stage value. The highest numbers will be on top, and they represent your critical asset list, sorted by privacy impact. Keep that list handy! It will guide many of your decisions, and it is a true-up test with your privacy counterparts, making sure that what you're protecting is also what they think is worth protecting.

There is one more thing left to do. You need to assign a financial value to all of these assets (systems, and others) that you have so painstakingly cataloged, indexed, assessed, inventoried, and reviewed. Typically, this solicits the response: "Good luck with that!" Unfortunately, that won't suffice here. We need to get some sort of valuation on the books.

Now, before you start running for the hills, consider this: We're not really looking for a formal, accounting, audit-proof valuation. Sure, that would be very nice to have (and in some cases required), but we can make do with an informal valuation. You may also ask, "Why now? Why couldn't we do this as we spent all those hours of uninterrupted fun doing the asset classification and business impact analysis work?" Well, the truth is that you could do it then, but I recommend that you don't. Instead, I recommend that you take the opportunity to do a presentation of your findings to date to all those involved. This will give you valuable feedback (in case something was missed), and give them a unique view of their world as seen through your eyes. That is when I feel is the best opportunity to talk dollars and cents.

So, corral your business unit owners and executive team and don't let them leave the room until they give you what you need: a number per asset. Some sort of quantifiable dollar value that answers the question: How much is the asset worth to you?

Replacement value is an easy starting point for most executives to grasp. What would it take to replace a particular asset? Think about it holistically: purchase or lease, equipment, licenses, expertise, staff time, the works. It's not that crazy of a calculation, really.

When you're done with the first pass, let's talk damages. What kind? Which assets or units are affected? All? Some? Which contracts? What services? Any products? Any regulatory implications? What about reputation? You should assess those costs as well. For example, your team will know the value of the contracts and the corresponding penalties and losses associated with failure to fulfill. They also will know any regulatory penalties that may ensue as a result of a loss or breach. Finally, you can estimate with the team the cost of rebuilding the firm's reputation when those emails that you called people all sorts of names leak out. You got this!

That's it. Now, you're done. You added the last field on your spreadsheet: impact, expressed in dollars. Take a well-earned break and get ready for the next step.

CHAPTER 15

Threat Assessment

The difference between theft and destruction is often a few keystrokes.

—Dmitri Alperovitch

Now that you have a solid understanding of not only what specific assets you're protecting but also what those assets are worth, it's time to consider who might be coming after them and how that might occur.

In order to get a handle on this, you'll need to perform some threat assessments. But before you start, there are four concepts you need to understand right away: threat, attack, vector, and payload.

- *Threat* refers to the potential of an agent to cause adverse effects on an asset.
- *Attack* is the realization of a threat.
- *Vector* is the pathway that a threat takes to compromise an asset.
- *Payload* is the actual way that the compromise is effected.

As outlined by the wise people at NIST: the threat source (also called an *agent*) initiates the threat event (or attack); the threat event exploits one or more vulnerabilities that cause adverse impact (you got hacked!); the end result produces organizational risk. And migraines. Painful, splitting migraines.

In terms of risk, a cyber threat has three main attributes: the kind of threat agent, the probability of occurrence, and, of course, its impact. During our threat assessment, our goal is to determine all three attributes on a per-asset basis. To do this, we'll need to know what the assets are (which we have already accomplished), what their value is to us (our definition of impact), who the threat agents might be (the bad people out to get you), their motives, and any pertinent threat intelligence and historical data out there.

As you recall from our earlier discussion of value, anything that is of value to you is also of value to someone else. If it is your PII that is of value, then someone else will also want it. If your corporate data is of higher value, then they're after that. The higher the value, the more attractive the target.

There are all kinds of items of value hackers might come after, but for our purposes here, we are focused as always on privacy issues first. The question is: Is there a specific, privacy-only threat that we need to account for?

The answer is, of course there are specific privacy-only threats, and it is these threats that a well-designed privacy program attempts to address. What about a privacy-centric cybersecurity program? Are there specific privacy threats that we need to focus on?

If you look again at the division of labor between cybersecurity and privacy programs, you'll quickly—and thankfully—realize that the privacy threat that we need to deal with is 100 percent in alignment with the threats we discussed above: the threat source (agent) initiates the threat event (attack); the threat event (attack) exploits one or more vulnerabilities that cause adverse impact. This adverse impact may well have a privacy component, and that is something that we must account for when we consider our defense-in-depth strategy and the layering of our controls, but this impact will not exist in isolation. Even if it is the privacy attributes of the data that is of interest to the attacker, it is the totality of the asset that will be compromised, and therefore, it is the totality of the asset that must be protected, albeit with the specific privacy impact considerations in the control selection.

What all this means is that the way we think about threats and vulnerabilities does not change when we're designing a privacy-centric cybersecurity program. Our threat assessment is enhanced by the privacy work we did during the assessment phase and the partnership that we have between cybersecurity and privacy programs. That, though, does not change what we need to know about threats and vulnerabilities to our specific business environment. The same threats and vulnerabilities that were there before you considered privacy are the same threats now that privacy considerations are at the forefront. Your view changes, but the threat itself is the same.

Another way of looking at this is "a breach is a breach" irrespective of whether what is being breached is PII or not. The effect to the business, of course, will change depending on what was breached.

Types of Threats

In the broad sense there are two, and only two, kinds of threats: external and internal.

An external threat originates outside your organization. We have a nice long list of those in Table 15.1.

An internal one? Well, are you familiar with the 1979 classic horror film, *When a Stranger Calls?* That's a perfect example of an internal threat: "The call is coming from inside the house!" Not surprisingly though, both external and internal threats can and do share the same motives, which include ideology, ego, and money.

What makes an internal threat particularly dangerous is that it has already bypassed your perimeter defense. The attacker is already in the system and needs only to bypass the internal controls in order to wreak havoc! Internal attackers also know where all the bodies are hidden: in other words, they know what's of value and what's not.

Who are these internal threats? What makes them so dangerous?

Internal Threats

There is no typical profile for internal threat actors except that they have the means, the motive, and the opportunity. They can be employees, either full-time or part-time. They can be contractors. They may be vendors that require temporary access to your system (e.g., a telephone system vendor). And God help you if they are "power users" or some sort of "administrators" of systems. Anyone who has access, whether on-site or remote, presents the possibility of an internal threat.

Their means can be many. They can physically exfiltrate the data by removing printouts of sensitive information, even taking pictures of screens with their mobile phones. If they have the right (or wrong!) privileges, they can copy data onto USB drives or transmit data to cloud storage. There have even been cases where in which "administrators" removed terabytes of data on removable hard disks!

Motives are equally varied. Internal threats are usually motivated by the same things that motivate external actors, but internal threats have easier access to your systems. Many are motivated by money. Indeed, they may have a pressing need for money for any number of reasons (family emergency, debt, drugs, gambling, etc.). Others may be motivated by ideology (disagreeing with company or state policies, a sense of "right versus wrong," self-righteousness, etc.). Others may have more personal motivations (disgruntled employees, various psychopathologies, just "the thrill of it," etc.). They may be recruited by the competition, a nation-state, or any other "organization." Or they themselves may be the victims of a crime, such as blackmail. No matter the motive, they will always find a way to rationalize their actions—be it to save the world, to save a loved one, to save themselves, or because "they deserve it."

It's even possible that your internal threat has no conscious motivation at all! Consider the accidental insider who sincerely "didn't know any better" and copied half the database to his private cloud so he could work from home! Or the one who fell for a phishing scam and clicked a link he shouldn't have or answered the fake call from "Microsoft" when that big-bad-red-alert sign popped up, and so on.

Regardless of whether the breach was deliberate or accidental, the damage is very real. But that doesn't mean you should apportion blame in precisely the same way. Yes, you can trace the data exfiltration to accidental credential leakage, but is it really the victim's fault? Is someone whose wallet was stolen responsible for the thief who used the access card? To be sure, a stolen card should be reported it in a timely way—but in the cyberworld, access is instantaneous. There is no "timely reporting" when you are a victim of social engineering and you click that link! Moreover, shouldn't you be looking closely at your own policies and procedures, your own training protocols, and your data loss prevention systems? I would!

This brings us to the final requirement: opportunity. Internal threat actors, whether intentional or not, require opportunity. How do they get it? If the organization has poor internal controls, that's all the opportunity they'll ever need. What do I mean by "poor internal controls"? The list is long! For example, if the employer has poor onboarding procedures or lax physical security, the employee may well be able to access data that they shouldn't. Similarly, there may be poor implementation of technical access controls, poor segregation of duties, or nonexistent data classification. Or the employer may have poorly trained or inexperienced managers in human resource–related matters (such as performance reviews, employee behavior monitoring and support, and confidential employee help resources) or the firm may lack a sophisticated human resource function altogether.

Who fits that last profile? The majority of small and midsized businesses who are focused—day in, day out—on simple survival. Unfortunately, it is these same businesses that frequently cannot even afford to retain cybersecurity expertise, much less roll out a data-loss prevention system (DLP). And yet they are the firms that need it most. Fortunately, there are sets of controls that can be deployed against insider threats, accidental or not. For example, you can train your people to be sensitive to employee behavior around data. If, say, John is suddenly interested in accessing the client master file although his job is in product development, that should raise a flag and it should be reported up the food chain.

For now, we need to focus on the threat itself. How does it manifest? What are the things we need to know about the threat going in? These are similar questions that we need to ask about all threats, but the human element of the insider threat makes this analysis unique.

The first question to ask is how can someone turn an employee into an insider threat? As it goes in the spy novels, so it goes with cybercrime: Nefarious agents turn your employees into assets. How are these employees identified and compromised? What are the signs you need to watch for?

Well, Mr. Bond, you need to think like a criminal to catch one! How would you go about it? You'd identify the weakest links. Employees who are having problems would be on the top of the list, followed by disgruntled ones. How do you identify them? Just monitor their social media! People offer up all this information for free and to all. Someone is getting divorced, someone else has cancer, a third person complains about her boss (you?) ... You'd be amazed what you can learn from people's blogs, Twitter feeds, poorly secured Facebook pages, and so on.

Need to get more sophisticated? Buy the information from any of the major data aggregators. They will gladly sell it, showing everything from credit status to health status and purchase trends. Remember, the adversary does not care about your or your employee's privacy. They will use whatever means necessary to achieve their nefarious goals.

As we continue to think like our enemy, consider that you must pick your asset wisely. You need someone who has enough privileges to get you what you need. Targeting the marketing associate because he just happened to be going through a nasty breakup will not do! You need to target the right asset for the job. Again, think like the bad guys: find the privilege, work the motive, ensure the opportunity.

Now reverse this strategy to protect yourself. Sensitize your employees to "abnormal behavior." Is someone who never worked late spending endless nights in the office? Or surfing the file server in areas outside their work scope? Is somebody constantly "making backups" on USBs or accessing cloud storage? Perhaps somebody with no history of working at home is suddenly accessing the site remotely all the time?

What about an employee who jumped ship from your competitor? Is the person still a bit too close with ex-colleagues? Could he or she be a "plant"? Does an employee seem stressed out of his mind, or exceedingly paranoid of the boss or others? Is someone "living large" on an associate's salary?

These are just a sampling of behaviors that may be signs of impending trouble. Some of these you can turn into controls by institutionalizing them, for example access controls, segregation of duties, multifactor authentication, geolocation sensitivity, behavioral patterning. Others are a matter of proper training and sensitivity towards your environment. All are important in managing the insider threat.

External Threats

According to a recent ISACA estimate, around 40 percent of the threats you may face will be internal, which leaves us with 60 percent coming from the outside. And, just like for their insider counterparts, you'll need all the intelligence about them that you can get. Who are they? What are their motives?

The main external threat actors have fairly predictable corresponding motives, as outlined in Table 15.1.

These threats all involve human actors (there is some debate if they represent the *best* of the species, but still ...), and they are all well within the scope of your cybersecurity program. If you were looking at this from a business continuity or disaster recovery perspective, you would include accidents, and the only nonhuman actor: think Mother Nature, pandemics, and related apocalyptic fun.

How does "motive" drive an actor in your case? This question is as simple as recognizing your place in the world.

Table 15.1 Threat Agents and Motives

Actor	Motive
Cybercriminals	Money
Online social hackers	Money
Cybers spies	Espionage
Hacktivists	Activism
Cyber fighters/army	Patriotism
Cyberterrorists	Terrorism
Script kiddies	Curiosity, thrill, fame, money

Are you a country? It's a safe bet that the threat agents are motivated by espionage, terrorism, activism, and outright warfare. Wouldn't it be fun, for example, for one country to hack another country's elections? Crazy talk, I know, but one can speculate!

Are you a utility or part of the national infrastructure? Same concerns! Crippling a utility can cause warfare-scale chaos. Rival nation-states and cyberterrorists can and do jump at the opportunity to interfere with these systems. For example, Ukraine's electrical grid suffered just this kind of attack in 2016, and it caused all sorts of chaos. The culprit? Well, the culprit remains officially unknown (but I'm looking at you, Vlad!).

Are you a Fortune 5000, a multinational, or massive conglomerate of some sort or another? You are fair game for espionage, sabotage, extortion, activism, and terrorism.

Are you in health care or education? Then the motive is more than likely data exfiltration for identity theft and money, although terrorism can't be ruled out, especially in large health care institutions and major universities.

Everyone else? Show me the money!

Cybercrime is expected to fetch upward of $2 trillion by 2020. For that matter, now that we are in the era of cybercrime-as-a-service, your competitor or a nasty nation-state can buy the services of hackers to achieve their ends. They may want to steal your intellectual property, sabotage your operations, or commit an act of terror—the hackers don't care as long as they get paid.

Given the absence of any other meaningful ranking, let's look at the main motives alphabetically.

Activism/Terrorism

This is very tricky. After all, one man's activism is another's terrorism and vice versa. Is Edward Snowden a patriot? A traitor? An activist? A terrorist? What about Julian Assange and WikiLeaks? What about Anonymous? Or what about the "Guardians of Peace," which hacked Sony Corporation?

They all framed their actions in some type of social-justice narrative, but we don't always know the true motives. In many big hacking cases, experts suspect that lurking behind expressed motives of activism (or terrorism) is a nation-state, terrorist organization, or clandestine service that funds and directs the attacks.

Are you a likely target of activists or terrorists? There is actually no easy answer. You need to carefully weigh your industry and your role in the world. Even then, what makes terrorism horrific is that they prey on unsuspecting civilians, who all too frequently pay the ultimate price.

Espionage

Tinker, tailor, soldier, spy? No more—those days are over. Today, most acts of espionage, be they corporate- or state-sponsored, are done over the Net. The motives behind espionage have not changed but the methods have. The type of attack motivated by espionage is typically advanced and persistent. The skill sets involved are many and complex. And the effects, when successful, can be catastrophic for the victims. Are you at risk? If your intellectual property PII is of value at the international level, then yes. If you are involved in critical infrastructure, communications, energy, or government, then absolutely.

Money/Extortion

From internal threats to ransomware to denial-of-service (DoS) attacks, take your pick! Money ranks as the highest motive behind the majority of cyber-attacks. The methods are many, the barriers to entry low and getting lower, especially with cybercrime-as-a-service. Are you at risk? One guess: Yes! You are.

Patriotism

Whether they are called "resistance fighters" or "commandos," the result is the same: These hacker armies perform what they believe to be their patriotic duty by developing and unleashing sophisticated, advanced, persistent threat-type attacks against "the enemy." Their activities are typically funded—overtly or covertly—by nation-states. If you have any nation-states that consider you the enemy, then of course you're at risk. But if you're even perceived to be "working with" or "working for" someone else's enemy, you are also at risk. For example, a small manufacturing facility that makes those pretty camouflage uniforms is definitely on the list.

Revenge

It's not business, it's personal—and frequently, very ugly. Hell hath no fury like an employee scorned, or one who is, as Freud might put, a bit "kooky." Who is at risk? Anyone with employees. In 2016, ISACA ranked insider threats second only to malware in terms of capacity to cause havoc! From what I have seen that ranking has not budged! Revenge, by the way, doesn't have to mean destruction of property. It may well mean data exfiltration and sale to your competitor, or leaking it out to the public. Be afraid, be very afraid.

Trolling/Cyberbullying

A very dark motive, indeed. These are typically individuals who target other individuals, frequently (but not always) famous or prominent in some way, and deliver attacks designed to besmirch their reputation or cause outrage. There have been cases in which this has jumped from the cyber world to the physical world, just as there have been cases of cyberbullying among young students with horrifying results. Are you at risk? There is no easy way to tell—worse yet, there aren't many effective controls against a personalized troll attack. If you are in the public eye, and depending on the extent and role, the chances are that you may fall victim of trolling.

Vanity

Typically, these are hackers who want to make, or maintain, their name and status in the media. Their goal is fame and notoriety. Their targets are not picked based on some ideology, although they may claim otherwise. The target is picked on their potential for making news or based on some real or perceived hacker challenge. Are you at risk? It depends on your visibility as a business or institution or—worse—personal fame. If your company or its staff is frequently in the spotlight, you should expect to attract vanity-driven hackers.

Warfare/Sabotage

Stuxnet was the first and best-known cyber weapon, used against Iran's nuclear facility, but there is little doubt that there are many more just like it in the arsenal of most nation-states. For example, recently Pakistani hackers have been waging cyberwarfare against India by buying up hundreds of Indian domain names and creating Twitter handles to spread misinformation and confusion, practices likely to increase in the region and around the world. Obviously, these are acts executed by well-funded, state-sponsored, and controlled hacker armies. You are at risk if you're in any business supporting critical infrastructure and, of course, if you are working in any government institution.

Threat Rankings

Your next task is to rank the preceding list in terms of which actors and motives are most likely to be engaged in your world. You already have a good sense of your assets, both at the enterprise level and at the business unit level; now spend some time and think: Who on this list is the most likely agent for an attack? Assign a numerical value from 1 to 4, ranging from "least likely," to "somewhat likely," to "very likely," to "extremely likely." In terms of my bias and recommendations? I'd consider the insider as a very likely agent and money/extortion as the primary motive.

You now have an understanding of the threat agents and their motives as they might apply to your organization. This is an excellent first step, but you're far from finished. Knowing the *who* and the *why* of cyberattacks is not enough. You also need to know the *how* and the *when*.

First, the *how*. One of the best places to look for this type of information is the European Union Agency for Network and Information Security (ENISA). They have been putting together an annual threat landscape and trends report since 2012. At this stage in your process, this document is required reading—succinct, and easily understood by both executives and cyber-professionals alike. At the time of this writing, the most recent report is the 2020 edition reviewing the threat landscape from January 2019 through April 2020. According to ENISA, the top threats were malware, web-based attacks, and phishing (see Table 15.2 for more).

Table 15.2   ENSIA Threat Landscape

Top Threats: 2019 to 2020	Assessed Trends	Change in Ranking
Malware	Stable	Same
Web-based Attacks	Stable	Going up
Phishing	Increasing	Going up
Web-application attacks	Stable	Going down
Spam	Declining	Going up
Denial of Service	Declining	Going down
Identity Theft	Increasing	Going up
Data Breaches	Stable	Same
Insider Threat	Increasing	Same
Botnets	Declining	Going down
Physician manipulation, damage, theft, and loss	Stable	Going down
Information leakage	Increasing	Going down
Ransomware	Increasing	Going up
Cyberespionage	Declining	Going up
Cryptojacking	Declining	Going down

From January 2019 to April 2020 The Year In Review ENISA Threat Landscape © European Union Agency for Cybersecurity (ENISA), 2020 Reproduction is authorised provided the source is acknowledged.

These reports and others like them offer you an understanding of the prevalent *how*'s in the previous year. You can extrapolate from that (who was at play last year, using which tool?) and make reasonable assumptions and decisions that will affect your choice and tuning of your cyber controls. What these reports do not give you is a sense of what is happening right now.

For that, you'll need the *when*.

Threat Intelligence

To get that information, you will need real-time threat intelligence, both from inside and outside your organization. External-threat intelligence provides you with clues about the types of likely payloads and who is currently using them. For example:

- What kind of malware has just been released?
- What new vulnerabilities have been discovered, and what's being done to address them?
- What attacks are in progress?
- What's the current "buzz" on the dark web?

Threat intelligence also gathers information from inside your organization and provides insight on everything from the state of equipment to who is accessing what and when, any abnormal behavior and traffic, and so forth.

As you can imagine, the amount of data involved in threat intelligence is massive. Moreover, processing and making sense of the threat intelligence data requires expertise and dedication. Someone in your staff with cybersecurity and technology training needs to be charged with making sense of the data and providing the necessary feedback and recommendations.

Doing this involves threat intelligence tools and feeds (both private and public). I highly recommend picking one of the top-tier vendors, installing (or subscribing to) their solution, and dedicating the right personnel to monitor and advise. Otherwise, you may find yourself trying to empty the ocean one teaspoonful at a time.

But if you really want to take a crack at threat intelligence on your own, you will find many places with public feeds, including:

- LookingGlass Threat Map: https://map.lookingglasscyber.com
- AlienVault's Open Threat Exchange: https://otx.alienvault.com
- Threat Intelligence Review's Cybersecurity Intelligence Feed Reviews: http://threatintelligencereview.com

Furthermore, most cybersecurity vendors produce free threat-intelligence reports on a regular basis. For example:

- CISCO's Security Advisories and Alerts: https://tools.cisco.com/security/center/publicationListing.x#~Threats
- McAfee's Threat Center: http://www.mcafee.com/au/threat-center.aspx
- Symantec's Security Response: https://www.broadcom.com/support/security-center/a-z

If a formal threat-intelligence solution is not appropriate to your size company, then, at a minimum, I recommend that you review these reports on a regular basis.

Threat Modeling

Is there some sort of organized methodology for all this? You bet! In fact, threat-risk modeling is a vast discipline. It's PhD-level stuff, with some of the best and brightest minds in risk management, cybersecurity, and technology working on it day and night. The following is a very, very small sampling of their work:

- "STRIDE": Several years back, Microsoft developed STRIDE, to replace their older threat classification DREAD. DREAD stood for: Damage potential, Reproducibility, Exploitability, Affected users, and Discoverability. But STRIDE stands for Spoofing (of a user's identity), Tampering, Repudiation, Information disclosure, Denial of service, and Elevation of privilege.
- "TRIKE," which doesn't stand for anything in particular, is an open-source threat-modeling tool created by Brenda Larcom and Eleanor Saitta. Their claim to fame is its granular, risk-based approach. TRIKE's great spreadsheet and help file are free to download from octotrike.org.
- Carnegie Mellon University's Software Engineering Institute, in collaboration with CERT, developed OCTAVE (Operationally Critical Threat, Asset, and Vulnerability Evaluation), which is currently considered to be one of the best threat-modeling frameworks and toolsets. OCTAVE comes in three sizes: the original OCTAVE for large enterprises, OCTAVE-S for smaller companies, and OCTAVE Allegro, which is a narrower, information-asset focused version.

When it comes to the total universe of frameworks, tools, and resources available for threat analysis, this list doesn't even begin to scratch the surface. The subject matter is vast, and unless you are at a minimum a cybersecurity professional—or better yet, a threat researcher—you can quickly become overwhelmed. Even the well-meaning, beautifully curated open-source community sites with the latest threat intelligence can quickly make you feel like you're trying to drink from a fire hose.

So what do you do? Take it a step at a time, use the resources at your disposal appropriately, and trust yourself.

I am hoping that by now I don't need to tell you that threat assessments are dynamic: what is a threat today may be moot tomorrow. You need to remain vigilant in your efforts to stay current with what is going on in cyberspace. Money and effort spent to protect yourself from one threat must be redirected to protect you from the new threats that have surfaced.

Neither privacy nor cybersecurity programs are "one and done." Both must always be present in your thinking and your planning. Much as we consider healthy living to include proper nutrition and exercise, good cyber-living includes proper privacy and cybersecurity practices.

Both are a way of life.

CHAPTER 16

Vulnerabilities

> **USBs are the devil. They just are.**
> —Overheard at SecureWorld Atlanta

As we've discussed, the ugly truth about vulnerabilities is that every system has them! Every single one. Worse: Each of these vulnerabilities has the capacity to destroy your privacy efforts all on its own!

And we're not just talking about a couple of vulnerability issues here and there. Think thousands upon thousands, with more being discovered every day. Our goal is to identify the ones applicable to our environment and deal with them. To do that, we'll need a list.

So off we go searching for vulnerabilities listings. It should be no surprise that one of the first entries that comes up is NIST's National Vulnerability Database (NVD). At the time of this writing, the NVD contained the following information:

- CVE Vulnerabilities: 143,438;
- Checklists: 513;
- US-CERT Alerts: 249;
- US-CERT Vuln Notes: 4,487;
- OVAL Queries: 10,286; and
- CPE Names: 500,344.

What do all these things mean?

- CVE stands for "Common Vulnerabilities and Exposures." It is a list of entries that contain an ID number, vulnerability description, and appropriate references for everyone to use.

- US-CERT is the Cybersecurity and Infrastructure Security Agency of the Department of Homeland Security.
- OVAL stands for "Open Vulnerability and Assessment Language" and it is an international effort to help standardize how to assess and report on the state of computer systems.
- And CPE stands for "Common Platform Enumeration." It is a dictionary containing a structured naming scheme for IT systems, software, and packages.

Who's Who in Vulnerabilities Tracking

Keep working the list and you'll run into all the usual suspects: MITRE, OWASP, CERT, and several security vendors. The situation can quickly become confusing and overwhelming. If you thought threat assessment was a bear, welcome to vulnerability assessments!

It is worth your while to understand the sources of vulnerability data, because you will need to refer to them as you apply them to your specific business.

Before we take the plunge, let's make sure we know what we are looking at. What exactly are these vulnerabilities? It's useful to refer back to NIST's definition once more:

> Vulnerabilities are weakness in an information system, system security procedures, internal controls, or implementation that could be exploited or triggered by a threat source.

The good news is that the vulnerabilities you need to be concerned about are limited to your world and your world only. In other words, we only care about *your* information system, system security procedures, internal controls, or implementations—not the universe of vulnerabilities out there. You have enough headaches as it is! More good news is that since you've done your asset classification, you know exactly which systems need to be tested against known vulnerabilities.

Of course, *your world* is a rather expansive term, one whose boundaries you'll need to decide ahead of time. Think about the now-famous hacking of Target in late 2013—it was the largest hack of a retail company to date. Something you may not realize unless you were following the situation closely: it wasn't the actual Target systems that were hacked! Instead, a Target vendor was compromised—a so-called trusted partner. Target didn't control the vendor's cybersecurity system, but boy did Target get the blame when that system failed. The question therefore is: what constitutes Target's cybersecurity world? If you answered, "Their own systems plus all the vendor partner systems," you get a cookie! You are correct! The same goes for your organization: *Your world* in cybersecurity terms is not limited to your own internal network.

The problem is, performing a vulnerability assessment on such an expansive definition of *your world* becomes unwieldy, not to mention legally tricky. For example: Do you, as a procuring organization, have the right to test the seller's systems? It depends on (a) what you are buying and (b) how good your lawyers are. What if you are buying something-as-a-service? What kind of vulnerability testing can you reasonably demand? Again, those are very tricky conversations.

What most organizations have settled on, and my recommended approach, is for the buyer to do the following: first, request that the seller complies with a reasonable cybersecurity operational standard (e.g., "Have you implemented <insert your favorite standard here> in your organization?") and second, demand the right to audit the vendor.

Whether or not you have the right to audit can be a matter of dispute. For example, what if the vendor serves multiple clients, some of which may be your competitors? If you have the right to audit, the other clients may object on the grounds of data confidentiality. You could descend into a legal rabbit hole defining exactly what system you'll audit, how you'll audit, and so on, but you get the picture.

Audit is a five-letter word that is best used sparingly and with profound respect. Fortunately, there are workarounds. For example, you may be able to demand the results of an independent audit, as opposed to performing one yourself.

Next question: how do you decide which vulnerabilities apply to your world? You start by matching your systems to known vulnerabilities. You know your systems. Now, you need to find the list of applicable known vulnerabilities.

What about the unknown ones, you ask? Those are the dreaded "zero-day exploits"!

Obviously, you can't test against an unknown vulnerability anymore that you can vaccinate against an unknown virus. But, just like in medicine, you can monitor your systems closely for any signs of abnormal behavior and respond accordingly. Most importantly? You are not alone in this! Thousands of dedicated cybersecurity professionals and cybersecurity companies make it their mission in life to scan for as-yet-unknown vulnerabilities, publish them, and recommend patches or mitigating controls.

Referencing back to our cybersecurity primer, you'll remember that zero day refers to nasty little bugs that exploit vulnerabilities in existing systems that are known only to the hacker. So your goal with zero day exploits is simple: Stay alert, stay informed, and have in place a defense-in-depth strategy that protects your organization as much as is practical.

The choice of the word *practical* here is key. It is not about protecting your organization to the outer limit of what technology allows—that would not be necessarily appropriate to your risk appetite. It is always about deploying protection in a practical and pragmatic way.

The first step is to use your asset classification to determine which type of vulnerabilities may apply. You know the drill. Break out your spreadsheet and get cracking! At a top level, you should be able to place your assets into the following buckets:

Operating Systems

This is the software that controls your hardware. Operating systems can be manufacturer-specific, such as Apple's and Microsoft's, or they can be open-source based such as LINUX. Operating system choices can be extremely polarizing, and I advise you to avoid those conversations like the plague. All you need to know is which systems are deployed in your organization. Leave the question of which one is better to be debated by the corresponding high priests of each tech religion. If you are interested in market share of operating systems, browsers, search engines, platforms, and so on, I recommend you visit the Global Stats site (http://gs.statcounter.com)—a free website of statistics happiness.

Servers

These are essentially applications that host (or enable) other applications. For example, database servers or web servers. You will need to know how many, what kind, the manufacturer, version, and so forth. Remember the one spreadsheet to rule them all from the Asset chapter? If you have gone granular enough, all this information will be in it.

Applications

These run either directly off the operating system (like a word processor), or in combination of operating system and some server (like a website.) For example, your accounting system is running both on an operating system, using a database server, and is itself an application for which you need to know all the fun stuff we've been cataloguing (manufacturer, version, etc.).

Services

When will the fun stop? It stops with services! Those are any information technology services that your company consumes from a third party. It could be storage. It could be infrastructure. It could be anything-as-a-service (infrastructure-as-a-service, firewall-as-a-service, software-as-a-service, etc.). And, yes, you need to know about it in as much detail as possible. In the case of as-a-service you will need to consult the agreements you have with the vendors, as well as contact their cybersecurity personnel to determine what their baseline posture is. Assuming you're dealing with a reputable vendor, they will be able to provide you with all the documentation you need.

Vulnerabilities: Mapping and Remediation

With your spreadsheet in hand, you will now research and develop a current known vulnerability list for each of the four buckets. To do this, you will need to consult with the following amazing, free, and hard-to-imagine-anything-more-useful services:

MITRE

According to their website:

> The MITRE Corporation is a not-for-profit company that operates multiple federally funded research and development centers (FFRDCs). We provide innovative, practical solutions for some of our nation's most critical challenges in defense and intelligence, aviation, civil systems, homeland security, the judiciary, health care, and cybersecurity.

I am here to testify that yes, they do, and I am one of their biggest fans! One of their many projects is the Common Vulnerabilities and Exposures Details, whose website is at: https://www.cvedetails.com. This is an amazing tool, where you can search by vulnerability, product, vendor, or anything else you can imagine and get meaningful, up-to-the-minute, actionable information. For example, searching for Microsoft SQL Server will return a table by year, number of vulnerabilities, type, and so forth, all of which link to more specific information. If you click on year 2015 "Code Execution" vulnerabilities, you will get two of them: CVE-2015-1763 and CVE-2015-1762. Clicking the second one, you'll get all the details about a remote code execution vulnerability for the specific product and what to do to mitigate it. What's not to love?

The National Vulnerability Database (NVD)

If you thought MITRE was hot, you haven't seen NVD yet! Originally the brainchild of the National Institute of Standards and Technology's (NIST) Computer Security Division, these days the NVD is brought to you by your friends at the Department of Homeland Security's National Cybersecurity Division. According to them,

> The National Vulnerability Database (NVD) is the U.S. government repository of standards-based vulnerability management data represented using the Security Content Automation Protocol (SCAP).

This data enables automation of vulnerability management, security measurement, and compliance. The NVD includes security checklists, security-related software flaws, misconfigurations, product names, and impact metrics.

When you visit their website (https://nvd.nist.gov) and click on the Vulnerability Search Engine link, you'll have a very powerful research tool at your disposal. For example, entering the CVE-2015-1762 vulnerability from our previous example, you will get a detailed report including description, impact, and references to advisories, solutions, and tools, to say nothing about all the technical details you can eat. Personally? You had me at "References to Advisories, Solutions, and Tools."

OWASP

Last but not least, we have the Open Web Application Security Project. OWASP is an international open community "dedicated to enabling organizations to conceive, develop, acquire, operate, and maintain applications that can be trusted. All of the OWASP tools, documents, forums, and chapters are free and open to anyone interested in improving application security." Their claim to fame is the periodic publication of the OWASP Top Ten 10 most critical web application security risks.

It is not only an incredibly useful and actionable tool, but it has also significantly contributed to cybersecurity awareness among developers and computer professionals as a whole. You will find this and many other tools and guidance at their website: https://www.owasp.org.

Is that it? Are these three sources all there is? Not even close. There are many more sources and resources out there for vulnerability research. Many are free; some are subscription-based. The three listed above here are simply a good start: They are all free, and they will suffice for most organizations' vulnerability identification needs. The trick to all this is vigilance. Like all things in cybersecurity, you do the task once and recheck on at regular intervals. How regular? It depends on your systems and assets: No two companies are the same.

Having identified and mapped the known vulnerabilities to your systems, the next step is remediation. Known vulnerabilities have, thankfully, known remediation steps. If you can, follow them to the letter!

Why did I say, "If you can"? Because, crazy as it may sound, you may not be able to plug a known vulnerability, because some application or workflow may actually depend on it. This typically happens when you are running obsolete applications that, for example, will not run on modern operating systems. You're stuck running them on old, vulnerable operating systems that are past their end-of-life and no longer supported. Therefore, their security vulnerabilities are not patched, and you cannot upgrade to the current operating system version because the jalopy app will not run on it.

Now you have a real problem: You know you're vulnerable, and you also know you can't fix it. What do you do? You apply controls around the known vulnerability to mitigate the risk until such time as the genius who wrote the application that's dependent on the vulnerability issues a fix.

Vulnerability Testing

After your vulnerability remediation, you'll need to confirm them as fixed. Your next step, therefore, is to perform a vulnerability test.

This is not to be confused with a penetration test, or "pen test" for short. A pen test, simply put, is a simulated cyberattack against your systems or company. Pen tests are used to assure that a cybersecurity program is working as intended. A vulnerability test, on the other hand, is a diagnostic test that will help in the development of your program.

Best practice, and my strong recommendation, is to retain a reputable third-party vendor to run vulnerability tests on your behalf. They would get the list of your assets and create sets of tests to check against all known vulnerabilities against those assets. Once done, the vendor will present you with a list of holes you need to plug.

A typical vulnerability test follows the steps discussed here:

1. **The vulnerability-test vendor will use your asset classification work as input.** This is a critical step, and it's where the quality of your earlier work gets to shine. The more detailed and prioritized it is, the easier this step becomes. For example, if your list of systems

and assets is long, you may be forced to prioritize and segment the test. You will do this based on the criticality of systems and assets that you established earlier. I strongly recommend that you test all systems, but I do understand that time and budgets may force a tiered-testing approach. That's fine, insofar as you don't make the mistake of thinking that the least important system doesn't need the test. In their attempts to be frugal, too many firms approach cybersecurity as if it were the Maginot Line—France's "impenetrable" defense against Germany that didn't extend along the Brussels border, enabling the Nazis to simply go around it. That is exactly what hackers hope you will do with your security. So even if you cannot test everything at once, make sure you do test everything and sooner rather than later. Otherwise, attackers will simply go around your hardened systems and compromise the least important one, using it as a staging point.

2. **Compare the list of assets against known vulnerabilities.** With the assets prioritized, the tester will use external resources to match each asset to its known vulnerabilities. For example, one question might be: "What are the known vulnerabilities for the asset Windows Server 2008?" There are automated applications that do these comparisons, making life easier for all. Nevertheless, that does not absolve you, or the tester, from double-checking that work, especially on critical assets. You want to make sure that any automated system is picking up the most up-to-date vulnerability list and does so from multiple sources and feeds.

3. **Test each asset against these identified vulnerabilities.** This can get tricky. In some cases, testing for the vulnerabilities is as easy as making sure that a security patch has been applied, or the system is running the most current version of software. In other cases, you may need to take the system off-line and check the underlying hardware for one specific vulnerability or another. Either way, you will need the help of at least two technical experts: the vendor performing the test and your in-house (or outsourced) IT team. Both must be in alignment about the goals, the methodology, and the desired end result. A critical thing to remember here is to avoid pointing any fingers at the asset's custodians (e.g., the IT team). You need to look at this exercise dispassionately—you simply need to know the truth of

the matter—but also with empathy toward the people charged with supporting the asset. Think of a patient going for a CAT scan: the radiologists are not there to judge whether you smoked or not. They want to perform a test and get a result. Even in an adverse diagnosis, one should never berate the patient. What is done is done. The goal after the diagnosis is only to apply the cure and the lessons learned.

4. **Recommend specific steps to either eliminate or mitigate vulnerabilities.** The results of the vulnerability tests tend to be fairly black-and-white: either the asset is vulnerable or it is not. If it is, then you hope that there is a clear path to eliminating the vulnerability. As discussed earlier, that may not always be the case, and the reasons may surprise you. There may not be a "fix" available for the vulnerability—yet! The manufacturer or developer may be currently working on it. A worse situation is if your system is no longer supported and there are no plans to fix the vulnerability (but in this case you might well wonder what you're doing running an antique system!). Another common problem is when the vulnerability does in fact have a fix, but if you apply it, your systems downstream may not work properly. The list goes on and on, but the good news here is that you have an answer: you either fix the vulnerability or you take mitigating action. Be aware, however, that the answer may be different for each vulnerable asset.

Prioritizing Vulnerability Remediation

Managing your vulnerabilities can feel like shoveling snow in the middle of a blizzard: Get the list of assets, research the vulnerabilities, plug the vulnerabilities, test the fix, start all over again. No matter how diligent you are, there will always be new ones that are discovered designed to make your life miserable.

The failure to keep up with vulnerability assessments is one of the most common problems I see as a consultant. It is boring work. It is overwhelming. It is constantly changing. And, for many firms, the job is just not as big as a priority as it should be. I know many good technologists who may well be aware of a vulnerability on a server but hesitate to apply the vendor patch. Oftentimes they are worried that something else may break downstream, and all of a sudden, what is a half-hour job turns into a two-day crisis.

I understand the hesitation, but I can't excuse it. According to White Hat Security, in 2016 the average vulnerability age—meaning how long the vulnerability has been around—was 339 days! And yet the average remediation rate is a paltry 42 percent. The time to fix? 117 days! That's almost four months from the moment someone knew about a vulnerability to the moment they addressed it. And that's just in the banking industry, which is supposed to be tight and regulated!

The excuses are many: overworked staffs, underfunded departments, competing priorities—I've heard them all, and I believe them. Most cybersecurity professionals and most IT shops truly are overworked, underfunded, and drowning in competing priorities. Unfortunately, that is not likely to change anytime soon. We therefore need to reprioritize vulnerability assessment and remediation. It truly represents relatively low-hanging fruit, and we are leaving it to rot on the branch because we are too busy to go get the step stool.

My recommendation is that you engage with your IT department (be it in-house or outsourced) and make sure that vulnerability identification and remediation, along with frequent testing, is someone's explicit responsibility. You should further insist on a monthly report that shows you the vulnerability status per system, and the remediation timeline. It is silly for us to keep trying to secure the fort if someone leaves the side entrance unlocked!

Speaking of locks, those are controls! The time has come for us to take a real close look at controls: how to select them, how to deploy them, and how to manage them.

CHAPTER 17

Environments

If security were all that mattered, computers would never be turned on, let alone hooked into a network with literally millions of potential intruders.

—Dan Farmer

I know you are chomping at the bit to get to the chapter about controls and how to use them to protect your assets. But before we get to controls, we need to think about where we are going to apply them. We apply them, of course, on our environments.

I use the term *environments* to mean three things, each of which has different cybersecurity and privacy needs. I will list them here briefly, and then we'll take a closer look at each environment in turn.

1. **Computing Environments.** There are four basic types.

    a. On-premises (in other words, the servers are under your direct control, literally in your office);

    b. Private cloud (the servers are elsewhere, but you still control them, as in, they live in someone else's building, but you have the only key to your own private office in that building);

    c. Public cloud (the servers are in someone else's office, many people have keys to that building, and you don't have a private office there); and

    d. Hybrid cloud (the servers are all over the place; some are in your private office, some are elsewhere).

2. **The Internet of Things (IoT).** For our purposes here, IoT means every device that is connected to the Internet, regardless of its location or function—from nanny cams to SCADA (supervisory control and data acquisition) systems. If it's not part of our standard end-point definition (computers, phones, tablets, etc.) but it's connected to the Internet, then it's IoT.

3. **Distributed Workforces.** Where are your employees located when they work? In the office? At home? On the road? Or increasingly, a mix of all three?

It's worth pausing a moment to talk more about that third item, distributed workforces. When I wrote my first book on cybersecurity, I discussed a forward-thinking treatment to this "oddity" called telework! Some companies were doing it and loving it, others hated it. Then the COVID-19 pandemic hit, and the world was turned upside down, kicked sideways, and slapped a couple of times for good measure. All of a sudden, *everyone* possible was working from home!

Even the most ardent detractors of telework noticed that their company could remain productive, competitive, even innovative, while everyone was working remotely. It didn't take long for the detractors to do the math—think of the real estate cost savings alone—and the next thing you know, leases were being cancelled and people were building out little corners of their bedrooms to be offices. "Zooming" became a verb, and everyone was trying to figure out how to "blur" their background and soundproof their children.

Now, as I said in the original book, I like huddling over a good watercooler conversation as much as the next person, but between the lessons of the pandemic and the cultural shift on what "work" really means, modern workspaces seem to be doing away with the very concept of the "office." Even before the horror of the pandemic, more and more people were taking advantage of the Internet to collaborate from locations all over the world. Sometimes, these arrangements mirror employer-employee relationships. Other times it is a collection of freelancers coming together for a project.

Like it or not, this is the new normal. The way we work is changing in a fundamental way, and the way we view privacy and cybersecurity over a distributed workforce needs to reflect this new and dynamic environment.

On-Premises Computing Environments

Most people are familiar with an on-premises computing environment. Depending on company size, this is basically your typical business office with a server room. These server rooms range in size from a cramped, dusty closet, to a large, air-conditioned, fireproofed data center. The commonality is that the server room is in the same physical space where the information technology services are being consumed. That said, a larger company with multiple buildings will still be considered to have an on-premises environment if they house their data center in one of their own buildings, despite distributing the services to multiple others, potentially across cities and countries.

On-premises environments afford you total control. You control access, you control what equipment is deployed, what software is installed, how the infrastructure is monitored, and so forth. It's all yours, no questions asked. If you want to decommission a server, you go right ahead. If you want to install a new firewall, knock yourself out! If you want to let your six-year-old kid bike around the environmentally controlled room, you can do that, too. Of course, total control comes with the corresponding price tag. More than just dollars, euros, or yen, the price tag also reflects the responsibility of maintaining this infrastructure from an IT point of view (installations, management, maintenance, end-of-life considerations, etc.) and, of course, protecting it.

Ay, there's the rub! Yes, you have total control on how you can protect the equipment, and as such you can be sure that it is always safe and sound, with the best and most appropriate controls at all times. But on the other hand, you're paying for all this infrastructure and associated headaches—including the likelihood of underutilizing your technology during a downturn, not to mention the challenges of scaling it up during a rapid growth cycle.

If you're a businessperson, you'll loathe both the expense and the rigidity. If you're a cybersecurity professional, you'll probably love it. But if you're an IT professional with vision—one who recognizes that you always need to align technology with business goals—then you will always recommend that any choices about IT architecture align with business goals as much as possible, even if that meant you'd miss looking at the blinking green lights in your server room.

So is an on-premises computing environment worth the headaches? How to decide? And who decides?

Remember, everything we do is based on this question: *What's it worth to you?* The only people who can answer that question are the business owners or their legal representatives. No one else! Not the IT team. Not the cybersecurity group. Not even the Privacy professionals.

IT must inform and advise on how best to generate value for the company by aligning with its business goals. Cybersecurity must inform and advise on risk and how best to protect company assets. Privacy must inform the team about what the company must do to protect PII. The business owners will evaluate and adopt the most suitable IT strategy and accept the appropriate risk. If that means 100 percent on-premises, that's what it will be, and if that means 100 percent carrier pigeons, so be it!

Private Cloud Computing Environments

Whatever its downsides (and there are more than a few), an on-premises computing environment does provide IT and cybersecurity professionals with lots of something they simply adore: control! Once you switch to cloud environments, that control starts to fade away, and that can make some IT and cyber folks nervous. One of the ways to talk a cybersecurity professional off the ledge when you're discussing the cloud is to promise that you'll be moving the IT infrastructure into a private cloud. What that means is the infrastructure will at least be located inside a dedicated, secure, access-controlled, and likely ISO-certified data center, and only you and your team will have access to it.

Private clouds try to deliver the benefits of scalability and on-demand provisioning of a public cloud solution while maintaining the sense of ownership and control of an on-site architecture. In other words, private clouds attempt to deliver the public cloud advantages, but they do so in an exclusive way for your organization. You are still responsible to maintain the resulting IT services footprint, just as you are responsible for protecting it, but now you have the advantage of not actually owning the infrastructure. You are, in essence, leasing on demand whatever it is you need at any time. You can provision and deprovision as much and as often as you like, thereby gaining the flexibility that on-premises infrastructure denies, while maintaining the tight control that a highly secure or mission-critical infrastructure demands.

It is important to note here that you should not think of a private cloud infrastructure as a bunch of dedicated physical computers. Although that may be a possibility, it is unlikely. The probability is that your private cloud solution will be virtually delivered to your company just as with a public cloud but with one key difference: The delivery of this infrastructure-as-a-service is done through proprietary, dedicated, single-tenant "pipes," in essence creating a physical separation tenant to tenant.

When you're running a private cloud, much like running your own on-premise infrastructure, you are entirely responsible for your private cloud's security needs. It's all you. Essentially, what you have gained is the flexibility of cloud infrastructure-as-a-service and perhaps software-as-a-service, while you have retained total control over cybersecurity. If that's worth it to you, then great! But again, the answer lies in aligning business goals with IT value delivery, and nowhere else. If that alignment results in a private cloud implementation, then cybersecurity will step up to the plate and protect it.

The catch is, of course, that any cloud choice, private, public, or hybrid, will introduce additional cybersecurity considerations to any on-premises infrastructure. For example, before you even contemplate procuring the service, you'll need to make sure that the provider of your private cloud is in compliance with several standards. These include all the usual suspects, such as CSA STAR, HIPAA, ISO27001, PCI-DSS, SAS-70, SOC-3, and TRUSTe. If you must pick only *one* certification, you should pick Cloud Security Alliance's STAR certification (it integrates ISO27001 with their own cloud controls matrix CCM). CSA STAR comes in three flavors: a level one self-attestation, a level two certification, and the in-development level three continuous monitoring implementation. Once you have that, you can investigate additional requirements such as Privacy Shield (if you're concerned with the European Union's General Data Protection Regulation [GDPR], which you should be), PCI, or HIPAA.

Public Cloud Computing Environments

The very idea of a public cloud makes most cybersecurity professionals hyperventilate. Sure, there are tons of certifications, the marketplace is maturing, there are appropriate controls, and so on and so forth, but we're talking risk-minded computer scientists. No matter what you say, for them the risk is just too much. Why is it too much? Because we're not a trusting folk! In a public cloud, cybersecurity is the responsibility of the provider, and simply put, we don't trust them. Some will call this paranoid and inappropriate. We call it prudent. Go figure!

So how can we all get along here? For one, you (as the acting cybersecurity executive) should fully understand the provider's policies and controls across several key variables and with privacy being a top driver: What are their privacy policies? Where are they compliant and where are they not? What are the issues with global data flow? And what is their transparency policy?

You should insist that your cloud-solution provider be able to articulate, demonstrate, and make available to you for audit-on-demand their security strategy, their controls, their business continuity and disaster recovery plans, staffing expertise and security clearances (including background check policies), staff training and certifications, cloud facility certifications and past audit results, their incident response plan, and communications policies. If they comply, then we're good. If they don't, then the risk is yours to accept or not.

What is that risk?

There are a few. If you don't know how your data is protected, then you may also not know if it has been stolen or altered until it is too late. Or since you're in a public cloud, an attacker may be targeting your "roommate" and trash your servers in the process. Or imagine that another tenant is hacked, but the landlord chooses not to communicate this fact to you (or anyone else), because it is not in their best interest to expose the breach. And so on and so forth.

There are also serious technical considerations that you will need assurances on: issues such as cotenancy, parallel processing, and process-memory segregation. We don't need to get into the weeds with this stuff here—that's why you should retain a cloud security certified professional. Suffice it to say that since everyone is in the same pool, you want to make sure that if the kid in the corner has an accident, you don't end up swimming in it!

Hybrid Cloud Computing Environments

You already have a hybrid cloud, even though you may not be formally acknowledging it. How do I know? Well, I think I'm safe in assuming that everyone in your organization has some sort of a smartphone or tablet. If so, they are already using the cloud whether you like it or not. All these devices typically connect to the cloud for backup and storage. If your users are using these for corporate email, it is possible that those messages are stored in the cloud. Of course, one can apply strict controls to all this, but then you're starting a war you can't win: a losing war with *Shadow IT*.

Shadow IT is defined as any information technology solution employed by your users that is neither approved nor maintained by your IT department. Shadow IT frequently results from user frustration with the rigidity of IT and their approved solutions. In search of speed, efficiency, or simple convenience, users will open up a Dropbox account, or use a work or private email address to bypass whatever organizational controls they perceive as onerous.

Smart organizations recognize this and get in front of it by training the users and allowing some (if not all) of the flexibility that this "IT on demand" allows. It's all about training and control. To the degree that the users understand the risk and the implications, and to the degree that appropriate controls are in place, let them go forth and conquer! Who knows? They may discover a solution that disrupts the company for the better, and that solution will become the adopted standard. But they can also discover the pits of hell, which is why the controls exist so that only a few users get scorched and the organization as a whole remains unharmed.

This brings us to the more conscious choice of a hybrid-cloud solution. The typical scenario is one in which a set of applications cannot be delivered over the cloud, requiring local infrastructure, while other sets can. Equally common is to see an on-premises private cloud–public cloud deployment. That's the ultimate hybrid. What does that look like? You have a set of applications that must be on-premises (let's say, for example, your accounting system). You have a data application that you need to scale on demand, and that's on a private cloud. You also have the company email coming from a public-cloud provider. There you go. Full-bore hybrid!

The security considerations, of course, don't change much. But they are additive. You need to make sure that each one of these environments is addressed properly, has its own cybersecurity strategy and controls, and is assessed regularly. You know all about the on-premise requirements, and now you have some sense of what you need to look at for both public and private clouds. Put them all in the mix, and you've got yourself the hybrid-cloud cybersecurity considerations.

Before we wrap up our computing environments review, I would like you to consider two things: First, evaluating a cloud solution is not the same as evaluating a technology solution. When you think about environments, you're evaluating a business solution. The work you need to do to satisfy yourself on its fit and applicability is closer to a business acquisition due diligence exercise than a technology assessment.

Second, it is highly probable that as you're starting down your cybersecurity journey, one or more cloud solutions will already be in place. That means we are looking at not just a business due diligence exercise, but an asset discovery one as well. There's data up in those clouds! And you need to discover them and treat them like the valuable assets they are.

Cloud Security Questions

Our friends at ENISA have a wonderful publication and a corresponding online tool that can help you with the first part: ENISA's Cloud Security Guide for SMEs—Cloud computing security risks and opportunities for SMEs—April 2015. I urge you to download and read it. There you will find an appendix labeled: E.3 Security Questions Form.

Their questions, repeated here but edited by me, should be your go-to in getting a sense of where your cloud provider stands:

1. How does the cloud provider manage network and information security risks?
2. Which security tasks are carried out by the provider, and which type of security incidents are mitigated by the provider?
3. How does the cloud service respond to natural disasters affecting data centers or connections?
4. How does the provider ensure that personnel work securely?
5. How is the physical and logical access to customer data or processes protected?
6. How do you ensure software security?
7. How is the physical and logical access to customer data or processes protected?
8. Which national legislation or foreign jurisdictions are involved—for example, because of the physical location of data centers or cables?

It's important to not fall in love with the provider's promises. Stay vigilant. If you don't like the provider's answers, look for a different provider.

When it comes to understanding what's already out there, you need to use all the asset discovery and classification skills that you already learned in our Assets chapter. You'll need to engage with stakeholders, identify the assets, understand the corresponding workflows, and document the full life cycle of the assets. What services are being used on the assets? Where from? Who controls them? Who monitors for incidents? What's the reporting like? What happens in regard to business continuity and disaster recovery? Who are the asset's custodians? Who's responsible for compliance? Who's responsible for any cross-border issues? And so on, and so forth! By now, you're an old hand at this!

The Internet of Things (IoT)

In January 2020, *Security Today* predicted that by 2025 there would be 75 billion devices connected to the Internet, with corresponding revenues exceeding one trillion dollars. In the business world, the primary drivers of this expansion will be operating efficiency and increased productivity. Meanwhile, a day doesn't go by when you don't read about the new smart home or smart office, the new smart cities, the connected cars, and, of course, wearables such as FitBit, Garmin, and Apple Watch.

Why is this important to you in our privacy-first cybersecurity context? Because if you have a smart thermostat in your office that is connected to your network and the device is not secure, then you might as well leave the door unlocked with a big neon sign welcoming anyone in.

The unfortunate reality is that these devices crept into corporate use while no one was looking. Certainly, the cybersecurity department wasn't informed that a smart refrigerator was being plugged in at the company cafeteria. IT wasn't notified either. Why would they be, right? Somebody at facilities spoke with the vendor and gave the vendor the Wi-Fi password, and they were razzle-dazzled by the pretty colors on the refrigerator's screen.

Given their pervasiveness, IoT devices represent a clear and present danger to your cybersecurity program. You will need to follow a rigorous set of steps to make sure IoT doesn't come back to haunt you later. Namely:

- **Extensive inventory of all IoT devices.** You'll need to get with both IT and relevant departments (for example, facilities, security, audiovisual) and go through every device that is Internet-enabled. What do they do? Why are they there? And, of course, where are they?

- **Configuration analysis of all IoT devices.** Depending on the number of devices in play, this task alone can be hours of uninterrupted fun. You'll need to know what exactly is running in your environment, but that's just the beginning. You also need the gory details, such as what sorts of data are going through the devices; what are the corresponding data-loss profiles; what are the risks of compromise to the devices; and how do these IoT devices fit into your incident-response, business-continuity, and disaster-recovery planning.

- **Securing the IoT devices.** Now that you know the nature, location, and configuration of the devices, you'll need to secure them. This sounds a lot easier than it is. Some of these devices do not have any security capabilities at all because the manufacturers, driven by low margins, couldn't care less about security, patching, and software configurations. That leaves you holding the bag. If the software on the device cannot be secured, you'll need to seriously think about either eliminating the device altogether or air-gapping it (meaning, not allowing it to connect to the network).

- **Rinse, lather, repeat!** Doing this exercise the first time sets the baseline IoT posture for your company. But that is not enough. You will need to stay on top of it, because new devices are introduced all the time. Some are even brought into the organization by unsuspecting users. Consider, for example, some new-fangled wearable (but unsecured!) device walking through the door and immediately connecting to your Wi-Fi through the user's cell phone credentials. It's like Bring Your Children to Work Day, but with electronics! You therefore must constantly be scanning the network for any unauthorized attempts to connect. Your default should be to deny all unless authorized at the media access control (MAC) address level.

Moreover, as part of your cybersecurity awareness program, you need to make sure that people understand the implications of IoT and how it can potentially become the company's Kerkoporta, which, unless you were really paying attention to your Byzantine history lectures, you may not know what it is!

Kerkoporta (Greek: Κερκόπορτα) was a small, unattended doorway along the fortified walls of Constantinople, which was allegedly left unlocked and unchecked, thereby allowing the Ottoman troops to enter and sack the city. Thus, no more Constantinople—we have Istanbul instead. Lesson learned: keep all your gates attended and locked.

There are currently a lot of efforts by both industry groups—such as the Industrial Internet Consortium (IIC), which has rolled out the Industrial Internet Security Framework (you guessed it: IISF)—and by both domestic and international regulators, all voicing their concerns about security and privacy in the IoT. For example, the US Senate introduced (and in 2019 reintroduced) S.2607, the Developing Innovation and Growing the Internet of Things Act, aka The DIGIT Act.

Bottom line? Expect to see a lot more action on this, especially as the growth path of IoT makes the infamous hockey-stick curve look limp by comparison.

Distributed Workforces

Once upon a time, before the pandemic of 2020, people used to get up and physically transport themselves to an office where they performed work. When they were done, they did the physical transport routine in reverse. Endless hours were wasted in transit, with tons of pollutants dumped into the environment.

People toiled for years and years under these conditions, until two things happened: First, Alexander Graham Bell invented the telephone, and Mr. Watson started to phone it in. Second, a virus got loose and sent the world into a tailspin.

Things went south from there.

According to Gallup, from 1995 to 2015 the percentage of workers in the United States telecommuting for work rose from 9 percent to 37 percent. That is more than one third of the workforce of the United States telecommuting at some point during the month, with 9 percent of those telecommuting half the time or more. There was some debate about whether the trend was leveling off or increasing and also about whether it's smart or counterproductive.

Then COVID-19 hit. All the stats and arguments about telework went out the window as the planet self-quarantined for months. We all watched in horror as the daily statistics ebbed and flowed region by region—lives lost, hospitalization counts, daily intubation numbers, infection rates. I don't need to remind you of any of this. I'd rather forget it myself.

Regardless, one thing remains clear: telecommuting is now a permanent reality, and it is likely to continue in one form or another, especially if work entails getting into an office and working on a computer. And this time it's not going to be for a few times per month. In the future, telework will increasingly be the rule, and office visits the rarity.

Of course, there will be companies and types of work that cannot be "teleworked." You need to have "boots on the ground" to perform construction, produce food, deliver healthcare, and so on. But if you're in a type of business that can create value through telework, there can be no excuse why you wouldn't.

Hence, a brand-new headache for anyone dealing with cybersecurity and privacy.

Why? Because unless your company is providing and controlling the equipment used to access corporate resources, you have a problem. A big problem. If your organization's corporate policy is BYOD (bring your own device), then it implies that a private piece of equipment is connecting to the corporate network, working with corporate assets and doing so over potentially unsecured connections, which could include someone's home, hotel, coffee shop, airport—anywhere an employee might go.

Moreover, neither your IT nor cybersecurity and Privacy departments have any legal standing with regard to accessing and controlling an employee's private computer or phone. That causes a serious legal headache if an employee is terminated, and IT and cybersecurity want to ensure that no corporate data is walking out the door. You cannot exactly take over the system remotely and wipe it. The individual may have personal data (for example, his or her personal contacts), which, may be commingled with their corporate contacts. What's more, if you have any reason to assume the employee may seek a new job with your competition, you can see how this can quickly become a serious problem.

What can you, the newly anointed cybersecurity czar to do? Assuming that you cannot persuade the company to provide equipment for all employees (local and remote), then your options are limited to creating a set of policies and standards to which employees must consent in order to access the network.

These policies and standards, translated into some form of an employee agreement or consent form, will not guarantee that your data won't fly out the door. But they may set minimum security standards and corporate rights that survive separation. It is absolutely critical that your attorney is involved in drafting these. It is the only way you can maximize your chances of making the policies enforceable following an event. Even then—I won't lie to you—enforcing these rules can become very time consuming and very expensive.

Remember our guiding principle to date: *What is it worth to you?* You must have a heart-to-heart talk with your executive team and your board to determine how far is far enough in regard to writing and enforcing security policies. It is only they who can accept the risk. There is no best practice when it comes to these issues. It's all about your risk appetite: What are you willing to accept and what are you not?

There are companies that will not accept this risk—mine among them. They recognize the reality of a distributed workforce. They even welcome the savings in physical plant costs, but they are not willing to accept the risk of their network being accessed by noncompany equipment. And so they provide everything: the equipment, the policies governing its use, and extremely tight controls on who, how, where, and when is accessing the corporate network and assets allowed. If an employee is separated, they immediately "brick" the equipment (a slang term meaning to render the equipment as useful as a brick) and provide for a mechanism for the equipment's safe return. Of course, all the corporate data across the board, local or remote, tend to be encrypted both in transit and at rest.

Obviously, this level of control does not come easily or cheaply. The systems, workflows, and personnel training required are complex and expensive in both time and money. Moreover, the message to the company is that Big Brother is watching. With both eyes squarely on you! Therefore, when discussing with your board such an approach, make sure that you sensitize them to all aspects of such an implementation. In some cases, there is no choice (e.g., you're working for the NSA, for crying out loud! What did you expect?). In others, there may be some give and take. As always, your role is to be there and inform the board, owners, or executives charged with accepting risk with all the pertinent details and then accept their decision.

On the other hand, there are other companies that fully, and perhaps cavalierly, accept the risk. Their position is that even if data is exfiltrated, it is useless without the company know-how with regard to generating value, so the corporate attitude is: "Let them have it!" In terms of the gaping cybersecurity hole that this allows (e.g., access by an infected computer), well, as we've discussed, "Ours is not to reason why!" You have informed the stakeholders of the risk, you made sure they understood it, and they have accepted it. Move on.

Then there are the companies that fall somewhere in between. Yours probably—hopefully!—is one of them. These companies are very concerned about the risks introduced by BYOD and distributed workforces, and as such, they mitigate the risks as best they can, through their defense-in-depth strategies. In practice, that looks something like this:

1. Create legally binding agreements with employees and their use of equipment accessing corporate assets.
2. Create and communicate clear policies, standards, procedures, guidelines for all information technology use and corporate systems access.
3. Have clear and timely onboarding and offboarding processes for all employees.
4. Provide cybersecurity awareness training to all employees, at least quarterly, and maintain awareness throughout the year.
5. Deploy a wide range of controls, including a well-tuned security information and event management system and a data loss protection system.

Like it or not, distributed workforces, freelancing, telecommuting, BYOD, and so on, are here to stay, likely to grow, and likely to have significant impacts on our definition of the workplace and to the new normal. The impact of these developments on IT, cybersecurity, and Privacy is equally profound. For cybersecurity, the concept of perimeter security is completely redefined. Indeed, some argue the perimeter no longer exists at all.

As for me, I argue that your current perimeter does exist, but it's not one or more campuses or offices.

Your perimeter is planet wide. Plan accordingly.

CHAPTER 18

Controls

There are risks and costs to a program of action—but they are far less than the long-range cost of comfortable inaction.
—John F. Kennedy

In the basic primer on cybersecurity in Chapter 11, we defined the four broad types of controls: preventative, detective, corrective, and compensatory. Some analysts include a fifth type, called a targeted control or a counter-measure, which addresses a specific threat or a specific vulnerability. But for simplicity's sake, I am going to include targeted controls as part of the four categories, depending on how they function.

What about Privacy controls? This is, after all, a privacy-centric cyberse-curity program. that's true—it is! But remember this?

We are operating within these boundaries—in other words, there are many aspects of a privacy program that are beyond the scope of a cybersecu-rity program. Consequently, we are also operating under the assumption that our colleagues across the hall doing the privacy program have established the necessary privacy controls and rolled them out across the enterprise and implemented them appropriately in all data processing areas.

That's not to say that we don't have a lot of collaborative work to do. For one, we need to understand where the boundaries are between the two programs. It's one thing to say we're dealing only with "cybersecurity-related privacy events"; it's quite another to define these for your specific organiza-tion. The boundaries between the programs are there, to be sure, but they are also nuanced and flexible. No two organizations are going to have the same boundary definition, just like no two organizations are going to have the same level of maturity in their privacy and cybersecurity programs.

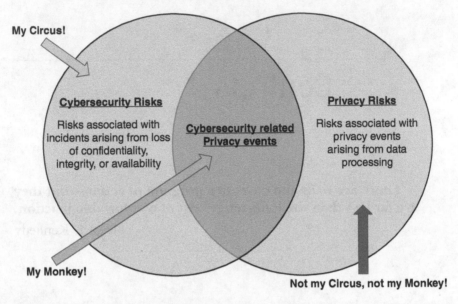

Figure 18.1   Cybersecurity and Privacy Program Boundaries

The way we will proceed here is as follows: First, we will assume that there is a privacy program in place, and that its creators have done their job in establishing the appropriate controls for their scope of work. Second, we will look at the pure cybersecurity controls that we must know and understand in order to have a solid, functional cybersecurity program. And finally, we will look at NIST's privacy control guidance from their famous NIST Special Publication 800-53, which undoubtedly you have and have read cover to cover.

First things first!

Assuming that our privacy controls are in place, we can proceed in examining our own cybersecurity controls. We'll look at each control class and give examples for each one.

Keep in mind that the examples that follow are just that, examples—not an exhaustive list by any means. New control products are developed almost daily as part of the constant arms race between hackers, cybersecurity vendors, developers, IT companies, end users, and governments.

Preventative Controls

Preventative controls are the road barriers of the information highway. They are designed to stop an attacker from getting to an asset. If the asset involves physical protection, then a good example of a preventative control would be security guards. Digital equivalents of the security guard include:

- **Antivirus and antimalware applications.** Typically lumped under endpoint protection systems, these are mostly signature-based applications that scan traffic, compare it against a known database of threats, and decide accordingly. What I mean by *signature* is that viruses and malware programs, once discovered, usually have a unique look, like a signature. That uniqueness makes them identifiable to the antivirus and antimalware applications. These applications are as good as their signature databases and their frequency of update, although the best-of-breed versions employ heuristic analysis to predict possible malware as well as sophisticated interfaces across applications (such as email, web browsers, and mobile apps). My recommendation: Don't turn on a computer without one installed and up to date.

- **Cybersecurity awareness training.** As discussed earlier, employee awareness is one of the most effective preventative controls. Training should consist of both on-site and on-demand training for all employees. The most effective versions employ a blend of delivery methods, repeat at least twice a year, and include follow-ups such as short quizzes to keep everyone on their toes.

- **Data loss prevention systems (DLPs).** Designed to ensure that sensitive data stays where it belongs, these systems operate across several layers in an organization. Depending on its configuration, a DLP will look for specific types of data (credit card numbers, Social Security numbers, account numbers, etc.) and make sure they are being accessed by authorized users only. A DLP can also inspect traffic to make sure that sensitive information is not on the move—be it on a network, an external storage device (e.g., a USB drive), or even a printer. DLPs are only as good as their configuration and upkeep, so you need to be particularly sensitive in making sure that they constantly know your data environment and your security policies. When correctly deployed, they can be a powerful preventative control, which plays well with others and is one of the few that can alert you to a possible insider threat.

- **Firewalls.** These are appliances meant to segregate the inside (company) network from the Internet. They come in several flavors that range in capabilities, configuration options, and complexity. There are firewalls that encrypt data as well as monitor traffic. Others monitor traffic and compare it against malware signatures. Still other firewalls do all of the preceding and more. Keep in mind that, as with DLPs, a firewall is only as good as its configuration. An erroneously configured firewall, or one that is poorly maintained, is useless. Your specific control requirements will dictate which kind and how many firewalls to deploy, as well as how they are configured.

- **Gateways.** Gateways monitor and control Internet traffic coming and going from your company servers. Let's say you call up a web page on a company computer. You can have a gateway that senses your request for a web page, segregates it from other traffic, disguises it, even encrypts it, and then sends it out. Why do this? Because if the request is intercepted, the intercepting person doesn't get your address; he or she only sees the gateway instead. In this example, this gateway would be called a (web) proxy server: a device designed to hide the other internal devices from the Internet by managing each session and exposing only itself to the outside world. You can have an application-level gateway, which is focused on services, or a circuit-level gateway that monitors, for example, a specific communications protocol across all services. Most firewalls and proxy servers perform network address translation (NAT), which is a way to map internal non-routable device addresses (that cannot be used on the Internet) to external Internet-acceptable addresses.

- **Intrusion prevention systems (IPSs).** These systems complement the panoply of firewalls, antivirus, and antimalware systems by introducing a systems-monitoring layer. Unlike IDS, which looks for a signature, an IPS will be tuned to what constitutes normal behavior on your networks. The moment something happens outside that frame, an IPS raises the alarm. An "alarm" in this context includes not only logging the event but also the ability to terminate connections. An example of a well-tuned IPS response would be the immediate termination of file-encryption activity taking place unexpectedly, usually the result of a ransomware attack. Of course, if your normal is all over the map and no baseline can be established, then the IPS may become difficult to tune and could produce many false positives as a result.

Detective Controls

If the preventative controls are the road barriers, the detective controls are the motion sensors that let you know that someone is in the room. The idea behind them is to detect abnormalities and raise the alarm. Some controls listed as examples under preventive controls work here as well—for example, antivirus and antimalware systems and intrusion prevention systems can be considered both preventive and detective. Other examples of detective controls include:

- **Intrusion detection systems (IDSs).** These are essentially antivirus and antimalware systems on steroids, using a combination of signature-based analysis (comparing traffic to not only known signatures of viruses and malware but to specific attack patterns), and anomaly analysis (comparing expected normal system behavior to current state). IDS can vary in intelligence and efficacy, depending on which system you deploy. Some use artificial intelligence applications to learn from their environment and therefore become better at detecting an attack. IDS integrate into the larger suite of controls by providing extensive event logging, automated responses and triggering of downstream controls, and organization security-policy enforcement. That last one is a set of rules that your cybersecurity department has painstakingly established to address control and notification behavior across systems.
- **Security information and event management systems (SIEMs).** These are applications that combine both detection and response management. They combine analysis of event logs across multiple systems, event correlation, abnormal event detection, notification, automated actions, and response event tracking. As you can imagine, the volume of logs and events has risen exponentially and can be properly managed only by a good SIEM. If forced to choose, I would deploy a SIEM before an IDS, because as far as I am concerned, a solid SIEM will provide greater insight and coordination across the enterprise than any IDS.

Corrective Controls

Like the name implies, these are controls that focus on repairing damage during or after an attack. Many targeted controls fall in this category: for example, vulnerability patching is a corrective control. Keeping your systems current—meaning, most recent operating system release as well as application releases—also represents corrective control, because it patches (corrects) known vulnerabilities.

But the ultimate corrective control is backup, and that's worth spending some time on. There is no substitute to the feeling of relief that you will have when you know that you have a good, solid, backup set from which you can restore your data. To get there, you need to understand the kinds of backup that are available to you, and when to use which kind.

There are three main kinds of backup: full backup, which as the name implies is a complete and total copy of all of your data; a differential backup, which copies only the data that has changed since your last full backup; and finally incremental backup, which involves only the data that has changed since the last backup of any kind. Which backup you use and when depends on the size of your organization, the amount and type of data, and the values that you established for your recovery time objective (RTO) and recovery point objective (RPO). Generally speaking, small organizations do a daily full backup, while larger organizations tend to employ periodic (e.g., weekly) full backups as well as a combination of differential or incremental backups.

A full backup has the benefit of the fastest restore time, since all the data is in one place and you don't have to go hunting among differential or incremental backups for that one file that's missing. On the other hand, if you're backing up several terabytes' worth of data, then, irrespective of method, you're using multiple and complex strategies to ensure timely restores.

There are additional considerations when it comes to your backup and restore strategy, most of which need to be covered by your business continuity and disaster recovery plan. There are different methodologies—such as mirroring, disk-to-disk-to-cloud, continuous backup, and hot failover—that may make sense given your specific requirements.

The one thing you need to be concerned about, no matter your size or strategy is: Make sure that your backups are absolutely solid and 100 percent verifiable. Check often! Trust me on this! You will thank me later.

Compensatory Controls

These are the types of controls you put in place when you know that all your other controls cannot mitigate one or more risks all the way down to a desired level—be that a level required by regulators or simply your own peace of mind.

In a perfect world, every company would address every vulnerability in a perfect way with perfect timing. But that's not our world. You may find, for example, that you cannot apply a necessary security patch or upgrade because doing so will cause havoc with your systems downstream. Or you may have a recovery-time objective that's so short, no backup strategy can meet it. Maybe you are dealing with such highly classified data that your system must be completely "air-gapped" (i.e., no Internet access ever).

Typical examples of compensating controls include hot failover sites (mirror sites where duplicate systems and facilities exist and can go live instantly), access controls (e.g., access depending on your clearance and the data's classification, function, geography, etc.), and the extremely important one, especially for insider threats: segregation of duties. Segregation of duties is a very powerful compensating control and one that you can easily implement.

Consider the following example: You have a mission-critical database application. As a result, you have some version of an application/database (DBA) manager, who may be in-house or a vendor. You also, of course, have a systems administrator. Again, that person may be in-house or outsourced. A good segregation of duties control implementation would be for the systems administrator to not know the database password, and for the application's manager to not have system administrative privileges. This keeps everyone honest. The administrator can always report on the DBA's actions from the logs, and the DBA can never erase those logs because they don't have the privilege, and vice versa.

Defense in Depth

The right way to use all of these controls is by deploying them across systems in a way that achieves defense in depth. This has the effect of putting multiple and diverse barriers (controls) between the attacker and the asset. This strategy looks different from case to case (e.g., cloud-based versus office versus mobile), but it has proven to be the best way to protect yourself and your assets.

If you recall an example from Chapter 11, people used to use lots of creative methods in combination to protect their castles. Translate that into the electronic realm and you've got your basic defense-in-depth concept down pat.

Back in March 2010, the NSA published a paper called "Defense in Depth," in which the authors pointed to three critical elements for success: people, technology, and operations. In my view, they nailed it! But not everyone agrees. There are many cybersecurity experts who question the approach. Some argue that defense in depth is dead and can no longer address the current asset realities and threat landscape. Their argument centers on two main—and very valid—points: first, the rapidly expanding network perimeter and second, the rapid adaptation and availability of attackers, attack vectors, and payloads.

What does this mean? The argument is that since everyone has a mobile device, and since applications and storage are increasingly consumed as cloud services, this new reality destroys the traditional notion of concentric castle-type defense-in-depth ideas. We can't build "walls" that are tall or wide enough to cover our users and their diverse technologies. Making things worse, attackers are faster and meaner, plus their tools (and themselves) are available as a service with guarantees! To say nothing of the insider threats (willing or not) who are already inside the castle, so ... defense in depth *that*!

I disagree. The arguments about the perimeter breakdown are sound, but I don't interpret defense in depth as simply meaning the creation of a multi-layered perimeter.

Quite the opposite: My view is that defense in depth applies at all levels and across all perimeters. It applies as much to the organizational perimeter—location by location, end point by end point—as it applies to its providers, partners and clients and as it applies to individual users, no matter where they may be.

In other words, defense in depth is not just a top-level "castle with five walls and three crocodile-filled moats" strategy. It is also a practice that needs to be applied at each asset point. Firms need to develop defense-in-depth strategies for physical (and virtual) offices, both local and remote, plus they should expect a defense-in-depth approach from their cloud services providers (trust but verify, always), and depending on scope, they need it from their trading partners as well. If you doubt the last one, talk to the folks at Target.

That is why I firmly believe that the NSA has it right. Defense in depth is not about any specific technology or topology. Defense in depth is truly about people, technology, and operations, no matter where, no matter how.

Privacy and Cybersecurity Controls

Having understood our cybersecurity control classes and the strategy for their deployment, the time has come for us to examine the partnership between privacy and cybersecurity controls.

There has been a lot of work in this field, going back several years. In 2013, NIST published the NIST Special Publication 800-53, Revision 4 titled "Security and Privacy Controls for Federal Information Systems and Organizations." This has been the gold standard for the past few years, but work has been far from static. Many worldwide organizations have been tirelessly working to create tools and refine existing frameworks marrying the two fields, including NIST.

In March 2020, NIST released for public comment the final draft of NIST Special Publication 800-53, Revision 5. The comment period ended in May 2020, and by the time you read this book NIST will have released their work as NIST Special Publication 800-53B.

Unfortunately, the book is being written during the comment period, so I do not have the final version to share with you. But the good news is that when NIST puts something out as "Final Draft" for comment, you can bet that what is in the draft will end up in the final publication pretty much unchanged. It is with that in mind that I am sharing with you the key elements of this draft that I consider absolutely essential to our work.

The first thing that the NIST introduces is the "Collaboration Index" between the Privacy and Cybersecurity program life cycle. They propose two options for this index (see Table 18.1).

My position on the index is that both cybersecurity and privacy programs, because of their inherent complexities and organizational nuances, are best served by the 5-tier option.

The draft goes on to present the enhanced "Security and Control Families" classification table that helps us categorize and organize privacy and cybersecurity controls (see Table 18.2).

Table 18.1 2020 NIST Special Publication 800-53, Rev. 5, Collaboration Index Options

Option 1		Option 2	
S	Controls are primarily implemented by security programs—minimal collaboration needed between security and privacy programs.	S	Security programs have primary responsibility for implementation—minimal collaboration needed between security and privacy programs.
Sp	Controls are generally implemented by security programs—moderate collaboration needed between security and privacy programs.		
SP	Controls are implemented by security and privacy programs— full collaboration needed between security and privacy programs.	SP	Security and privacy programs both have responsibilities for implementation—more than minimal collaboration is needed between security and privacy programs.
Ps	Controls are generally implemented by privacy programs—moderate collaboration needed between security and privacy programs.	P	Privacy programs have primary responsibility for implementation— minimal collaboration needed between security and privacy programs.
P	Controls are primarily implemented by privacy programs—minimal collaboration needed between security and privacy programs.		

Table 18.2 2020 NIST Special Publication 800-53, Rev. 5, Security and Privacy Control Families

ID	Family	ID	Family
AC	Access Control	PE	Physical and Environmental Protection
AT	Awareness and Training	PL	Planning
AU	Audit and Accountability	PM	Program Management
CA	Assessment, Authorization, and Monitoring	PS	Personnel Security
CM	Configuration Management	PT	PII Processing and Transparency
CP	Contingency Planning	RA	Risk Assessment
IA	Identification and Authentication	SA	System and Services Acquisition
IR	Incident Response	SC	System and Communications Protection
MA	Maintenance	SI	System and Information Integrity
MP	Media Protection	SR	Supply Chain Risk Management

The real meat and potatoes of the publication rests with the subsequent 20 tables for each one of these control families. Obviously, I will not present them here, but I think you will be well served by reviewing them yourself (the draft is available at: https://doi.org/10.6028/NIST.SP.800-53r5-draft).

Remember, by the time you're reading this, the document will no longer be in draft mode, but I expect that URL to take you to the live document. My strong recommendation is that you get the NIST document and use the tables to create the corresponding spreadsheets for your company that can then show you who has implemented which control, why, and how.

Why go through all this trouble? There are a couple of reasons. First, because failing to do so will leave you exposed to subsequent audits. And second, because not knowing who has implanted which control, why, and how will lead to confusion and possible duplication of effort between your privacy and security programs.

For now, as you're getting ready to do the work, I want you to take a look at the 2013 version of the "Summary of Privacy Controls by Family" table, and use that as a template to confirm and assure that you have these controls in place in your organization (see Table 18.3).

This table is based on the Fair Information Practice Principles (FIPPs; remember those from our regulation section?). The goal is to demonstrate that the organization is taking privacy seriously. I like using this as an onboarding exercise when a client engages us to take a look at how to transform their cybersecurity program into a privacy-centric one. Sit down with your executive committee and go through this short table line by line. The goal is to identify what is in place and get a scope of what the integration of these two programs will entail.

Remember: The only way that you will be successful in both cybersecurity and privacy program development is with (a) complete transparency and collaboration among divisions and (b) complete support and evangelism by the board and executive team. Anything less will not do! It is therefore critical that everyone, from the board down, sets these programs as a strategic priority, as key elements to the organization's survival and future success, and takes the time to be involved, informed, and engaged.

Part of your job is to partner with your privacy counterparts and "sell" your programs up and down the organizational food chain. You (both) have the responsibility to communicate clearly, to demonstrate the return on investment, to engage your company, even shift its culture!

Table 18.3   2013 NIST Special Publication 800-53, Rev. 4, Summary of Privacy Controls by Family.

ID	Privacy Controls
AP	**Authority and Purpose**
AP-1	Authority to Collect
AP-2	Purpose Specification
AR	**Accountability, Audit, and Risk Management**
AR-1	Governance and Privacy Program
AR-2	Privacy Impact and Risk Assessment
AR-3	Privacy Requirements for Contractors and Service Providers
AR-4	Privacy Monitoring and Auditing
AR-5	Privacy Awareness and Training
AR-6	Privacy Reporting
AR-7	Privacy-Enhanced System Design and Development
AR-8	Accounting of Disclosures
DI	**Data Quality and Integrity**
DI-1	Data Quality
DI-2	Data Integrity and Data Integrity Board
DM	**Data Minimization and Retention**
DM-1	Minimization of Personally Identifiable Information
DM-2	Data Retention and Disposal
DM-3	Minimization of PII used in testing, training, and research
IP	**Individual Participation and Redress**
IP-1	Consent
IP-2	Individual Access
IP-3	Redress
IP-4	Complaint Management
SE	**Security**
SE-1	Inventory of PII
SE-2	Privacy Incident Response
TR	**Transparency**
TR-1	Privacy Notice
TR-2	System of Records Notices and Privacy Act Statements
TR-2	Dissemination of Privacy Program Information
UL	**Use Limitation**
UL-1	Internal Use
UL-2	Information Sharing with Third Parties

You also have the right to expect the active support of the organizational hierarchy. This responsibility-and-right coupling cannot be separated and cannot be broken. Absence of either component will translate to program failure.

People, Technology, and Operations

Of this triad, the people component is in my view the most critical element of a successful privacy-centric cybersecurity program. As we mentioned, support from the board on down is essential. This support must be emphatic, clear, and actionable. There can be no doubt anywhere in the company that cybersecurity and privacy is a mission-critical organizational practice: It needs to be supported with clear policies, standards, procedures, and guidelines.

At each level of the organization, these policies, standards, procedures, and guidelines must be actionable, complied with, measured, tested, and reevaluated at least annually. All members of the organization must receive regular cybersecurity and privacy awareness training, with mandatory attendance and follow-up quizzes. Specifics of compliance, metrics, and reward and penalty policies will vary from company to company, but ultimately one thing must be unambiguously clear to all: These cybersecurity and privacy policies are mandatory, and just like any human resource policy, for instance, nondiscrimination, are enforced rigorously across the board.

When it comes to the technology part, things can be both complicated and complex. Anna Murray, in her excellent book *The Complete Software Project Manager*, explains the difference between simple, complicated, and complex projects—her example is the difference between snowplowing (lots of hard work but relatively simple), assembling an IKEA desk (it's complicated—trust me!), and performing open-heart surgery (complex, really complex!). In our case, developing and deploying a defense-in-depth strategy for the privacy-centric cybersecurity component, we will have to deal with both the complicated and the complex.

I'll go on record by saying that I believe that you can deal with the complicated: I am confident that you can put together an IKEA desk. I do, however, feel that you'll need to partner up with a surgeon for the open-heart surgery part. There is no escaping it. The subject matter becomes very specialized and it requires experience and expertise.

Your role will be to review and prioritize the assets that need to be protected by privacy and criticality. The role of your surgeon will be to match those up with a set of controls based on threat surface (how vulnerable is the asset) and control resilience (how well can the control protect it). And don't forget, you'll have a second attending physician throughout all this: your Privacy program team. They are critical to this operation!

The goal is to have several controls protecting each asset. These controls will be placed either in sequence (Control-A → Control-B → Control-C → Asset, that is, the concentric circle view) or layered across system function (User Controls → Operating System Controls → Application Controls → Database Controls → Hardware Controls).

You will also need both to think about using overlapping controls. What this means is that you want to place different controls in parallel, protecting the same asset.

Then you should consider asset segregation. That is when specific assets "live" segregated from one another. The accounting systems are on an isolated server on an isolated network segment from the file servers, and those are separated from the human resources systems, and so forth.

When you are done with asset segregation, you need to think about segregation of duties. This is very important. You should confirm that the custodians of your critical assets do not have unnecessarily elevated privileges. For example, there is no reason why the database administrator needs to have system administrator privileges and vice versa.

Speaking of privilege, the same kind of thinking applies for your users. At a minimum, you should implement least-privilege, role-based access. For instance, the accounts payable person cannot run the accounts receivable module. Different roles mean different access privileges. The more secure and sensitive the site, the more elaborate this can become. For example, there are mandatory access controls, context access controls, discretionary access controls, rule-based access controls, location-based access controls, and so on and so forth. The majority of businesses will be well served with clearly defined and religiously maintained simple role-based access. The religiously maintained part means that when the aforementioned accounts payable employee gets promoted to accounts receivable, her role is to be immediately changed by first eliminating the accounts payable rights, and then granting the accounts receivable ones. Were you to simply add the additional rights, you would have a user with unnecessarily elevated access privileges, creating an opportunity for mischief!

Finally, be aware that the introduction of controls themselves may introduce unplanned vulnerabilities. After all, you are introducing all sorts of technology layers, and we all know that not all technologies play well with one another. There are cases that one control rendered another one inoperative or ineffective. Make sure you test, check, and retest. Avoid the deployment of any control that depends on another one.

And don't forget: What happens when a control does fail? (Yes, think in terms of when, not if.) You need to decide how they behave not only while working but also while dead. Do your controls fail open or fail secure? As an example, consider that failing secure can be life-threatening in certain circumstances: If, say, your access doors to the computer center fail secure (i.e., all doors automatically lock) while there is a fire, and you're inside!

Ideally, all these practical considerations need to be addressed before any control is turned on. But this is not an ideal world. The possibility exists that you are not starting from a blank slate and that some, or many, controls are already in place. You will therefore need to examine each control and how it measures up to both the defense-in-depth strategy and to the practical considerations previously discussed. Learn from what you discover and adjust accordingly. Repeat this review at least annually. Controls become obsolete, threats change, systems and people change, and so does risk appetite, strategy, privacy requirements, and company needs.

The thing to always remember, your go-to safe bet, is to have as many independent and automated controls as necessary. Nothing more and nothing less. The main reason you should strive for automation and independence of controls is the third item in the people-technology-operations triad.

No two companies operate alike, but companies' operations share a common set of responsibilities that ensure the smooth running of the value-producing engine. Operations are the heartbeat of your company. You always want it to be nice and steady, never erratic and, God forbid, never arrested!

For your defense-in-depth strategy to be an operational success, you need to keep things as simple as possible, not overburdening operations with anything more than what they are already doing, and make sure you have the following one key ingredient:

Communications

As you can imagine, operations people have a tall order to fill. Depending on the size of your company and in terms of privacy and cybersecurity, operations will include members of risk management, audit, IT, cybersecurity, and HR.

If you are a company of one, well, the good news is your environment is simpler! The bad news is, you still need to make sure you have your finger on the pulse of all this, which will typically mean being diligent with the vendors that provide you all these services.

The larger the company, the more complex the operational food chain. The more complex the operations, the more essential the need for proper change management, strong communications, and cross-departmental engagement. If there is one takeaway that I can offer you from my experience evaluating different companies' operations, it is this: The minute you uncover a communications block in operations, pull the emergency break and address it. If you don't, your attackers will.

In the absence of solid, dependable communications, there can be no successful business strategy implementation, much less a successful privacy and cybersecurity defense-in-depth strategy. You should need to be comfortable in sitting down with your operations teams and discuss options, explain issues, and engage them directly in developing your specific defense-in-depth strategy.

Once that is done—once you are confident that the people-technology-operations triad has been properly engaged, issues addressed, and concerns satisfied—you are ready to document your defense in depth and let your people know what's expected of them.

Policies, Standards, Procedures, and Guidelines

In my original book, *Cybersecurity Program Development for Business*, I dedicated a full chapter to governance. As much as I wanted to bring it over to this book unchanged, the space constraints wouldn't allow it. That said, we need to discuss a few aspects of governance that become essential to the success of our privacy-centric cybersecurity program.

As always, we'll start with our definitions:

- **Policies** are the highest-level directives in an organization (or government agency, and so on). They originate with either the board or top management. Policies are both definitive and general. For example, a policy of a company might be: "This company is always headed north." It is definitive (we're going north), but it's also general (we're heading north but not necessarily on I-95).

- **Standards** set the ecosystem of a policy. They create a mandatory and meaningful framework for understanding and implementing the policy. In our northward policy example, the corresponding standard would specify which modes of transportation should be used (planes, trains, and automobiles), what types of compass are acceptable in determining true north, and any other metrics that can be used to verify that the policy is being followed.
- **Procedures** are listings of actions that, if and when they are followed, satisfy the standards and thereby implement the policy. People frequently merge standards (which are mandatory) and procedures (which are optional) into a mandatory procedure—hence the frequent reference to policies and procedures. An example of a procedure would be: "When using a car to go north, you must: (a) make sure you have fuel, (b) make sure you have insurance, (c) make sure you have your license with you, (d) make sure the GPS is on," and so on.
- **Guidelines** further clarify procedures. They, too, are optional, and may be specific to a department or function. In the example we have been using, a guideline would be: "You can only use the mail room truck if you are transporting boxes; otherwise, you should don your leather jacket and use the facility's Harley."

When it comes to privacy and cybersecurity program development, you and your privacy counterpart are on the hook for developing and disseminating policies and standards. They must, of course, be approved by the executive team and, ultimately, by the board or its equivalent.

Procedures and guidelines will be the responsibility of each department downstream. As the one charged with developing the cybersecurity program, you will advise and consult, but you cannot—and should not—be drafting departmental procedures and guidelines. Ownership of those must be local, or they will be unenforceable.

The first policy you will commonly create is the one that announces the existence of the privacy and cybersecurity programs, along with their standards. I recommend that the structure of all your policies and standards follow a consistent format. You should always check with your HR and legal departments to make sure that you are following internal templates, but in the absence of one, I'm partial to the following list and recommend it as an excellent starting point for your work:

1. **Policy title:** This is where you announce to the company what this is about. My recommendation, across all these fields, is that old standby, "Less is more." Keep it short and to the point. For example, "cybersecurity policy" is enough. (No, your company name is not needed. If the people reading this don't know which company they are working for, you have a much bigger problem than privacy and cybersecurity.)

2. **Policy description:** What is this policy about? Be specific without being verbose. For example, "This policy establishes the intent, provides direction, and sets expectations of conduct with regard to cybersecurity." Remember: Your privacy counterpart is drafting a separate policy dealing with the privacy program. Do not combine them. Keep them separate and keep them simple.

3. **Why are we doing this?** This question, along with the next, have proven extremely helpful for two reasons: Answering the questions will force you to communicate a well-thought-out policy and second, answering the questions will help set transparency expectations. Everyone needs to understand why a policy has been created and why it makes sense for the organization to have it. Finally, providing this information goes a long way in creating buy-in by all involved, and trust me, without buy-in, there can be no cybersecurity program. A good entry in this field should read something like, "We take the security of our people, our clients, and our data very seriously. As a direct result, we have decided to create and rigorously maintain our cybersecurity program, which we have based on based practices and proven cybersecurity frameworks."

4. **Why does it make sense?** As I mentioned already, the great Peter Drucker said, "There is nothing so useless as doing efficiently that which should not be done at all," and this is your opportunity to explain why this cybersecurity program does makes sense. Keep it brief. For example, "Having evaluated our assets, threats, and our risk tolerance, we understood that unless we take concrete, measurable action in cybersecurity, we would be exposing everyone

to unacceptable risks. This program is our answer in minimizing and mitigating this risk as much as possible."

5. **Who does it affect?** The answer here is simple: everyone. Cybersecurity, and of course Privacy, affects everyone in an organization. It is also everyone's responsibility. It should be no surprise to hear that my recommendation in introducing a cybersecurity policy would be to answer this question in exactly that way: "Cybersecurity affects everyone in the organization. Moreover, cybersecurity is everyone's responsibility."

6. **What are the applicable standards?** Here you have some choices. If you prefer to stick with just policies and procedures, then skip this entry altogether, replacing it with a list of mandatory procedures. My recommendation is to stay with the standards because the idea behind a policy is that it rarely changes. It is a top-level directive. For example, you wouldn't expect our go-north policy to change anytime soon, but you might expect the occasional change on the standards supporting the policy (for example, the addition of GPS to acceptable compasses). And you certainly expect the procedures and their guidelines to be changing as often as necessary. If you do choose to implement standards, then this is where you list them. For example, because you're all over the NIST cybersecurity framework, you could say, "The standards supporting this policy are: identify, protect, detect, respond, and recover." You would then produce and publish each standard, allowing for each department to develop procedures to support it. So, for example, accounting might set their own procedure for user access, while the IT department would determine their procedure for endpoint protection.

7. **What is your responsibility under this policy?** This is where the rubber meets the road. Remember all the buy-in talk earlier? This is where you find out whether it worked or not. If you have done a great job in getting everyone's feedback, incorporating their concerns, responding to their questions, engaging with them across levels, then they will be happy to integrate this policy into their lives and operations. If not, nothing you write here—even if it's blind and unquestionable obedience—will help. I suggest something like, "You are responsible to understand, disseminate, and comply with this policy, its associated standards, and the specific procedures and guidelines as applicable to your job function in the organization."

Putting It All Together

After all this work, what have we achieved? Let's review!

You are responsible for developing an organization-wide, privacy-centric, cybersecurity program. You have done your work, you identified your assets, the threats, and your possible vulnerabilities. You thought things through, partnered with your Privacy program counterpart, and developed a defense-in-depth strategy that has identified the necessary controls and how they must be placed to protect the organization. You have communicated all this, trained your people, and created the necessary policies and standards. You have also contributed to the creation and rollout of the applicable procedures and guidelines.

But none of this exists in isolation of geography and the local regulatory frameworks. You must take this work and tweak it so that the local applicable laws are respected. That means that it is entirely possible that your German office will have different standards from the one in Austin. They may have the same policy, but the standard needs to reflect the local regulatory constraints. If those constraints span continents, then you will need to have standards that address that as well.

Do you have to, though? Do you *really* have to meet each and every local regulation?

Well now, you rebel! It depends!

What is our number-one yardstick that we've used throughout our privacy-centric cybersecurity program development? What is the question we always need to have a definitive answer to?

How much is it worth it to you?

And as usual, that is a question for the board. The board may decide not to comply with one local regulation or another. The board may decide that it is worth it to them to pay any fines they may incur. In short, the board is accepting this risk. You do not have to agree with that decision. And it is not yours to make.

You can, and should, advise the board on what you think is possible in regard to controls, strategy, and so on, to mitigate this risk, and you should do it objectively and clearly. Terrorizing executives and boards with, *"Do you feel lucky, punk?"* kind of questions never works! Stick to the facts, present alternatives, educate, and ultimately, accept their decision and move on!

And so will we. Onward to incident response!

CHAPTER 19
Incident Response

> The best way to get management excited about a disaster
> plan is to burn down the building across the street.
>
> —Dan Erwin
> Security Officer, Dow Chemical Company

We've been through quite a journey thus far! From improving our understanding of privacy and looking at privacy and data protection regulations around the world to tweaking our cybersecurity program into a privacy-centric one.

Along the way, you may have noticed that this last piece, the tweaking, was not evenly applied to every part of your program. Critically, the area of cybersecurity program development most affected by privacy concerns is asset discovery. There, we underwent a discovery-in-depth exercise to make sure that we captured the necessary privacy variables necessary to formulate our control and defense-in-depth strategy. This discovery-in-depth is truly at the core of a privacy-centric cybersecurity program. The rest of the program remains largely unchanged: you still need to get a handle on threats, vulnerabilities, environments, controls, and so on. But the critical piece is the asset discovery work. At the end of the day, what does a good cybersecurity program do? It protects your assets! And, what does a good privacy-centric cybersecurity program do? The same thing! It protects your assets, only in this case, the assets are "sensitized" with the privacy dimension.

Which brings us to incident response. How different is incident response for a program that's privacy-centric vs. one that is not? It turns out, not very!

You still must develop and integrate your business continuity plan, your disaster recovery plan, and your incident response plan. You still have to break it down in phases: Identify the incident, contain the incident, treating the incident, recovering from the incident, and learning from it. The core difference in our privacy-centric program is that we must include the privacy program team throughout all its phases, from incident response planning, to testing, training, and executing. Much as asset discovery was transformed by our privacy focus, so will incident response need to adjust, prioritizing privacy-impact response while also attending to the cybersecurity incident at all other levels: technical, legal, and human.

In some ways, incident response is both anticlimactic and depressing! After all, you have spent endless hours getting to this point, only to turn around and develop a plan for when all you've done proves inadequate to the task. You've built a defensive perimeter around your castle, but you still need to make a plan for what happens when the enemy crosses the alligator moat anyway. What a joy!

In the 2015 movie *The Martian*, the main character teaches a group of aspiring astronauts. He tells them:

> At some point, everything's gonna go south on you … Everything's going to go south and you're going to say, "This is it. This is how I end." Now you can either accept that, or you can get to work. That's all it is. You just begin. You do the math. You solve one problem … and you solve the next one … and then the next! And if you solve enough problems, you get to come home!

Honestly, if there is a better description about what an incident response plan looks like, I have not found it!

Incident Response Planning: Not Just a Good Idea—It's the Law!

You may have heard of FISMA. It stands for Federal Information Security Management Act. It was signed into law in 2002, and it essentially requires all federal agencies to develop an incident-response plan.

I know what you're thinking—"But my company is private, so why should I care about federal regulations?" The reason is similar legislation requiring your firm to do the same is already here. For example, New York State passed 23 NYCRR 500, a regulation requiring most financial and insurance firms to retain a chief information security officer (CISO), have a robust cybersecurity program, perform risk assessments and testing, roll out two-factor authentication, and report incidents within the first 72 hours. And, of course, develop an incident-response plan.

Today, having an incident-response plan is either mandated by regulators or most certainly expected by your vendors and clients. If you don't have one, you will either lose business or fail to gain business.

Consider seatbelts! Once considered optional, the current policy on seatbelts is "Click it or ticket." Having an incident response plan is like a seatbelt for your business. It may not prevent an attack (that's what all the other stuff is for), but if one happens anyway, it will help limit the damage and recover the business.

Another reason why governments are likely to get increasingly intrusive by requiring incident response plans is that insurance companies and governments are not prepared to shoulder the hits from an attack alone. The cost of a breach is going up by the day, and with privacy regulations being what they are, you should expect these costs to continue to rise for the foreseeable future. In some cases, this cost has been terminal to the business.

The good news is that there are plenty of resources to help you develop an incident response plan. The bad news is that developing an incident response plan can be fairly complicated. In a sense, it's similar to building a hospital. The basics are obvious: You know it must have an emergency room, diagnostic facilities, intensive care units, operating rooms, patient rooms, offices, and so forth. But that's just the beginning! You also need to know the community that this hospital will be serving. Is it a metro area? Is it a small town? A group of isolated villages? Is the hospital in the tropics? The Arctic? And more questions follow: Who's funding it? The community? A wealthy donor? Is this a private company or government-owned? What kind of specialties will it have?

You get the idea. Your preexisting knowledge of minimum essential services plus demographics, geography, and budget will go a long way in deciding size and scope. For example, maybe your hospital can handle most everyday types of medical care, but when it comes to transplants, you'll need to refer the patient to a more specialized facility.

The same is true with your incident-response plan. Your firm's size, location, and budget will determine how sophisticated the plan will be. A small company may have an incident response plan that calls for identifying an incident and immediately calling in outside expertise. A larger firm may have multiple incident response specialists in-house. As you can guess, the most critical step in developing your incident response plan is going into it prepared to answer these questions, with the privacy impact questions at the top of the list! What happens when the PII you so carefully guard are exposed? How do you recover? What is the liability?

The answer to all these questions will guide your incident-response plan. Some of the answers will come from your asset discovery-in-depth exercise and the resulting spreadsheets. Other answers will come from your risk register that ingests information from your cybersecurity and privacy programs. The rest of the answers will come from your board of directors (or equivalent corporate authority); they are the governance body that is most informed about risk, and they alone can set the risk appetite and tolerance.

Incident-Response Plan Phases

When it comes to disasters of one kind or another it seems that each year is competing with the one before. In 2020, as this book is being written, we had a pandemic, riots on the streets, and "murder hornets"! Eight years before, August 2012 was, for its time, a record breaker. Much warmer than average in New England, 63 percent of the states suffered droughts while Florida was getting drowned from Hurricane Isaac and a bunch of tropical storms.

Also back in 2012, the National Institute of Standards and Technology (NIST) in Gaithersburg, Maryland, was hard at work releasing "NIST Special Publication 800-61 Revision 2: Computer Security Incident Handling Guide." You have to hand it to them; their titles are killers! But that's nothing compared to what's inside.

Currently, NIST 800-61r2, as it's known, is required reading for anyone in the cybersecurity field. It is a beautiful piece of work, and if you plan to get hands-on with incident management, you need to get to know it. You should also get cozy with other reports with captivating titles such as "ISO/IEC 27035-2 Information Technology—Security Techniques—Information Security Incident Management—Part 2: Guidelines to plan and prepare for incident response." (No, I am not kidding. That's the title. Fantastic work, too.) And while you're at it, you should also consult ENISA's "Actionable Information for Security Incident Response" and "Strategies for Incident Response and Cyber Crisis Cooperation," as well as their "NCSS Good Practice Guide—Designing and Implementing National Cyber Security Strategies." Not enough for you? Well, you incident-response animal, you—there are more relevant entries in the bibliography waiting for you!

What do you need to understand from all this? What are the essential elements of an incident response plan that you need to own in order to complete your own privacy-centric cybersecurity program?

The first critical thing to understand is that incident response is a program in and of itself. As such, it has its own distinct phases, and much like the overall cybersecurity program, it, too, is a living program. It's not one and done; it's a continuously managed program.

What are the phases? Have you heard of Elisabeth Kübler-Ross's five stages of grief: denial, anger, bargaining, depression, and acceptance? Many people go through them during an incident: "No! This can't be happening to us!" followed by choice expletives, then by the desire to pay to make this go away, quickly replaced by depression about having to face the music, and finally acceptance of the fact that you, like millions of others, are a victim of a cybercrime.

Thankfully, the core phases of incident-response planning are less gloomy. They are: preparing for incidents, identifying the occurrence of an incident, containing the incident, treating the incident (e.g., killing the virus, disabling access, etc.), recovering from the incident, and post-incident review, aka the "lessons learned" phase. That last one is key and should never be omitted.

To properly prepare for an incident you need to have four things in place:

1. an active privacy program;
2. an active cybersecurity program;
3. a business-continuity plan; and
4. a disaster-recovery plan.

The first two are rather obvious: you can't develop a privacy-centric cyber-security incident response plan unless you have both an active privacy and cybersecurity programs going.

The business-continuity (BC) plan is the document that the business has prepared to ensure continuity of operations and value delivery in case of disruption. A business disruption could involve a natural disaster such as a hurricane, an earthquake, or a disease outbreak such as the most recent COVID-19 pandemic. Or it could a man-made disaster such as a terrorist attack or a cyberattack. It could even involve a simple human failure, like if Julie from Accounting gets food poisoning from the cafeteria's tacos, and she's the only one who can get people paid!

The BC plan has all sorts of useful information that feeds into the incident response plan. For example, it has a defined business-continuity organizational structure, policies, and workflows, as well as information about who can trigger the BC plan and how that occurs, detailed contact information, including emergency contact numbers, client and vendor information, relocation strategies, recovery procedures, and the like. The benefit of the BC is that if and when it is invoked, different parts of the business execute different workflows designed to protect people, communicate effectively with all affected, and initiate as rapid a business recovery as possible.

The disaster-recovery plan (DR) is technology-centric. Its focus is in recovering the technology infrastructure of the company. This is where you will find all our favorite acronyms and their values per system: recovery time objectives (RTO), recovery point objectives (RPO), and the maximum tolerable downtime (MTD). All directly influence the incident response plan.

Consider, for example, if your MTD is zero. Who has such zero tolerance for downtime? Trading systems. Banking systems. Air-traffic control systems. Utility systems. (And, for some of us, Uncle Bob's Bagel and Pastrami Paradise.) How do their incident response plans address this requirement, keeping in mind that a cyberattack on a trading system may well have serious regulatory implications, which means preserving evidence, forensics, and so forth? You would need to plan for a zero MTD and remain compliant with regulations, which means you can't just kill the intruder, reboot the system, and be back in business. As a matter of fact, shutting down an infected system would wipe its volatile memory, destroying any forensic data that may be there.

Do you see now why planning ahead is so important? You need to take this a step at a time. Also, it is in the DR plan that you will find the pertinent privacy metrics that apply to your information technology ecosystem. The reason for that is straightforward: The technology ecosystem is the one that both hosts, processes, and shares PII internally and externally. Therefore, its DR plan addresses the recovery steps necessary for all digital PII.

Preparing Your Incident-Response Plan

Notice the use of "your" in the subhead—it doesn't say "Preparing an Incident-Response Plan." Why? Because no two IR plans are alike. They depend on many variables, from the size of the company, the scope of business, regulatory needs, to the company culture.

You might be surprised to hear that culture plays a role in incident response, but it does. An active, engaged, and educated user community in both privacy and cybersecurity is an important asset in detection, communications, and remediation. A passive, disengaged, and generally privacy- and cyber-ignorant culture frequently contributes to the incident and may even hinder its remediation.

By now, I expect you have a solid understanding of your firm's privacy and cybersecurity programs. By understanding your business-continuity and disaster-recovery plans, though, you will gain the necessary solid footing in framing your incident response plan.

Similarly, the absence of either of these two plans speaks volumes about the company's priorities and risk-management capabilities. It is your job to confront this reality head-on, starting with engaging the executive team, whose active support is a requirement in all privacy and cybersecurity program development efforts and is critical in developing IR capabilities.

In-house or Outsourced?

Remember back to our hospital building analogy? All previous aspects of cybersecurity program development were akin to building the different wards and wings of the hospital. Incident response is the surgical center. Question number one, therefore, is: Do you need a surgical center, or are you shipping your patients to a different facility altogether? In other words: Do you need, can you afford, and will you keep engaged an in-house incident response team? Or do you need to enter into an agreement with an outside incident response services provider?

For the majority of small to midsized businesses, the answer will be to outsource the IR function (at a minimum). The current lingo describing these providers is *managed detection and response vendor*, usually shortened to *MDR vendor*. If this were a hospital, that would mean you keep the internists (or at least the nurses) in-house but outsource the surgeons. It is highly unlikely that a small business will be able to both afford and to keep engaged a team of highly skilled and specialized privacy and cybersecurity incident response people. But that doesn't get you off the hook from designing your incident response plan appropriately!

Remember, you can outsource *responsibility*, but you cannot outsource *accountability*. You still need to work with the service provider in designing and owning the plan. For your cybersecurity program development effort to succeed, you must always maintain accountability and full ownership. You are the one responsible for being knowledgeable enough and engaged enough to be able to successfully complete a cybersecurity handshake with your vendors. And you're the one whose head is on the block should the company be found ill prepared.

Businesses that use an in-house team for incident response need to also recognize that they must provide a complete governance ecosystem for that team to succeed. An in-house IR team should report directly to the chief information security officer (CISO) and should have unfettered access to the privacy and risk management teams, as well as the information technology, human resources, legal, and communications departments. The minimum size of an IR team will always be two: an IR manager and an IR engineer. One interfaces with the organization and directs the incident response, while the other is deep in the weeds doing forensic and remediation work. The larger the organization, the larger the IR team, and the more specialized and complex its structure.

Organization

Irrespective of size and scope of company, be it in-house or outsourced, your IR plan will need to address several key components, starting with a detailed description of your policies, standards, procedures, and guidelines as they relate to cyber incidents. These, thankfully, will be derived to a considerable extent from your privacy and cybersecurity programs, the business continuity and disaster recovery plans, and with the added input of at least risk management, legal, and communications. These policies will introduce organizational structure and will essentially define the who-does-what-when part of the IR workflow.

With regards to the organizational structure, you'll need to adopt the one that best reflects the organization's needs. If you are decentralized, you may need decentralized IR teams. If not, perhaps a single centralized team is best. Depending on size and scope, you may decide to introduce a blended approach, where some IR capabilities are in-house, while the rest are outsourced. This works well when there is a large, headquarters-type of facility with smaller satellite offices scattered around the planet. In this case, you're probably better off having a centralized IR team at headquarters, with several vetted and contracted IR vendors at the remote locations. All involved get a copy of the plan, ideally saved in a big red binder with "Don't Panic" written all over it.

Communications

In addition to a clear organizational structure, a strong IR plan will also have clearly defined communications protocols. Think of this as the who-*says*-what-to-whom-when part of the plan. This is key. For one, you don't want to instigate a panic among users by screaming through the speakerphones, "Incident Alert! Incident Alert!" And you certainly don't want to broadcast to the bad guys that you have detected an incident. So avoid emails and nonsecure messaging platforms, all of which may have been compromised. In fact, consider that even unsecured telephone lines may also have been compromised. To the degree possible, stick with personal, one-on-one, secure communications on a need-to-know basis. Needless to say, this is not the time to get social! This is the time to carefully assess your situation: what exactly is happening; what is its potential impact on privacy, the business, clients, and vendors; and, of course, is there a need to notify law enforcement and regulators. The last thing you want to happen is to have someone from the press calling you with, "I got a tweet about you folks having been breached and three million PII records have been compromised ... Can you comment on that?" That's definitely not a good place to find yourself!

The "whom" in the "who-says-what-to-whom-when" workflow can be long, complex, and dynamic. It will change regularly and likely involve several third parties, such as your own insurance company, business vendors, cloud solutions providers, and your Internet services providers, as well as a slew of IT vendors and their own IR teams. You may be required to notify law enforcement—my go-to is always the FBI and the local district attorney's office. If you happen to be a multinational, then the contact list becomes substantially longer, since you may need to comply with local regulations on incident reporting on a country-by-country basis. On top of all these, you should consider sharing the information that you have with the US Computer Emergency Readiness Team (US-CERT) and other industry-specific IR organizations.

The fun part of notifications, of course, is letting your clients know about the breach. To be clear: There is no avoiding this, and the experience will not get better with time. The last thing you want is to have your clients learn about the situation from the news media. You need to be prepared and well rehearsed. Privacy, legal, insurance, and communications departments must all be in complete alignment on (at a minimum) what happened, who did it, why it happened, what you are doing in response, and how you're making sure it will not happen again. You may not know all the facts (such as who's behind the incident), but you need to be as proactive in your communications as due care and prudence will allow. Nothing destroys trust in a company faster than a poorly communicated privacy cyber incident. Get in front of it as soon as is practical—engage the news media and be as forthcoming as possible.

Integration and Updates

The next step in your IR plan creation is to integrate the wonderful results of your work to date in threat analysis, environments, and defense in depth and control deployments. The plan needs to reference all these, with specific clarity on where your threat intelligence is coming from and how you can leverage that in case of an incident, your environments at risk (clouds, Internet-connected devices, and your distributed workforce), and your defense in depth and controls deployment. These will be critical in both the detection of an incident and the response to it.

Remember, all these entries in your plan need to be kept current. If you learned anything from our earlier discussion of threats, it's that the threat landscape is highly dynamic. For your plan to be useful, it needs to reflect the appropriate level of changes over time. What does this mean for you? Get comfortable with two words: change management.

Tools and Personnel

To complete your incident response plan, you will need two more entries. First, you will need to identify your incident response toolkit. This is a set of mostly software tools (there are some hardware tools as well), that are specifically built for forensic and incident response work. Please note: These are surgical instruments, and they need to be handled by experts.

Moreover, the toolkit, like all else, evolves over time; in fact, toolkits are the fastest-evolving component of your response, because software is constantly updated. It is therefore critical that the plan reflect the most up-to-date toolkit in use, its locations (yes, there needs to be more than one), and any access credentials necessary. You do not want to be scrambling for USB keys in the middle of an attack. You need to know where your toolkit is, what is in it, and who are the right people to use it.

I can't emphasize enough the importance of the right people. Forensic and incident response work is very complicated and requires highly skilled specialists. Even the best-intentioned and expert IT professional can wreak havoc if she attempts to use forensic tools without specialized training and experience. There are any number of case studies where IR professionals walked into a site under attack only to find the well-meaning IT team having turned off the servers and already restoring systems from backup. This common mistake destroys the evidence, leaving you with no way to know who attacked and why, no way to learn how to prevent it in the future, and so on.

Training

The last component of your incident response plan is the training. And by that I don't mean the company-wide cybersecurity awareness training I discussed earlier. Here I mean war games. Full, all-out incident response exercises, conducted frequently and analyzed exhaustively. Just like the old joke about how do you get to Carnegie Hall, the only way to get to be good at incident response is practice, practice, practice. The higher your dependence on your IR team, the more and rigorous your practice exercises must be—think Red Teams and Blue Teams; the works! The exercises need to be comprehensive across all your environments, including your executive team, staff, and all key vendors. Some should be well planned, rehearsed, and announced, while others should be out-of-the-blue surprise drills. Everyone, from executives on down, should be aware and sensitized to incident response. They all have a role to play.

Meanwhile, your IR team should never rest. I know, that may sound harsh or over the top. But, that's the job. It's what they do. Constant training and practice are the only things that will make the final difference during a real attack.

Now, get to it!

Identifying Incidents

Armed with your up-to-date, shiny "Don't Panic" folder, you're ready to exercise your IR plan. All you need is an incident! If you're lucky, you'll wait for a nice, long time, giving you all the training opportunities your team needs. But if you're not …

How do you identify an incident? You monitor your environment. And by that I mean 24-7-365. Every system. Every action. Every event. Monitor. Monitor. Monitor. For the average company, monitoring will produce several thousand lines' worth of log entries and alerts from half a dozen systems (servers, firewalls, antivirus and antimalware software, switches, end points, etc.) or more. If your company is an above-average technology consumer, you will be dealing with potentially millions of log entries and events. Attempting to catalog all this, much less make sense of it all, is not something humans can manage on their own.

To be clear: Identifying an incident is far from trivial. Many have gone undetected for weeks and even months! It's not about interpreting alerts, reading logs, or processing user feedback. Hundreds of events in the course of doing business can be mistaken as a security incident. An application may modify a configuration file, and you get an alert: is it an incident or a normal function? A file server is slow: incident or just a heavy traffic load? Access to the Internet is spotty: incident or ISP errors? A file modification alert has been issued: malware or normal use? An email with a threat alert: is it mere spam or a sign of things to come? Unfortunately, all these will need to be looked at through your cybersecurity glasses, even if they end up being little else than routine bugs.

Enter SIEM. Security Information and Event Management systems ingest all this information (logs, threat feeds, etc.), correlate it, and issue alerts about abnormal events in your environment. What's not to love? Nothing. Except that not all SIEMs are alike, and, like all relationships, you need to put work into it to get the benefits out of it.

First, you should do your due diligence and select the right SIEM for your environment. They come in all sorts of sizes and flavors, including MDR/SIEM-as-a-service options. Second, depending on which system you deploy, you may have to fine-tune it. Make your SIEM too paranoid, and every alert issued becomes a ticket to be investigated. But tune it to "apathy" and you won't be notified until your data center has been pounded into fine silicon dust.

Once tuned, a good SIEM will be your best friend and cybersecurity partner. You'll be working hand-in-hand in processing the alerts, creating tickets, documenting trends, correlating with threat intelligence, and escalating to containment and treatment. All this beautifully orchestrated work will also be feeding into your cyber documentation tools, which your reporting workflows can use to notify authorities, incident information sharing organizations, wikis, and late-night glee clubs.

The catch, of course, is that to reach this level of incident-detection bliss will require not only the right SIEM properly configured, plus the right systems-management practices (e.g., documentation, normalization, synchronization) but also the right defense-in-depth strategy to begin with, which—you will recall—is the one that resulted in the deployment of the right controls being monitored in the first place.

And how did you get to the right defense-in-depth strategy? You got there because you did all the hard work during the asset, threat, vulnerabilities, and environments phases.

Who's better than you? No one, that's who!

Containing Incidents

ALERT! ALERT! This is not a drill!

You have an alert that was identified as legit, was pressure-tested, checked, and escalated to containment. Something is truly up! Now what?

- **Step one:** *Do not panic!* Heed the advice on the front of your binder! Do not panic! You've got this!
- **Step two:** *Identification.* What are you dealing with? What are your detective controls telling you? Trust your controls! Don't second-guess them.
- **Step three:** *Analysis.* This is elbow-grease work, requiring unique skills and specialized tools. Your team of experts will be asking a lot of questions: What is the payload? What is the vector? What does the threat feed tell us? How did it get in? What is the payload doing? How is it doing it? Why is it doing it?
- **Step four:** *Action.* Once you know who, how, and what, you need to be ready to act. Do you want to maintain the evidence for possible future actions (for example, prosecution)? Or do you want to get back to operations as soon as possible, with little regard to evidence preservation? That is, of course, a business decision and can only be taken at the board level. Do you want to tolerate the infection while you develop workarounds? These are decisions that you should have thought out ahead of time, and with board approval, and practiced with both your incident team and your top-level management.

Let's look more closely at step four, action. Action essentially means containment. To properly contain the incident, you'll need the results of Step 3—analysis. We need to know who, what, how, and if possible, why.

- **Who:** Who is behind the attack? Is this an accident? Is this an insider? Is this an act of terrorism? What do the threat feeds say about who's behind it? What is the motive? Understanding the *who* will help you develop methods of containment and treatment.
- **How:** What is the attack vector? Malware, and if so, which kind? Is this the result of a virus? A Trojan? A worm? Did someone plug in an infected USB somewhere? Did someone click a link in an email? Or

was this a "drive-by shooting," such as malware dropped on a computer while someone was just browsing? Or was the breach perhaps the result of stolen credentials? It may be one or more of these things or none of them. There could be some entirely other, more unusual method that the attacker used to compromise your systems. Your team will need to identify the *how* in order to contain it and potentially identify ways to preserve forensic data.

- **What:** What part of your system was hit? A single endpoint or multiple? Servers? Applications? Networks? Your forensic people will need to do a detailed end-point analysis on the affected systems to collect evidence. This will include any kind of tracks that the attacker left behind, including a bit-by-bit copy of what is in the volatile memory (not just the permanent storage [e.g., hard disk, SSD]). They will need to establish the incident timeline: When did the attack start, how did it propagate, what did it leave behind, what are the effects? Part of this process involves highly technical work that may include isolating the malware on a system for observation, or reverse engineering the malware to understand what the code is doing. Once all this is understood, then all systems across the company will need to be forensically verified that they have not been infected as well.

- **Why?** What made you a target? Are you just a random victim of greed? Are you a political target? Why exactly were you attacked? Are you collateral damage of a much larger attack? Roadkill on the information highway? Know this, and you may be able to learn a lot more about your adversary and build better future defenses.

It bears repeating that in the incident containment phase, knowing what not to do is as important as knowing what to do. If your company does not have the resident expertise, a panicked executive or IT person being flooded by alerts may be tempted to pull the plug of the infected computer, try to use some I-got-it-from-the-Internet-malware-removal-tool, or—worse yet—log in as the administrator to investigate it or call your friend in the FBI.

This is why it is so critical to have a plan in place before the incident and to practice, practice, practice! Knowing what to do and how to do it gets you halfway toward resolution.

Treating Incidents

When it comes to treatment, I have bad news and bad news. First, the bad news.

Sometimes, you may have to live with the disease. You may need to live with it because critical business considerations prohibit you from isolating or rebuilding one or more systems. Or you may need to keep the infected systems running so that the attackers don't realize that you are aware of them while shielding more valuable assets or sending Delta Force over to kick in their doors. Similarly, there may be upstream or downstream dependencies that require you to get creative. For example, because of business requirements of nonstop use, you may need to restore the infected system onto brand-new hardware and then reinsert it into production while taking the infected system out. That can prove about as easy as replacing an aircraft engine while it's in flight. It's doable but very, very windy.

Other times, you may be required to preserve the infected systems for evidence. That's all fine and good if you have one server that's infected; it's a whole other story if you have 50 of them sneezing and wheezing with a virus. Complicating things further is virtualization. These days, you can have multiple virtual computers running on a physical computer. Despite ironclad assurances from virtualization vendors that there can never be cross-contamination across virtual machine boundaries, I remain a skeptic. I am a firm believer that if one person can build it, another can break it. So I would not be surprised if a virus was created that could jump the virtualization boundary, despite whatever assurances you've been given. Remember the favorite saying of Dr. House: Everyone lies.

Once the evidence has been preserved, requirements have been met, all the t's crossed and all the i's dotted, next comes the fun part of coordinating one or more infected systems. Not only do you need the IR team on the same page, you need the whole organization to know which systems may need to go offline, for how long, what the impact may be, and so on and so forth. Depending on the number of systems, this can be an expensive, resource-intensive exercise. Plus, you'll make a whole new set of friends when you announce that all the passwords have been changed.

Which brings us to the bad news.

The only way to ensure that an infected system has been cured is to go to "bare metal." This means that you need to completely and thoroughly wipe the infected system and rebuild it bottom-up from clean installation media. There is no sugarcoating this. If you need to be 99.99 percent sure that the infection is gone, the only way to do it is by "burning the box" and reinstalling everything new.

Why only 99.99 percent sure, even after a clean wipe? Because word on the street has it that some agencies have developed malware that infects the actual hardware itself. Allegedly, this type of malware can infect the BIOS (basic input/output system) of a computer or certain EPROM (erasable programmable read-only memory) chips, such that even after you wipe the computer, the malware can reinstall itself. As unlikely as this may sound today, do keep it in the back of your mind. That way, you won't be surprised if the unlikely happens!

Of course, even wiping a single system is a time-consuming exercise. Not only do you need to have the clean installation media at hand, you also need to account for configuration settings, clean backup availability, data synchronization when the system gets reinserted into production, and so on and so forth. Now, multiply this by the number of infected systems.

Let's end with a *tiny* bit of good news: this moment is where your disaster recovery planning will shine. Having clean, recent, whole-image air-gapped backups for each system will go a long way toward a rapid recovery.

Incident Recovery

With the incident treated, you are ready to bring your systems back online. There are several questions that need answering here, bridging the incident-treatment process and final incident recovery.

First, long before any incident, you must have considered whether you will need to preserve any evidence. If you are required to do forensic preservation, then you cannot wipe the infected equipment and rebuild. You'll need replacement gear. Moreover, the documentation needs and requirements for evidence preservation are extensive. Your team will need to be familiar with all the laws and requirements for evidence handling, chain of custody documentation, proper evidence gathering, and so on. Your best bet is to retain a forensic firm to help you. They will interface with your attorney and your incident response team and make sure that all the evidence is taken care of properly.

Second, your incident recovery strategy hinges on your previously determined values of MTD (maximum tolerable downtime), RPO (recovery-point objective), and RTO (recovery-time objective). You have documented all of this before any incident, and they have governed your disaster recovery strategy. Here and now is where all this will be tested.

As with all things, recovery from an incident will fall on a spectrum. There will be companies whose MTD is practically zero and will therefore have hot failover sites, air-gapped (i.e., non-Internet accessible) backup and archives, and multi-timeline mirrors. (This refers to a mirroring strategy and equipment that creates isolated versions of mission-critical systems over predefined timelines—for example a real-time mirror, a day-old mirror, a week-old mirror, a month-old mirror, and so on.) Those companies will be using an army of resources to recover, because that's what it's worth to them and frequently is what is required of them (think utilities, national security installations, water purification, air traffic control, etc.).

Then, there are the majority of companies that can afford an MTD of hours or days. Their strategy is more appropriate to that timeline, meaning that the team has some runway to be able to restore systems to production. That is not to say that there is a company out there that doesn't want the absolute minimum MTD. This is to say that the majority of companies are smart enough to not overpay for disaster recovery when they can tolerate a few days' worth of an outage. There may be a question about whether those smarts are developed from proper risk management–centric thinking or from "Are you crazy? I am not paying all this money for backup!" reactions. Either way, most IT departments have in place a budget-appropriate solution that has also been implicitly accepted as recovery-appropriate.

Lastly, there are (hopefully) a minority of companies that have not thought through any of this. For them, incident recovery is … challenging. Some may never recover and go out of business (consider malware that destroys all data in the absence of a backup). Others will survive but pay a dear price in both time and money and get only a partial recovery. Either way, if you are reading this book, and have realized that this paragraph describes your company, you have a lot of work to do, and you'd best hurry up!

In our case, I am confident that you have evaluated and vetted your disaster recovery strategies and solutions as appropriate to your risk appetite, cybersecurity exposure, and so on, so we'll accept that your environment falls squarely into the smart group of companies! While your team is restoring your production environment, you are making sure that they are following a prerehearsed checklist that affirms proper and normal operation of all systems, following the communications and notifications protocols. All departments should be working together in incident response harmony. At the same time, you are making exhaustive notes on the incident that will help you in your post-incident review and action plan.

Post-Incident Review

There will be incidents and there will be INCIDENTS! Both will require your careful review. People call post-incident review many different things (lessons learned, postmortem, etc.), but no matter what you choose to call it, the review process is essential to the evolution of your cybersecurity program and team skills. To begin with, you need an answer to a whole list of questions, starting with:

- Who's responsible for this outrage? You should be able to answer this with confidence. And yet the question is more complex than it seems. It's not about merely assigning a name to the attacker; it is about building a complete profile. Sometimes getting a name will be impossible. You will still be able to glean quite a bit from the tools used, origin, threat intelligence feeds, and plain old Internet searching. Try to build as good a profile as possible. Understanding your attackers, their motives, and their methods will help you prepare for the next attack.
- Just the facts, ma'am! After the *who*, you need to document the *how*, and you need to do it in excruciating detail. You need to know exactly what happened, when it happened, how it happened, what vulnerabilities were exploited, how it was discovered, which alerts were triggered, and which were not. You need all the facts about the incident, in as much detail as possible. This will help you tune your defenses and identify holes in your control deployment.

- Knowing now what you didn't know then, what do you need to change? This is the introspective component of the exercise. You need to look inward and understand how your organization reacted to the incident. Look at everything and leave no stone unturned. How did the incident response team act? Were procedures followed? Were internal communications effective? Was the response time adequate? Were the response actions timely and adequate? Did you meet MTD, RPO, and RTO targets? How did the executive team support the effort? How did the staff react? How was the Privacy/IT/Cybersecurity partnership performance? Once these questions are answered, you can collectively sit down and tune your incident response plan such that next time you can perform better.
- How do you stop this from happening again? Having understood the organization's and team's performance, plus all about the incident itself, you need to plug the hole that allowed the incident to occur in the first place. This sounds a lot easier than it is. If the breach was due to a phishing incident, for example, your options may be limited to better email sandbox tuning and targeted cybersecurity awareness training. Neither of those will plug the hole completely. They may narrow it, but there is no guarantee that another member of the staff will not fall victim to such an attack. In which case, you're going back to layered defenses (sandboxing, role authorities, monitoring, training, etc.).

Do It All Over Again!

As we discussed earlier, privacy-centric cybersecurity program development in general and incident-response planning specifically are living programs. They change over time, they change with your environment, the market, the technology. They also change because you change: you learn, you grow, you adapt.

The good news is that as you learn, grow, and adapt, you can apply your knowledge, experience, and adaptation to your privacy, cybersecurity, and incident-response plans. You get a second chance! And a third, and a fourth …

Change is the only constant here, and it represents a wonderful opportunity to keep your privacy and cybersecurity program constantly tuned. Embrace this and take advantage of it. The alternative is catastrophic: an obsolete privacy, cybersecurity, and incident response program are just as bad as not having any.

CHAPTER 20

Welcome to the Future! Now, Go Home!

> We desire to bequeath two things to our children; the first
> one is roots, the other one is wings.
>
> —Sudanese proverb

I wrote *Cybersecurity Program Development for Business: The Essential Planning Guide* in 2018. The closing chapter of that book was titled "Living Cybersecure," and in it, I emphasized the need for readers to stay informed and current. The topics I wanted them to focus on were:

- *Scientific developments:* What's going on in the cybersecurity and information technology fields?
- *Regulatory developments:* What are the different legislative bodies enacting that affects your cybersecurity program?

Today, 2018 seems very far away, both in time and in how the world looked.

This book is being completed in the early summer of 2020 in New York City. We've been locked up for three months trying to deal with the COVID-19 pandemic, with no clue about second and third possible waves.

Last night, there were riots in many major cities across the country, the result of the police killing of Mr. George Floyd in Minneapolis. Some rioters took advantage of the demonstrations to loot stores, including the one on the ground floor of my apartment building.

Meanwhile the daily news reads like a bad science fiction novel: apocalyptic, confusing, and distressing. Foreign governments are actively engaging in cyberwarfare, unleashing worldwide campaigns of misinformation and voter manipulation.

In the midst of all this—and because of it!—with sirens wailing outside my window, I need to ask you to focus on privacy, regulations, cybersecurity, value creation, and protection! It may seem like a tall order, but there's nothing like a dystopian landscape to focus the mind!

So what are the things we as business owners, executives, professionals, consumers, and citizens need to pay attention sixty seconds into the future? I divided the list into three broad categories to consider in the context of our cybersecurity and privacy work: social transformation, technological transformation, and business transformation.

Social Transformation

The time is always right to do what is right.
—Martin Luther King Jr.

This is certainly not a book about politics, social injustice, or futurism. So what is a section on "social transformation" doing here?

Technology both drives social transformation and is affected by it. In our case, we need to consider the long path that technology has carved in enabling a global community to produce value in a geographically agnostic way and its implications on privacy and cybersecurity.

For decades now, we have been outsourcing value generation to information workers worldwide. You might sit in an office in downtown Des Moines while your analysts are doing work in India and the Philippines. And it's not just the tech industry that has been globalized: legal and financial services, administrative support, data entry, customer support, you name it—if it can be outsourced, then it has been.

Before the pandemic of 2020, we were used to this type of outsourcing. We understood the technology requirements behind it, and we even outsourced that, too! In terms of privacy and cybersecurity, our original position was "out of sight is out of mind" until the regulators descended, and we had to reconsider. Even then, it was compartmentalized. What happened in India stayed in India—except, of course, for the value that was transmitted back to headquarters in London, New York, or wherever they may be.

We would all wake up in the morning and go to work in our offices and integrate the benefits of outsourced value creation with our own. From our western point of view, this was a spoke-hub distribution. The hub was our office. The spokes were information pathways from all over the world coming into us.

What about physical goods? Outsourced as well! Practically everything was being made somewhere else where the labor was cheaper and the conditions favorable.

This is a natural point for some social commentary about the have and have-nots, the wealth inequity, and poverty gap, the opportunity lost, and the increasing polarization that has dominated the beginning of the 21st century, but I will not engage in this! It's neither my place nor is it appropriate for this book. I'll leave such reflections to you and just focus on what happened next.

COVID-19 is what happened next.

Overnight, it seemed, the world turned on its head. The skyscrapers of the world emptied out. Businesses shuttered, and the streets were left deserted. As of this writing, in summer 2020, about seven million people worldwide had been infected, with over four hundred thousand dead from the disease. Time was sharply divided into pre-COVID—or, in the words of *Mad Max*, "the before times,"—and post-COVID. People started talking about a new normal in trying to describe the post-COVID world of both business and personal life.

According to the Pew Research Center, pre-COVID, only 7 percent of Americans could work from home. This is in stark contrast to Europe where for the northern countries it hovered around 20 percent.

Post-COVID, the numbers in the United States changed dramatically. A Gallup poll found that by mid-March about 31 percent of Americans were working remotely. By the end of March, the number had jumped to 62 percent. Moreover, about 60 percent of workers said they would prefer to continue working from home, even after the COVID restrictions are lifted. America is not unique in this. Similar results are expected worldwide.

The implications to privacy, cybersecurity, and information technology needs are immense. Consider what an overnight transformation to a distributed workforce does to a company's threat surface! Consider the privacy implications of using a personal computer from home doing work when the employer insists on constant monitoring. Consider the bandwidth and connectivity requirements necessary to make telework happen. And so on, and so forth.

We don't yet know how permanent this state of affairs will be. Will more and more people choose to telework, even after restrictions are lifted? Will more and more companies side with the reduced pollution, reduced office expense, and reduced wasted time? Or will they side with the *"Unless you're here where I can see you, you're not working!"* approach of a few managers quoted in the popular press? Studies suggest that changes forced upon people due to a disruption tend to stick even after the disruption is removed. Will that hold true in this case as well?

For me, one thing is certain: We need to plan for an increased teleworking society. The benefits are just too many to ignore. But this means careful planning and understanding where we draw the personal/professional boundaries, understanding the privacy implications of telework, and protecting both the business and teleworker from cyberattacks.

My recommendation is to try to keep things as segregated as possible: Provide the teleworker with company equipment that you control and that can only be used for work. After all, you used to provide them with the same equipment in the office! You need to just allow for them to take that equipment home. Have proactive discussions with your teleworkers about the ground rules for privacy and conduct. Understand their environments and provide for secure connections between their locations and your office. And finally, make sure that the social aspect of work—the community and culture of your company—is preserved and enhanced, even when a large number of employees become teleworkers. The character and spirit of your company is at stake!

The effects of such a dramatic social change are not only felt in our professional lives. Our personal lives have been equally affected. Set aside the psychological effects of weeks-on-end quarantine. Consider instead how most people are facing the reentry to a new normal. Even after restrictions are lifted, there are many people that choose to socialize virtually, foregoing personal contact due to fear of the virus. Certainly, this will change as vaccines and cures become available, but for many the fear may never go completely away.

I am a cancer survivor, and the words of my oncologist are still with me to this day: "Chris," he said, "welcome to the cancer survivor's club where you won't have a headache in peace ever again!" He was right, and I now see the same trepidation on people's masked faces when someone walks by and coughs. There is no doubt: The world has changed, and so have we.

Dealing with the pandemic raised a whole set of personal privacy and technology issues as well. People were required, or at least strongly urged, to get tested. If the test was positive, they were required to provide a list of contacts that they feel they may have been in close proximity with. Then, an army of tracers would call each one of these contacts and ask them to get tested and to self-quarantine. Additionally, there is the reporting of the sick and deceased. How do you ensure that the reporting is at once comprehensive while preserving the privacy of the patients? Finally, both Apple and Google released technology that would allow their respective phone ecosystems to talk to one another—allegedly anonymously—so that people would receive an automated alert if they were in close proximity to an infected person. The question of balancing the common good with individual privacy collided head-on, and many fear that privacy lost out.

Just as you were thinking that the story couldn't get any worse, it did.

On May 25, 2020, Minneapolis police officers arrested Mr. George Floyd, a 46-year-old African American man, and in the process killed him by pinning him down, with one officer choking him with his knee while the other two watched. The murder was filmed and went viral on social media and broadcasted worldwide. What followed was weeks of international protests, and sometimes riots, in several major American cities, with a forceful response by many local police departments.

It is very difficult to write about the possible outcome of these historic events while simultaneously living through them. The question for us and this book remains "What is the impact of these dramatic events on privacy and cybersecurity?" The answer is complex and daunting and raises even more questions on how we practice privacy and implement cybersecurity.

Just as we considered the changed work parameters when moving, seemingly overnight, to a distributed workforce, we need to consider the implications of surveillance technology against the citizens of any country, the use of technology to spread disinformation, and the "looting" of personally identifiable data by governments and hackers alike during times of crisis. How we deal with this today will define the world we live in tomorrow.

In summary, we need to carefully study both telework and telelife needs in this moment in history and come up with ways to navigate them successfully.

Technology Transformation

It's still magic even if you know how it's done.

—Terry Pratchett

In December of 2019, with the pandemic lurking around the corner, Spiceworks published their excellent State of IT 2020 report. In the list of Top IT Challenges facing organizations in 2020, "Convincing business leaders to prioritize IT" was ranked fifth. This would typically produce little much other than a yawn for most people involved in IT management—the struggle to get "the suits" interested in tech has been a persistent problem since Alexander Graham Bell called Watson to come on over and help. Business leaders don't understand IT, IT people don't understand business, and so organizations hire this elusive of species called a CIO or CTO who they hope will translate between the parties, albeit not always successfully.

I am willing to bet the royalties from this book that after the pandemic, "Convincing business leaders to prioritize IT" will be much less of a problem! COVID-19 proved to be the singularity that changed the way business sees technology and cybersecurity forever. If your technology was not adaptable to telework, you were out of business.

For that matter, if your business was not adaptable to telework, no technology could keep you alive, either—as hospitality, transportation, sports and entertainment, and retail faced the devastating reality of consumers locked in their houses. Alongside these somewhat obvious victims of COVID lies another one: financial services, including FinTech. Transactions plummeted, currencies shifted, and credit dried up as companies ran to draw down their credit lines to survive.

For those firms that could make the transition to telework the key realizations were two: First: *"Thank you IT! You're my favorite essential worker!"* and second: *"Hmmm ... Why am I paying so much rent for this office when we can all work from home?"* Although it will take months and years to sort out the effects on commercial real estate, it is the ascension of IT that matters to us.

Seemingly overnight, IT priorities became business priorities: keeping IT infrastructure up to date, balancing IT tasks and improvement projects, updating outdated software, and following security best practices (Spiceworks' top 4 Top IT Challenges) were front-and-center, becoming top items for discussion on the daily Zoom call with management. And it's safe to assume that this trend will continue. The world has changed, and no one will forget what we all went through. To be sure, there will be leaders and laggards in this, but no matter where your company falls, you need to be aware of what will drive this transformation forward.

One hint: it's not hardware.

What is it then? Is it fast Internet? Is it the cloud? Is it the Internet of Things (IoT)? Is it artificial intelligence (AI), edge computing, or blockchain? What is the one thing that will have the biggest impact on business? Software.

Practically everything on the list above is made possible because of software. Yes, to be sure, software needs hardware to run, but that's saying that a piece of paper is of greater value that the poem written on it. It is not. It is always about the poem.

And today, it is always about software! That is where your money should go, and that's where your focus should be: Software, software, software! Your own, custom built or off the shelf: It's about software!

Artificial intelligence? Brought to you by software!

Edge computing? Brought to you by software!

Hyperconverged infrastructure? Yup! Brought to you by software!

Blockchain? Software it is!

Before we go too deep into the rabbit hole, let's at least know what we're talking about. Here are the definitions for my top ten business software disruptors that you need to know about, in alphabetical order:

1. **Artificial Intelligence:** There are several definitions for AI, from machines that demonstrate cognitive skills, to machines that can learn and problem solve. AI requires tremendous computing power to perform these cognitive tasks, and in years prior the cost of the associated hardware stymied its growth. Today, hardware has become so cheap

and powerful that AI systems are not only being developed at an alarming pace, but whole countries are investing billions of dollars toward the development of AI in what is called the AI race. I prefer to call it "the AI Wars," since countries don't invest billions to enhance their academic world standing but rather to solidify their power: My AI can beat your AI, so you best behave!

2. **Automation Systems:** These are software solutions that automate the majority of the interaction between human IT professionals and the systems themselves. Think of it as, for example, automatic provisioning of infrastructure, on demand and directly by the user, as opposed to having IT involved in spinning up computers, storage, networks, and so forth.

3. **Blockchain Technologies:** In their simplest form, blockchain technologies are implementations of decentralized and distributed ledgers that can record pertinent data about an asset. The important thing to understand is that while blockchain tech may have been developed for financial instruments, it can be used for anything. An "asset" can be anything you need to keep track of, and all sorts of assets can be recorded via blockchain technologies. For example, you can have an art blockchain that unmistakably traces both provenance and value of all paintings listed on it.

4. **Container Technologies:** These are software containers that wrap around an application and isolate it from other environments such as operating system differences or hardware configurations. This allows, for example, the creation of an app that, once containerized, can run identically on any platform that can accept the container.

5. **Edge Computing:** This refers to the methodology of pushing both the application and the data right to where they are physically needed as opposed to consuming bandwidth and resources to fetch it from servers or the cloud. This dramatically improves performance because the travel time is reduced, and work is performed locally at the device. For example, the more data and processing power is embedded on your smart digital assistant, the less time and bandwidth it needs to go to the cloud to respond to your request for a "Wake up alarm to 'Manic Monday' on Tuesday at 4:00 a.m." (What are you doing up at that time, anyway?)

6. **Hyperconverged Infrastructure:** This takes the concepts of edge computing and container technologies and makes them into one big happy software bundle. Processing power, communications, storage, and so forth, are all bundled in one software integrated solution and delivered to the users. This reduces cost and increases performance, as compared to larger data center deployments.

7. **Internet of Things (IoT):** We discussed this extensively in Chapter 17. IoT is essentially one big interconnected insecure mess, made possible by cheap hardware and (usually bad) software, plus some brilliant mind who exclaimed "I know what I want! An Internet-connected toaster oven!" The ensuing petabytes of data traffic can be harvested, analyzed, manipulated, sold, and ultimately deliver intelligence on everything from traffic patterns and energy use, the state of your nuclear reactor, how far your planes are flying apart from each other, and, of course, to how dark you like your bread toasted in the morning.

8. **Machine Learning / Big Data:** Those two terms go together by the nature of the application, although they mean different things. Machine learning is an AI application that specifically refers to the ability of the system to learn from the data (i.e., experiential learning). It is particularly powerful in pattern recognition, which is where Big Data comes in. That refers to extremely large sets of data that once analyzed, they reveal—you guessed it!—patterns! Those can be as "innocent" as purchasing and consumer behavior patterns, to increasingly "darker" analysis that can inform, for instance, credit card companies when your marriage is about to devolve into a nasty divorce (use prepaid cards, Karen!) if you're having a drug problem in the family, all the way to voting patterns of minority populations.

9. **Serverless Computing:** This is essentially server infrastructure as a service. You provision a server on-demand through a cloud provider, run your application, process your data, and when you're done you de-provision the server and you're done! No more maintenance costs, electricity costs, and so forth. This is particularly useful because the on-demand part can be extended to include computing power on demand, such that the server ramps up its processing power as the

application and data warrant and ramps it back down when it is no longer needed.

10. **Virtualization:** This includes everything from virtualized computing environments to virtual reality. In the first case, virtualization software runs on a set of hardware making it appear as multiple physical machines, thereby maximizing the use of a single physical resource. On the latter case, virtualization may include anything from the creation of a simulated world, to augmentation of the real world with layers of data visible to the user. That is also known as augmented reality, which is what the people who wear those clunky looking glasses experience when they are not tripping over the sidewalk.

Each one of these entries is a field of study on its own right, so it is not particularly fair that you are saddled with the need to understand them enough to wrap a privacy-centric cybersecurity program around it. But then again, life is not fair. So what do you do?

You build alliances. You will need to interface with the resident (or outsourced) expert that is in charge of the deployment and maintenance of these systems. Together you will be able to understand the risks and start to devise a plan to protect these assets against attacks. Of course, it goes without saying that not only does your privacy team need to be fully onboard, but so does the rest of the executive team and the board.

Keep in mind that the introduction of AI into your business is inevitable. It's not "if you get an AI system," it is "when." These systems may arrive disguised as harmless sounding applications such as "business intelligence" and "data analytics." Do not be fooled! These are complex, powerful AI applications, and they will need to be thoroughly understood and vetted for privacy and cybersecurity risks.

Various combinations of these disruptors are a natural fit to telework and are potentially already in use at your company:

- Virtual reality, for example, can allow teams to "walk" around models as they build them, provide telemedicine and tele-education solutions, or hold those boring meetings you thought you escaped "in person."
- AI systems can, and do, facilitate and optimize the delivery of goods and services all over the world, including your telework office in your cabin in Vermont.

- Personal assistants such as Alexa, Siri, Google, and Cortana are learning more by the day and can perform more and more tasks by directly controlling IoT-connected devices.
- Smart cameras and security systems can keep you safe and alert for help in case of fire or unwanted intrusions. They can also seriously violate your privacy, especially if your boss decides that in order for you to get paid for telework you must enable your computer camera so you can be supervised!

If these systems are deployed in your organization, they become part of your possible attack surface and must be catalogued and treated as the critical assets that they are. Overlooking any such "peripheral" systems can be deadly for both privacy and cybersecurity programs alike. It is your job to make sure that any and all of such solutions are catalogued, accounted, and protected.

Business Transformation

When digital transformation is done right, it's like a caterpillar turning into a butterfly. But, when done wrong, all you have is a really fast caterpillar!
— George Westerman, MIT Sloan Initiative on the Digital Economy

The year 2020 has been world-changing, and I predict it will be viewed as such by historians. I am not only referring to the tsunami of digital transformation already in motion, the privacy laws being enacted worldwide, or the active cyberwarfare and cybercrime dominating daily life. I also refer to the social transformations already discussed, and the changes to the ways of doing business that followed.

All these forces continue to feed on each other, much like a hurricane over warm water. We don't know if the forces will peter out or strengthen. But we do know that wherever this "hurricane" makes landfall, the landscape will not be the same. Our lives will be changed forever.

Physics students are taught that although you can think outside the box, you really cannot directly observe it if you are in it! For example, we all know that the earth is careening around the sun at 67,000 miles per hour, while spinning at about 1,000 per hour around its axis, but we can't observe it: for us, it feels motionless. The same goes for all of us living through, and trying to make sense of, the changes around us. We can only do our best to adapt, predict, and manage, and hope that what we don't know won't kill us!

We also have different priorities as people toward our family and friends, different priorities as citizens, and different priorities as professionals. These priorities need not be at odds with one another. At the end of the day, we all want to take care of our own, live in a just society, and make an honest living. The first two, I'll leave to your reflections. For the last one, I'd like you to consider your role in implementing and managing the changes to your business in such a way so that you can *continue* making an honest living. What does this mean?

We spoke of the social changes and the transformative potential of tele-work. We also discussed the many mature and maturing technologies that are transforming the value-creation chain. In the first part of this book we reviewed how privacy has evolved and continues to evolve and its impact on our thinking. In the second part we reviewed what society thinks of what we must do to preserve the integrity of our private information. And in the third part we went over the ways we can implement a privacy-centric cybersecurity program to protect the ways we generate value.

Now we need to stretch our thinking and consider how we can continue to protect this value in a shifting landscape. We can use edge cases and case studies for this, and you should build your own for your specific business, since as we've said time and again, no two businesses are alike. A law firm is a very different business than a manufacturing business, which is a very different business from a hospital, which is a very different business from a restaurant, and so on. It is therefore important that you look at your own world to come up with case studies to model.

To get you started, I will present a fictionalized case (based on real clients of mine) and take a look at the potential impact of these changes on the way that firm does business.

The Story of ACME

Let's imagine a business called ACME Corp, which delivers both manu-factured products and services. It is a midsized concern, employing about

400 employees worldwide. The majority of ACME workers are at its New York headquarters, but it also has offices in Chicago, Atlanta, Dallas, and San Diego. ACME imports goods from China and Korea and has a manufacturing/assembly plant in Nashville. It also has a development office in India and a small presence in London, Milan, Nairobi, and Singapore. The company's revenue is split evenly between design and fulfillment services provided to other businesses (B-to-B) and revenue from its online catalog to consumers (B-to-C). Its big sellers include the "Do-It-Yourself Tornado Kit," "Dehydrated Boulders," and "Exploding Tennis Balls."

Before the pandemic, ACME was doing very well. Revenues were climbing year to year. Business was good. Their IT infrastructure was a hybrid between on-premises servers and cloud services. They had their own custom application that gave them a competitive edge when it came to customer service and fulfillment. The development team was split between New York and India, while the product team was out of Atlanta. Research and Development was out of San Diego, and customer service was spread across the several regional offices. The offices were all connected with high-speed VPN, and there was a dedicated in-house IT team supporting the company, an outsourced cybersecurity firm providing cybersecurity, and an in-house legal and compliance team that was charged with privacy. The company culture was strong and collaborative. The board and executive team were highly engaged, and everyone was on the same page in terms of mission and priorities.

Then the pandemic hit. The first signs of trouble were shipment delays and cancellations from China and Korea. Then, the Italian office closed, all 11 team members quarantined, with 2 of them getting sick. That was followed by the London office closure. Headquarters was getting very alarmed. Orders were not getting fulfilled, many canceled. Clients were starting to complain. Their largest client, Wile E. Coyote, was livid! The Board was getting involved in emergency meetings. Then, the other shoe dropped. New York closed down. Nairobi followed, then India. Within a month, all ACME offices worldwide were ordered closed, and employees were asked to work from home. The future looked bleak and uncertain.

Thankfully, ACME had a few things going for it—most importantly, its culture and its great IT team. The minute the trouble began, IT mobilized. Even before the first emergency meeting, the CIO had presented a plan to the executive team on how she could keep all the employees connected and workflows moving. They leveraged their cloud applications to the max and shifted to a strong messaging and collaboration platform that had been available to them but underutilized. IT knew the challenges ahead: How to manage access? How to manage resource allocation? How to manage storage?

They engaged the cybersecurity team. Their first step was to immediately roll out multifactor authentication company-wide. It had been in place as a pilot program for the executives, but now, it became mandatory for all. Overnight, it was rolled out to the entire ACME workforce. Then, the teams analyzed the new environment. They realized that the computers that will be used to access corporate resources were a blend of brands, capabilities, and most important, ownership. Over 85 percent of the computers that will be used to connect to the corporate network were individually owned. So the cyber team got to work: they developed a security profile that included a minimum set of configurations and an endpoint intrusion detection/intrusion prevention control. IT took it and ran with it. Within days, all computers accessing the resources remotely were running on this configuration.

However, the legal department took a dim view of these actions. They had been burned before, when Wile E. Coyote demanded his data under CCPA! They said that the firm could be in violation of privacy statutes in different countries because they were installing corporate apps on private computers. Working with HR they came up with a temporary workaround: have the employees sign a consent form, allowing the company to install applications that enabling their personal computers to access the corporate network. The idea was to bridge the time until such point when the employees could return to the office and these applications would be removed.

These actions took care of the majority of the employees on the service side. They were able to work from home and their productivity—to management's surprise—was even better than when the employees were in the office! Unfortunately, the manufacturing side of the business ground to a halt. The plant in Nashville went dark, and the impact to the business was significant. Aside of the painful labor impact, there were pallets of goods left at loading docks, complex equipment idled and in need of maintenance, utility bills mounting, and chemicals that needed proper storage and disposal. Costs were climbing by the day while revenue was tanking, with several ACME clients unable (or unwilling) to pay their invoices.

ACME was hanging from a thread. Government help went only so far. Drawing down the credit line helped some more, but the bank was cranky and not in a particularly giving mood. Financing dried up. By the second month of the pandemic, whispers of layoffs started making the rounds. To make things worse, the CEO contracted the virus and was on a ventilator in a New York hospital. Everyone was terrified, glued on the television watching the news, wondering if they'd have a job tomorrow, wondering what would happen if they got sick.

Fortunately, ACME proved more resilient than feared. Its culture and people saved the day. With the service employees continuing to produce, the executive team in daily strategy sessions mapped a course to recovery. They cut expenses to the bone; all save payroll. They kept everyone on the books and continued to pay salaries and benefits. That action, plus the consistent messaging that they were all in this together, galvanized the company. Creative solutions started to come from all corners. Better ways of doing things, optimized workflows, and sometimes radical changes in the way the approached their business. The product team in San Diego took their robotic assembly pilot project and scaled it up. They had a plan ready the minute Nashville could reopen to roll out automation across the entire floor in such a way as to implement the mandatory social distancing and minimize employee exposure. The management team surveyed all employees on what they felt about telework, and the vast majority were in favor of a blended telework program. The company quickly realized this blended telework approach—in which employees come to the office only as needed or on a limited basis—could save millions of dollars in rent per year, money that could be redirected to restructuring the manufacturing plant and pay for company-owned computers for remote employees. IT presented their plan of "cloud first" solutions, whereby the primary data processing across all departments will be a cloud/edge solution, while the on-premises infrastructure would be either decommissioned or used as a secondary backup until its end-of-life. Legal, the COO, and CFO negotiated with landlords and banks all over the world and delivered restructured leases and creative financing. And in another set of good news, the CEO after an incredible eleven days on a ventilator was released from the hospital and was on a long road to recovery.

As the countries began to cautiously open up, the management team charged the CIO to come up with a plan to add resiliency to their operations and reduce costs. She came back with several pilot projects, including what she called "Individualized IT," a hyperconverged infrastructure approach that could deliver customized and decentralized solutions on demand to users all over the world. Cybersecurity developed plans to protect the distributed solutions through layers of controls across each major touch point: The local endpoint, the communications pipe, and the cloud solutions. They integrated this with identity management and layered two distinct data loss prevention AI controls that would protect the company's intellectual property no matter where it was.

As of this writing, ACME is still transforming. How will it look in the end is anyone's guess, but one thing is certain: ACME's people and culture saved the day by daring to transform, daring to change, and by working together, pushing not only technology but themselves to visualize a new company for a new normal. I am convinced that ACME will not only survive but it will thrive. Wile E. Coyote will be getting back to testing its products in no time!

Final Words

> **The world changes according to the way people see it, and if you can alter, even by a millimeter, the way people look at reality, then you can change the world.**
>
> —James Baldwin

I feel that I have used the word "transformation" a thousand times in this book. Digital transformation, privacy transformation, business transformation, IT transformation, cybersecurity transformation, society transformation … everything transformation!

Perhaps it is a sign of the times. Certainly, I have been transformed in the writing of this book. Challenged as a person, a citizen, and a professional. Challenged to think differently, to act differently, to deliver value differently, to respect differently.

Change, said Heraclitus, is the only constant. We tend to forget that. We get comfortable in our lives, narrow-focused in our work, isolated in the torrent of information around us. We get angry at change because it is scary, uncomfortable.

But change is life. All aspects of it, personal and professional. This book included. It is about how we change a cybersecurity program from its narrow asset-protection mindset to a more expansive, people-centric view by including privacy.

On a fundamental level, cybersecurity programs are … cybersecurity programs! In other words, there is no change in the way you look at asset protection. Stay focused, apply controls, monitor, remediate, and repeat!

Nevertheless, as James Baldwin so eloquently said, change it even by a millimeter, and the conversation shifts. Privacy is "the" millimeter for this book. It is "the" millimeter for your cybersecurity program, your company. It is the way you alter your world to be more inclusive, more engaged, more respectful of what matters.

It is my hope that this book will help you in adding your millimeter and changing your sliver of your world by a mile!

BIBLIOGRAPHY

I n preparing for this book, the sequel to *Cybersecurity Program Development for Business: The Essential Planning Guide* (Wiley 2018), I have consulted with, attended, read, and visited thousands of primary sources, be they in the form of books, seminars, workshops, classes, conferences, vendors, or cybersecurity professionals of every specialty that you can imagine (and some that you cannot!). It is—clearly—impossible to list all the material that I consulted and influenced my thinking, and I therefore apologize in advance for any omissions from the following bibliography.

The bibliography is first organized topically, followed by selected bibliography from *Cybersecurity Program Development for Business: The Essential Planning Guide*, whose material has been used extensively throughout the cybersecurity part of this book.

History, Case Law, and Legal Analysis

Abigail M. Roberson, an Infant, by Margaret E. Bell, her Guardian ad Litem, Respondent, v. The Rochester Folding Box Company et al., Appellants. Court of Appeals of New York, 171 N.Y. 538; 64 N.E. 442; 1902 N.Y. LEXIS 881, February 13, 1902, Argued June 27, 1902, *Decided.*

Cohen, Julie E. "What Privacy Is For." 126 *Harvard Law Review*, 1904. May 20, 2013. https://harvardlawreview.org/2013/05/what-privacy-is-for/.

Cooley, Thomas McIntyre. *A Treatise on the Law of Torts: Or the Wrongs which Arise Independent of Contract.* Second Edition. Chicago: Callaghan, 1888.

DeCew, Judith. "Privacy." *The Stanford Encyclopedia of Philosophy* (Spring 2018 Edition), Edward N. Zalta (ed.). https://plato.stanford.edu/archives/spr2018/entries/privacy.

Elliot, David. "*Understanding Privacy* by Daniel Solove." Book Review. *Philosophy in Review XX.* 2010.

Epstein, Richard. "Privacy, Property Rights, and Misrepresentations," 12 GA. L. REV. 455 (1978). https://chicagounbound.uchicago.edu/cgi/viewcontent.cgi?referer=https://www.google.com/&httpsredir=1&article=2233&context=journal_articles.

European Data Protection Supervisor. "The History of the General Data Protection Regulation." https://edps.europa.eu/data-protection/data-protection/legislation/history-general-data-protection-regulation_en.

Ferenstein, Greg. "The Birth and Death of Privacy: 3,000 Years of History Told Through 46 Images." The Ferenstein Wire. November 24, 2015. https:// medium.com/the-ferenstein-wire/the-birth-and-death-of-privacy-3-000-years-of-history-in-50-images-614c26059e.

Freude, Alvar, and Trixy Freude. "Echoes of History: Understanding German Data Protection." Bertelsmann Foundation. October 1, 2016. http://www.bfna.org/research/echos-of-history-understanding-german-data-protection.

Glees, Anthony, and John C. Schmeidel. *Stasi: Shield and Sword of the Party*, Intelligence and National Security, 27:1, 165–166. (2012) doi: 10.1080/02684527.2011.628530.

Hartzog, Woodrow, and Neil M. Richards. "Privacy's Constitutional Moment and the Limits of Data Protection. *Boston College Law Review* 1687. August 24, 2019. Last updated June 1, 2020. https://papers.ssrn.com/sol3/papers.cfm?abstract_id=3441502.

Holvast, Jan. "History of Privacy." http://opendl.ifip-tc6.org/db/conf/ifip9-6/fidis2008/Holvast08.pdf.

Iannaci, Nicandro. "Katz v. United States: The Fourth Amendment Adapts to New Technology." National Constitution Center. December 18, 2018. https://constitutioncenter.org/blog/katz-v-united-states-the-fourth-amendment-adapts-to-new-technology/.

Igo, Sarah. *The Known Citizen: A History of Privacy in Modern America*. Cambridge, MA: Harvard, 2018.

International Network of Privacy Law Professionals. "A Brief History of Data Protection: How Did It All Start?" January 6, 2018. https://cloudprivacycheck.eu/latest-news/article/a-brief-history-of-data-protection-how-did-it-all-start/.

Jablonka, Ivan. "The Origins of Mass Surveillance: Interview with Sophie Coeuré." books & ideas (Arianne Dorval trans., Mar. 17, 2016). http://www.booksandideas.net/The-Origins-of-Mass-Surveillance.html. [https://perma.cc/M8AM-T7UW].

Kirchhoff, Ulrich, and Tobias Schiebe. "The Reform of the Japanese Act on Protection of Personal Information: From a Practitioner's Perspective." https://www.arqis.com/wp-content/uploads/ZJR_44_13_Kirchhof_Schiebe_7_HB.pdf.

Lane, Julia, Victoria Stodden, Stephan Bender, and Helen Nissenbaum, eds. *Privacy, Big Data, and the Public Good*. Cambridge, MA: Harvard, 2014. https://www.cambridge.org/core/books/privacy-big-data-and-the-public-good/1ACB10292B07EC30F071B4AD9650955C.

Lessig, Lawrence. "The Code of Privacy." Proceedings of the American Philosophical Society. Vol 151, No. 3, September 2007. 283–290. https://www.jstor.org/stable/4599071?seq=1.

Moore Jr., Barrington. *Privacy: Studies in Social and Cultural History*. 1984. Reissue. New York and Oxford: Routledge, 2018.

National Constitution Center Staff. "Olmstead Case Was a Watershed for the Supreme Court." June 4, 2020. National Constitution Center. https://constitution center.org/blog/olmstead-case-was-a-watershed-for-supreme-court.

Nissenbaum, Helen. "Respecting Context to Protect Privacy: Why Meaning Matters." https://nissenbaum.tech.cornell.edu/papers/Respecting%20Context%20to %20Protect%20Privacy%20Why%20Meaning%20Matters.pdf.

Pekgozlu, Ilker, and M. Kemal Öktem. "Expectation of Privacy in Cyberspace: The Fourth Amendment of the US Constitution and an Evaluation of the Turkish Case, Sanal Ortamda Mahremiyet Beklentisi: Amerikan Anayasası'nın Ek Dördüncü Maddesi ve Türkiye'deki Durumun Değerlendirilmesi. Sosyoekonomi." 2012. https://www.researchgate.net/publication/283316511_Expectation_of_Privacy_in _Cyberspace_The_Fourth_Amendment_of_the_US_Constitution_and_an_Evalu ation_of_the_Turkish_Case_Sanal_Ortamda_Mahremiyet_Beklentisi_Amerikan_ Anayasasi'nin_Ek_Dorduncu_Maddesi_ve.

Posner, Richard. "The Right of Privacy." 12 *Georgia Law Review* 393. 1977. https://chicagounbound.uchicago.edu/cgi/viewcontent.cgi?article=2803&context =journal_articles.

Post, Robert C. "Three Concepts of Privacy." 89 Geo. L.J. 2098 2000-2001. https://digitalcommons.law.yale.edu/cgi/viewcontent.cgi?article=1184&context= fss_papers.

Post, Robert C. "The Social Foundations of Privacy: Community and Self in the Common Law Tort." *California Law Review*. Vol 77, No. 5. October 1989. https://digitalcommons.law.yale.edu/cgi/viewcontent.cgi?article=1210&context= fss_papers.

Post, Robert C. "Data Privacy and Dignitary Privacy: Google Spain, the Right to Be Forgotten, and the Construction of the Public Sphere." 67 *Duke Law Journal*. 981. 2018. https://scholarship.law.duke.edu/dlj/vol67/iss5/2.

Rothman, Jennifer E. *The Right of Publicity Reimagined for a Public World*. Cambridge, MA: Harvard University Press, 2018.

Solove, Daniel J. "A Taxonomy of Privacy." *University of Pennsylvania Law Review*. Vol 154:477. January 2006. https://www.law.upenn.edu/journals/lawreview/articles/ volume154/issue3/Solove154U.Pa.L.Rev.477(2006).pdf.

Solove, Daniel J. "A Brief History of Information Privacy Law" in *Proskauer on Privacy: A Guide to Privacy and Data Security Law in the Information Age* (2006). https://scholarship.law.gwu.edu/cgi/viewcontent.cgi?article=2076&context=facul ty_publications.

Solove, Daniel J. *Information Privacy Law*. 6th Edition. New York, NY: Aspen Publishing, 2018.

Sprenger, Polly. "Sun on Privacy: Get Over It." Wired. January 26, 1999. https://www
.wired.com/1999/01/sun-on-privacy-get-over-it/.

Warren, Samuel D., and Louis D. Brandeis. "The Right to Privacy." *Harvard Law Review* 4, no. 5 (1890): 193–220. doi:10.2307/1321160.

Waxman, Olivia B. "GDPR Is Just the Latest Example of Europe's Caution on Privacy Rights." *Time.* May 24, 2018. https://time.com/5290043/nazi-history-eu-data-privacy-gdpr/.

Wessler, Nathan Freed. "The Supreme Court's Groundbreaking Privacy Victory for the Digital Age." ACLU. June 22, 2018. https://www.aclu.org/blog/privacy-technology/location-tracking/supreme-courts-groundbreaking-privacy-victory-digital-age.

Westin, Alan F. *Privacy and Freedom*, 25 *Wash. & Lee L. Rev.* 166 (1968), https://scholarlycommons.law.wlu.edu/wlulr/vol25/iss1/20.

Wilheim, Ernst-Oliver. "A Brief History of General Data Protection Regulation." IAPP Resource Center. https://iapp.org/resources/article/a-brief-history-of-the-general-data-protection-regulation/.

Zimmerman, Diane L. "Requiem for a Heavyweight: A Farewell to Warren and Brandeis's Privacy Tort," *68 Cornell L. Rev.* 291 (1983). http://scholarship.law.cornell.edu/clr/vol68/iss3/1.

Legislation, Regulation, and Analysis

"Amended Act on the Protection of Personal Information." Version 2, December 2016. Personal Information Protection Commission of Japan. https://www.ppc.go.jp/files/pdf/Act_on_the_Protection_of_Personal_Information.pdf.

Agencia de Acceso a la Información Pública (Argentina). "Protection of Personal Data." Last accessed on September 10, 2020. http://www.jus.gob.ar/datos-personales/english-version/regulation.aspx.

Allende and Brea. "Data Protected—Argentina." Linklaters. February 2020. https://www.linklaters.com/en-us/insights/data-protected/data-protected---argentina.

APEC Secretariat. *APEC Privacy Framework.* 2005. https://www.apec.org/Publications/2005/12/APEC-Privacy-Frameworkhttps://www.apec.org/Publications/2005/12/APEC-Privacy-Framework.

Brazil. "Law No. 13,709, of August 14, 2018—Provides for the protection of personal data." Translated by Ronaldo Lemos et al. https://iapp.org/media/pdf/resource_center/Brazilian_General_Data_Protection_Law.pdf.

Colombia. Constitution of 1991 with Amendments through 2015. https://www.constituteproject.org/constitution/Colombia_2015.pdf?lang=en.

Congressional Research Service. "Data Protection Law: An Overview." March 25, 2019. Federation of American Research Scientists. https://fas.org/sgp/crs/misc/R45631.pdf.

Coos, Andrada. "All You Need to Know About Brazil's New Data Protection Law." End Point Protector. March 8, 2019. https://www.endpointprotector.com/blog/about-brazils-new-data-protection-law/.

Coos, Andrada. "Data Protection Regulations in Latin America." March 18, 2019. Endpoint Protector. https://www.endpointprotector.com/blog/data-protection-regulations-in-latin-america/.

Creemers, Rogier, Paul Triolo, and Graham Webster. "Translation: Cybersecurity Law of the People's Republic of China." New America. June 29, 2018. https://www.newamerica.org/cybersecurity-initiative/digichina/blog/translation-cybersecurity-law-peoples-republic-china/.

Cultural Secretariat of Japan. "Act on the Protection of Personal Information. (Act No. 57 of 2003)." http://www.cas.go.jp/jp/seisaku/hourei/data/APPI.pdf.

Dentons. "Data Protection: Colombia." https://dentons.cardenas-cardenas.com/en/insights/articles/2017/july/28/-/media/e968e3912aed44358393bd7cb32b0d56.ashx.

Department of Homeland Security. "DHS Handbook for Securing Sensitive PII." December 4, 2017a. DHS Privacy Office. https://www.dhs.gov/sites/default/files/publications/dhs%20policy%20directive%20047-01-007%20handbook%20for%20safeguarding%20sensitive%20PII%2012-4-2017.pdf.

Department of Homeland Security. "Privacy Handling Incident Guidance." December 4, 2017b. DHS Privacy Office. https://www.dhs.gov/sites/default/files/publications/047-01-008%20PIHG%20FINAL%2012-4-2017_0.pdf.

DLA Piper. *Data Protection Laws of the World: Full Handbook.* February 20, 2020. www.dlapiperdataprotection.comwww.dlapiperdataprotection.com.

Economic Community of West African States (ECOWAS). "Directive on Fighting Cyber Crime Within ECOWAS." http://www.tit.comm.ecowas.int/wp-content/uploads/2015/11/SIGNED_Cybercrime_En.pdf.

Economic Community of West African States (ECOWAS). "Supplementary Act on Personal Data Protection Within ECOWAS." February 16, 2010. http://www.tit.comm.ecowas.int/wp-content/uploads/2015/11/SIGNED-Data-Protection-Act.pdf.

EUR-Lex. "Protection of Personal Data (From 2018a)." https://eur-lex.europa.eu/legal-content/EN/LSU/?uri=CELEX:02016R0679-20160504.

EUR-Lex. "Protection of Personal Data (From 2018b)." https://eur-lex.europa.eu/legal-content/EN/LSU/?uri=CELEX:02016R0679-20160504.

European Data Protection Supervisor. "Preliminary Opinion on Privacy by Design." May 31, 2018. https://edps.europa.eu/data-protection/our-work/publications/opinions/privacy-design_enhttps://edps.europa.eu/data-protection/our-work/publications/opinions/privacy-design_en.

"Federal Act on Data Protection." https://www.admin.ch/opc/en/classified-compilation/19920153/201903010000/235.1.pdf.

Fernandez, Diego. "Argentina's New Bill on Personal Data Protection." October 2, 2018. https://iapp.org/news/a/argentinas-new-bill-on-personal-data-protection/.

Gawad, Mohamed Abdel, and Yomna Elewa. "Data Protection in Egypt: Overview." 2019. http://sharkawylaw.com/wp-content/uploads/2019/02/Data-Protection-in-Egypt-Overview-W-009-2180.pdf.

Greenleaf, Graham. "The Influence of European Data Privacy Standards Outside Europe: Implications for Globalisation of Convention 108 (October 19, 2011)." *International Data Privacy Law*, Vol. 2, Issue 2, 2012; UNSW Law Research Paper No. 2011-39; Edinburgh School of Law Research Paper No. 2012/12. https://ssrn.com/abstract=1960299.

Lovells, Hogan. "New Bill Imposing Increased Fines for Violations of Russian Data Protection Laws Under Consideration." Chronicle of Data Protection. June 2019. https://www.hldataprotection.com/2019/06/articles/international-eu-privacy/new-bill-imposing-increased-fines-for-violations-of-russian-data-protection-laws-under-consideration/.

Mabika, Verengai. "Privacy & Personal Data Protection: Guidelines for Africa." Internet Society. https://www.itu.int/en/ITU-D/Capacity-Building/Documents/IG_workshop_August2018/Presentations/Session%207_Verengai%20Mabika.pdf.

Maine legislature. "An Act to Protect the Privacy of Online Customer Information. https://mainelegislature.org/legis/bills/bills_129th/billtexts/SP027501.asp.

Matthews, Kristen J., and Courtney M. Bowman. "The California Consumer Privacy Act of 2018." July 2018. https://privacylaw.proskauer.com/2018/07/articles/data-privacy-laws/the-california-consumer-privacy-act-of-2018/.

Michaelsons. "Data Privacy or Data Protection in South Africa." January 28, 2018. https://www.michalsons.com/blog/data-privacy-in-south-africa/150.

Ministry of Electronics and Information Technology, Government of India. "The Personal Data Protection Bill, 2018." https://meity.gov.in/writereaddata/files/Personal_Data_Protection_Bill,2018.pdf.

Ministry of the Interior, Mexico. "Decree Issuing the Federal Law on Protection of Personal Data Held by Private Parties." July 5, 2010. https://www.duanemorris.com/site/static/Mexico_Federal_Protection_Law_Personal_Data.pdf.

National Informatics Centre. "Personal Data Protection Bill of 2019." http://164.100.
47.4/BillsTexts/LSBillTexts/Asintroduced/373_2019_LS_Eng.pdf.

National Information Technology Development Agency. "Nigeria Data Protection
Regulation." 2019. https://nitda.gov.ng/wp-content/uploads/2019/01/Nigeria
%20Data%20Protection%20Regulation.pdf.

Office of Australian Information Commissioner. "Australian Privacy Principles—A
Summary for APP Entities." March 12, 2014. https://www.oaic.gov.au/assets/pri
vacy/guidance-and-advice/app-quick-reference-tool.pdf.

Office of Australian Information Commissioner. "The Privacy Act." 1988.
https://www.oaic.gov.au/privacy/the-privacy-act/.

Palker, Stacey. "Data Privacy Laws Across Latin America." April 5, 2019. TMF
Group. https://www.tmf-group.com/en/news-insights/articles/2019/april/data-
privacy-laws-across-latin-america.

Presidência da República (Brazil). "Lei N° 13.709, de 14 de Agosto de 2018." August
14, 2018. http://www.planalto.gov.br/ccivil_03/_Ato2015-2018/2018/Lei/L13709
.htm.

Presidente de la República de Colombia. Decreto (acerca de la Protección de Datos
Personales). June 27, 2013. http://www.lasallecucuta.edu.co/infopdf/decreto1377
.pdf.

Privacy International. "State of Privacy Egypt." January 26, 2019. https://
privacyinternational.org/state-privacy/1001/state-privacy-egypt.

Privacy International. "The Keys to Data Protection: A Guide for Policy Engagement
on Data Protection." August 2018. https://privacyinternational.org/sites/default/
files/2018-09/Data%20Protection%20COMPLETE.pdf.

PwC Middle East. "Egypt: A New Data Privacy Law." 2019. https://www.pwc.com/m1/
en/services/tax/me-tax-legal-news/2019/new-egyptian-data-privacy-law-nov
-2019.html.

Reilly, Brandon P. and Scott T. Lashway. "The California Privacy Rights Act Has
Passed: What's In It?" November 11, 2020. https://www.manatt.com/insights/news
letters/client-alert/the-california-privacy-rights-act-has-passed.

República Argentina—Poder Ejecutivo Nacional. "Mensaje: Ley de Protección de
Datos Personales." September 19, 2018. https://www.argentina.gob.ar/sites/
default/files/mensaje_ndeg_147-2018_datos_personales.pdf.

Rich, Cynthia. "Privacy Law in Latin America & the Caribbean." Bloomberg BNA
Privacy and Security Report. 2015. https://iapp.org/media/pdf/resource_center/
Privacy_Laws_Latin_America.pdf.

Russian Federation. "Federal Law No. 152-FZ of July 25, 2006 on Personal Data."
http://wko.at/ooe/Branchen/Industrie/Zusendungen/FEDERAL_LAW.pdf.

Secretaría de Gobernación, Presidente de los Estados Unidos Mexicanos. January 26, 2017. "Decreto por el que se expide la Ley General de Protección de Datos Personales en Posesión de Sujetos Obligados." http://www.dof.gob.mx/nota_detalle .php?codigo=5469949™fecha=26%2F01%2F2017.

Sheng, Wei. "One Year After GDPR, China Strengthens Personal Data Regulations, Welcoming Dedicated Law." Tech Node. June 19, 2019. https://technode.com/ 2019/06/19/china-data-protections-law/.

Shi, Mingli, Samm Sacks, Qiheng Chen, and Graham Webster. "Translation: China's Personal Information Security Specification." New America. https:// www.newamerica.org/cybersecurity-initiative/digichina/blog/translation-chinas- personal-information-security-specification/.

South Africa. "POPI Act Compliance." http://www.popiact-compliance.co.za/popia- information/16-offences-penalties-and-administrative-fines.

South Africa. "The Constitution of the Republic of South Africa, 1996." https://www .justice.gov.za/legislation/constitution/SAConstitution-web-eng.pdf.

South Africa, Information Regulator. "Protection of Personal Information, 2013." https://www.justice.gov.za/inforeg/docs/InfoRegSA-POPIA-act2013-004.pdf.

University of California, Irvine, Office of Research. "Privacy and Confidentiality." https://research.uci.edu/compliance/human-research-protections/researchers/pri vacy-and-confidentiality.html.

World Wide Web Foundation. "Personal Data Protection in Nigeria." March 2018. http://webfoundation.org/docs/2018/03/WF_Nigeria_Full-Report_Screen_AW .pdf.

Information Technology, Design, and Privacy

32nd International Conference of Protection and Privacy Commissioners. "Resolution on Privacy by Design." October 27-29, 2010. https://edps.europa.eu/sites/edp/files/ publication/10-10-27_jerusalem_resolutionon_privacybydesign_en.pdf.

Buttarelli, Giovanni. "Privacy by Design—Privacy Engineering." CPDP 2018—EDPS side event. January 25, 2018. https://edps.europa.eu/sites/edp/files/publication/ 18-01-25_privacy_by_design_privacy_engineering_cpdp_en_3.pdf.

Cavoukian, Ann. "Privacy by Design: The 7 Foundational Principles." August 2009. Information and Privacy Commissioner of Ontario. https://www.ipc.on.ca/wp- content/uploads/Resources/7foundationalprinciples.pdf.

Cavoukian, Ann. "Privacy by Design: The Definitive Workshop." May 18, 2010. https://rd.springer.com/content/pdf/10.1007%2Fs12394-010-0062-y.pdf.

Cavoukian, Ann. Biography. Ryerson University. https://www.ryerson.ca/pbdce/about/ann-cavoukian/.

Colesky, Michael, Jaap-Henk Hoepman, and Christian Hillen. "A Critical Analysis of Privacy Design Strategies." Institute for Computing and Information Sciences, Radboud University. 2016. http://www.cs.ru.nl/~jhh/publications/iwpe-privacy-strategies.pdf.

European Data Protection Supervisor. "Preliminary Opinion on Privacy by Design." May 2018. https://edps.europa.eu/sites/edp/files/publication/18-05-31_preliminary_opinion_on_privacy_by_design_en_0.pdf.

Hartzog, Woodrow. *Privacy's Blueprint: The Battle to Control the Design of New Technologies*. Cambridge, MA: Harvard, 2018.

Joint Task Force Transformation Initiative. "Security and Privacy Controls for Federal Information Systems and Organizations." NIST Special Publication 800-53, Revision 4. April 2013. https://nvlpubs.nist.gov/nistpubs/SpecialPublications/NIST.SP.800-53r4.pdf.

Karlstads University. "Properties of Privacy Controls." https://kau.instructure.com/courses/5337/pages/properties-of-privacy-controls.

Kupritz, Virginia W. "Privacy in the Workplace: The Impact of Building Design." *Journal of Environmental Psychology*. Elsevier, 1998.

Marshall, N.J. "Privacy and Environment." *Hum Ecol* 1, 93–110 (1972). https://doi.org/10.1007/BF01531349.

Michota, Alexandra, and Sokratis K. Katsikas. "Designing a Seamless Privacy Policy for Social Networks." PCI '15 (2015).

Threat and Incident Reports

AlienVault's Open Threat Exchange. https://otx.alienvault.com.

Bitdefender's E-Threats Landscape Reports. http://www.bitdefender.com/site/view/e-threats_reports.html.

CISCO's Security Advisories and Alerts. https://tools.cisco.com/security/center/publicationListing.x#~Threats.

Cisco Security Reports. https://www.cisco.com/c/en/us/products/security/security-reports.html.

European Union Agency for Network and Information Security (ENISA). Annual Incident Reports. https://www.enisa.europa.eu/topics/incident-reporting/for-telcos/annual-reports

LookingGlass Threat Map. https://map.lookingglasscyber.com.

McAfee's Threat Center. http://www.mcafee.com/au/threat-center.aspx.

Symantec's Security Response. https://www.symantec.com/security_response.

Threat Intelligence Review's Cybersecurity Intelligence Feed Reviews. http://
threatintelligencereview.com.

Future Trends

Bocci, Fabrizio. "Digital Transformation and Technological Debt." Being Better Matters. February 28, 2020. https://www.beingbettermatters.net/digital-
transformation-and-technological-debt/ (accessed: September 2020).

Bocci, Fabrizio. "Digital Transformation and Technological Debt." Being Better Matters. February 28, 2019. https://www.beingbettermatters.net/digital-
transformation-and-technological-debt/.

Brenan, Megan. "Workers Discovering Affinity for Remote Work." Gallup. April 3,
2020. https://news.gallup.com/poll/306695/workers-discovering-affinity-remote-
work.aspx.

Collins, Sean. "Why These Protests Are Different." Vox. June 4, 2020. https://
www.vox.com/identities/2020/6/4/21276674/protests-george-floyd-arbery-
nationwide-trump.

Desilver, Drew. "Working from Home was a Luxury for the Relatively Affluent
Before Coronavirus—Not Anymore." World Economic Forum. March 21, 2020.
https://www.weforum.org/agenda/2020/03/working-from-home-coronavirus-
workers-future-of-work/.

Dumalaon, Jane. "Working from Home, Even When the Coronavirus Crisis Has
Passed." DW. May 5, 2020. https://www.dw.com/en/working-from-home-even-
when-the-coronavirus-crisis-has-passed/a-53290644.

Electronic Information Privacy Center (EPIC). "Privacy Issues: Hot Topics and New
Resources." https://www.epic.org/privacy/.

Fitzgerald, Louisa. "Top Emerging Technologies Making an Impact in 2020."
CompTIA. June 10, 2020. https://www.comptia.org/blog/emerging-technologies-
impact-2020.

Future Today Institute. "Tech Trends Annual Report." 2020. https://futuretodayinsti
tute.com/2020-tech-trends/.

Maayan, Gilad, David. "The IoT Rundown for 2020: Stats, Risks, and Solutions."
January 13, 2020. Security Today. https://securitytoday.com/Articles/2020/01/13/
The-IoT-Rundown-for-2020.aspx.

McGowan, Heather E. Home page. https://www.heathermcgowan.com/writing.

McGowan, Heather E. "The Coronavirus is Creating an Inflection Point in the Future
of Work. Forbes. April 16, 2020. https://www.forbes.com/sites/heathermcgowan/

2020/04/16/the-coronavirus-is-creating-an-inflection-point-in-the-future-of-work.

McGowan, Heather E. "The Coronavirus Pandemic Accelerates the Future of Work." Forbes. March 23, 2020. https://www.forbes.com/sites/heathermcgowan/2020/03/23/the-coronavirus-pandemic-accelerates-the-future-of-work-and-provides-opportunity/#7c4d9ec8317f.

"The 2020 State of IT: The Annual Report on IT Budgets and Tech Trends." Spiceworks. https://www.spiceworks.com/marketing/state-of-it/report/.

Tufekci, Zeynep. "Think You're Being Discreet Online? You're Not." New York Times. April 21, 2019. https://www.nytimes.com/2019/04/21/opinion/computational-inference.html.

Selected Bibliography from *Cybersecurity Program Development for Business: The Essential Planning Guide* (Wiley 2018)

Americans and Cybersecurity. 2017. Washington, DC: Pew Research Center.

Atluri, Indrajit. "Managing the Risk of IoT: Regulations, Frameworks, Security, Risk, and Analytics," *ISACA Journal*, vol. 3, 2017, https://www.isaca.org/Journal/archives/2017/Volume-3/Pages/managing-the-risk-of-iot.aspx.

Bandos, Tim. "Incident Responder's Field Guide." 2016. Waltham, MA: Digital Guardian, Inc.

Barlow, Mike. *Governing the IoT—Balancing Risk and Regulation*. 2016. Sebastopol, CA: O'Reilly Media, Inc.

Blue Skies Ahead? The State of Cloud Adoption. 2016. Santa Clara, CA: McAfee, Inc.

Board Briefing on IT Governance, 2nd ed. 2013. Rolling Meadows, IL: IT Governance Institute.

Bonime-Blanc, Andrea. *Emerging Practices in Cyber Risk Governance*. 2015. New York: The Conference Board, Inc.

Borg, Scott, and John Bumgarner. *The US-CCU Cyber-Security Matrix*. (Draft Version 2). 2016. Washington, DC: United States Cyber Consequences Unit.

Bostrom, Nick. *Superintelligence: Paths, Dangers, Strategies*. 2014. Oxford, UK: Oxford University Press.

Bosworth, Seymour, M.E. Kabay, and Eric Whyne (eds.). 2014. *Computer Security Handbook*, 6th ed. Hoboken, NJ: John Wiley & Sons, Inc.

Brenner, Susan W., and Leo L. Clarke. 2010. "Civilians in Cyberwarfare: Casualties," *SMU Science and Technology Law Review*, vol. 13, 2010. http://works.bepress.com/susan_brenner/3.

Cameron, Kim, and Quinn, Robert. *Diagnosing and Changing Organizational Culture—Based on the Competing Values Framework*. 2006. San Francisco, CA: Jossey-Bass.

Cappelli, Dawn. *The CERT Top 10 List of Winning the Battle Against Insider Threats*. 2012. Pittsburgh, PA: CERT Insider Threat Center, Software Engineering Institute, Carnegie Mellon University.

Carnegie, Dale. *How to Win Friends and Influence People*. 1936, 1964, revised 1981. New York, NY: Simon & Schuster.

CGEIT Review Manual 2015. 2014. Rolling Meadows, IL: ISACA.

Characterizing Effects on the Cyber Adversary—A Vocabulary for Analysis and Assessment. 2013. Bedford, MA: MITRE.

Cichonski, Paul, Tom Millar, Tim Grance, and Karen Scarfone. 2012. *Computer Security Incident Handling Guide*. Gaithersburg, MD: National Institute of Standards and Technology.

Cisco 2017 Annual Security Report. 2017. San Jose, CA: Cisco Systems, Inc.

CISO Board Briefing 2017. 2017. Rolling Meadows, IL, ISACA.

Clinton, Larry. *Cyber-Risk Oversight—Director's Handbook Series*. 2017. Washington, DC: National Association of Corporate Directors.

Closing Security Gaps to Protect Corporate Data: A Study of U.S. and European Organizations. 2016. Traverse City, MI: Ponemon Institute.

Cloud and IoT Threats Predictions, McAfee Labs. 2017. Threat Predictions. Santa Clara, CA: McAfee, Inc.

COBIT—A Business Framework for the Governance and Management of Enterprise IT. 2012. Rolling Meadows, IL: ISACA.

Cole, Eric. *Insider Threats and the Need for Fast and Directed Response—A SANS Survey*. 2016. Bethesda, MD: SANS Institute.

Council Decision. "Security Rules for Protecting EU Classified Information" (2013/488/EU), *Official Journal of the European Union*. September 23, 2013. Brussels, Belgium.

Cyber 7—Seven Messages to the Edge of Cyber-Space. 2015. Heraklion, Crete: European Union Agency for Network and Information Security (ENISA).

Cybercrime: Defending Your Enterprise How to Protect Your Organization from Emerging Cyberthreats. 2017. Rolling Meadows, IL: ISACA.

Cybersecurity Fundamentals Study Guide. 2014. Rolling Meadows, IL: ISACA.

Defense in Depth—A Practical Strategy for Achieving Information Assurance in Today's Highly Networked Environments. 2010. Fort Meade, MD: National Security Agency.

Dekker, M.A.C., and Dimitra Liveri. *Cloud Security Guide for SMEs*. 2015. Heraklion, Crete: European Union Agency for Network and Information Security (ENISA).

Drucker, Peter F. *Classic Drucker—Essential Wisdom of Peter Drucker from the Pages of Harvard Business Review*. 2006. Boston, MA: Harvard Business School Publishing Corporation.

Drucker, Peter F. *The Essential Drucker*. 2001. New York, NY: HarperCollins.

ENISA Threat Landscape—Top 15 Cyber Threats 2015. 2016. Heraklion, Crete: European Union Agency for Network and Information Security (ENISA).

ENISA Threat Landscape 2015. 2016. Heraklion, Crete: European Union Agency for Network and Information Security (ENISA).

ENISA Work Programme 2017 (Draft). 2016. Heraklion, Crete: European Union Agency for Network and Information Security (ENISA).

EU-US Privacy Shield Framework—Key New Requirements for Participating Companies. 2016. Washington, DC: US Department of Commerce.

Evolution of Incident Response. Enterprise Management Associates, Inc. 2017.

Flynn, Lori, Carly Huth, Randy Trzeciak, and Palma Buttles. *Best Practices Against Insider Threats in All Nations*. 2013. Pittsburgh: CERT Division, Software Engineering Institute, Carnegie Mellon University.

Framework for Improving Critical Infrastructure Cybersecurity—Draft Version 1.1. 2017. Gaithersburg, MD: National Institute of Standards and Technology.

Gottfredson, Linda S. "Mainstream Science on Intelligence," *Wall Street Journal*, December 13, 1994.

Grance, Tim, Joan Hash, Marc Stevens, Kristofor O'Neal, and Nadya Bartol. *Guide to Information Technology Security Services*. 2003. Gaithersburg, MD: National Institute of Standards and Technology.

Grance, Tim, Tamara Nolan, Kristin Burke, Rich Dudley, Gregory White, and Travis Good. *Guide to Test, Training, and Exercise Programs for IT Plans and Capabilities*, 2006. Gaithersburg, MD: National Institute of Standards and Technology.

Guide to Sound Practices for Cyber Security, Version 2.0. 2017. London, UK: The Alternative Investment Management Association, Ltd.

Hanson, Tom, and Birgit Zacher Hanson. *Who Will Do What by When? How to Improve Performance, Accountability, and Trust with Integrity*. 2005. Longwood, CA: Power Publications Inc.

Herzog, Peter. *The Open Source Cybersecurity Playbook*. 2016. Cardedeu, Spain: ISECOM and BARKLY.

Hovland, Carl I., and Walter Weiss. "The Influence of Source Credibility on Communication Effectiveness," *Public Opinion Quarterly*, vol. 15, 4, January 1, 1951, 635–650.

Implementing Cybersecurity Guidance for Small and Medium-sized Enterprises, 2015. Rolling Meadows, IL: ISACA.

Implementing the NIST Cybersecurity Framework. 2014. Rolling Meadows, IL: ISACA.

Industrial Control Systems Cyber Emergency Response Team. *Recommended Practice: Improving Industrial Control System Cybersecurity with Defense-in-Depth Strategies.* 2016. Washington, DC: Department of Homeland Security, Office of Cybersecurity and Communications.

Information technology—Security techniques—Information security incident management—Part 2: Guidelines to plan and prepare for incident response (ISO/IEC 27035-2). 2016. Geneva, Switzerland: ISO (International Organization for Standardization) and IEC (the International Electrotechnical Commission).

Information technology—Security techniques—Information security management systems—Overview and vocabulary. 2016. Geneva, Switzerland: ISO (International Organization for Standardization) and IEC (the International Electrotechnical Commission).

Insider's Guide to Incident Response—Expert Tips. 2017. San Mateo, CA: Alien Vault.

IS Audit/Assurance Program—Data Privacy. 2017. Rolling Meadows, IL: ISACA.

Janis, Irving L., and Bert T King. 1952. *The Influence of Role Playing on Opinion Change.* New Haven, CT: Yale University.

Kaplan, Robert S., and David P. Norton. 1996. *The Balanced Scorecard: Translating Strategy into Action.* Boston, MA: Harvard Business School Press.

Kissel, Richard (ed.). 2013. *Glossary of Key Information Security Terms.* Gaithersburg, IL: National Institute of Standards and Technology.

Klahr, Rebecca, Jayesh Navin Shah, Paul Sheriffs, Tom Rossington, Gemma Pestell, Mark Button, and Victoria Wang. 2017. *Cyber Security Breaches Survey 2017.* London, UK: Crown.

Kohen, Isaac. "ISACA Cyber Security Articles," *5 Layers of Defense that Prevent Insider Threats.* 2017. Rolling Meadows, IL: ISACA. https://www.isaca.org/cyber/cyber-security-articles/Pages/5-layers-of-defense-that-prevent-insider-threats.aspx.

Kral, Patrick. *The Incident Handlers Handbook.* 2016. Bethesda, MD: SANS Institute.

Lacey, David. *A Practical Guide to the Payment Card Industry Data Security Standard (PCI DSS).* 2015. Rolling Meadows, IL: ISACA.

Leventhal, Howard. "Findings and Theory in the Study of Fear Communications," *Advances in Experimental Social Psychology,* vol. 5, 1970, 119–186.

Lynden K., Shalm, et al. "Strong Loophole-Free Test of Local Realism." *Physical Review Letters,* 115, 250402, December 16, 2015.

McFarlan, Warren F., and Richard L. Nolan. "Why IT Does Matter," *Harvard Business School—Working Knowledge,* August 25, 2003. http://hbswk.hbs.edu/item/why-it-does-matter.

McMillan, Rob. *Gartner Security and Risk Management Summit Security 2020—The Future of Cybersecurity.* 2016. Stamford, CT: Gartner Inc.

Moar, James. *Cybercrime and the Internet of Threats 2017*. 2017. Basingstoke, UK: Juniper Research Ltd.

Moen, Ronald D., and Clifford L. Norman. *Circling Back—Clearing Up Myths about the Deming Cycle and Seeing How It Keeps Evolving*. 2010. Milwaukee, WI: Quality Progress.

Mortakis, Georgios. *Cyber Security and Information Assurance Controls Prevention and Reaction*. 2013. Coral Gables, FL: Enterprise Risk Management.

Moschovitis, Chris; Erica Pearson, Hilary W. Poole, Tami Schuler, Theresa Senft, and Mary Sisson. *The Internet: A Historical Encyclopedia—Chronology*. 2005. Santa Barbara, CA: ABC-CLIO, Inc.

Murray, Anna P. *The Complete Software Project Manager—Mastering Technology from Planning to Launch and Beyond*. 2016. Hoboken, NJ: John Wiley & Sons Inc.

NACD Advisory Council on Risk Oversight. *Cybersecurity Oversight and Breach Response*. 2015. Washington, DC: National Association of Corporate Directors.

Needle, David. *Business in Context: An Introduction to Business and Its Environment*. 2010. Mason, OH: South-Western Educational Publishing.

Northcutt, Stephen. *"SANS Technology Institute—Security Laboratory" Security Controls*, September 1, 2009. https://www.sans.edu/cyber-research/security-laboratory/article/security-controls.

Operational Levels of Cyber Intelligence. 2013. Arlington, VA: Intelligence and National Security Alliance.

Overview of Digital Forensics. 2015. Rolling Meadows, IL: ISACA.

Overview of the General Data Protection Regulation (GDPR). 2016. Brussels, Belgium: Information Commissioner's Office.

Patel, Hemant. "IoT Needs Better Security" *ISACA Journal*, vol. 3, 2017. https://www.isaca.org/Journal/archives/2017/Volume-3/Pages/iot-needs-better-security.aspx.

Paulsen, Celia, and Patricia Toth. "Small Business Information Security: The Fundamentals." 2016. *NISTIR7621 Revision 1*. Gaithersburg, MD: National Institute of Standards and Technology.

People and Technology in the Workplace. 1991. Washington, DC: National Academies Press.

Petty, Richard E., and John T. Cacioppo. *The Elaboration Likelihood Model of Persuasion*. 1986. Cambridge, MA: Academic Press.

Proctor, Paul E., and Katell Thielemann. "Gartner Security and Risk Management Summit" *to the Point: Implementing the Cybersecurity Framework (CSF) and the Risk Management Framework (RMF)*. 2016. Stamford, CT: Gartner Inc.

Read, Opie Percival. *Mark Twain and I*. 1940. Chicago: Reilly and Lee.

Responding to Targeted Cyberattacks. 2013. Rolling Meadows, IL: ISACA.

Review of Cyber Hygiene Practices. 2016. Heraklion, Crete: European Union Agency for Network and Information Security (ENISA).

Rogers, Everett M. *Diffusion of Innovations*. 1983. New York, NY: The Free Press.

Ross, Ron, Stu Katzke, Arnold Johnson, Marianne Swanson, and Gary Stoneburner. *Managing Risk from Information Systems—An Organizational Perspective*. 2008. Gaithersburg, MD: National Institute of Standards and Technology.

Schafer, Robert B., and John L. Tait. *A Guide for Understanding Attitudes and Attitude Change*. 1986. Publication 138, Reprinted August 1986. Ames, IA: North Central Regional Extension.

Shackeford, Dave. *The SANS State of Cyber Threat Intelligence Survey: CTI Important and Maturing*. 2016. Bethesda, MD: SANS Institute.

Smallwood, Robert F. *Information Governance—Concepts, Strategies, and Best Practices*. 2014. Hoboken, NJ: John Wiley & Sons, Inc.

Snedaker, Susan, and Chris Rima. *Business Continuity and Disaster Recovery Planning for IT Professionals*. 2014. Waltham, MA: Elsevier, Inc.

Snyder, Joel. *Six Strategies for Defense-in-Depth*. 2007. Tucson, AZ: Opus One.

Standards for Security Categorization of Federal Information and Information Systems (FIPS PUB 199). 2004. *Gaithersburg, MD: Computer Security Division*, Information Technology Laboratory, National Institute of Standards and Technology.

State of Cyber Security 2017. 2017. Rolling Meadows, IL: ISACA.

Symantec Corporation. "2017 Internet Security Threat Report." 2017.

Talent.oecd—Learn. Perform. Succeed—Competency Framework. 2014. Paris, France: The Organisation for Economic Cooperation and Development (OECD).

The 2016 Cyber Resilient Organization Executive Summary. 2016. Traverse City, MI: Ponemon Institute.

The Alien Vault Incident Response Toolkit: Putting the OODA Loop to Work in the Real World. 2017. San Mateo, CA: Alien Vault.

The Current State of Cybercrime 2014—An Inside Look at the Changing Threat Landscape. 2014. Hopkinton, MA: EMC Corporation.

The Cyberresilient Enterprise: What the Board of Directors Needs to Ask. 2015. Rolling Meadows, IL: ISACA.

The Importance of Cyber Threat Intelligence to a Strong Security Posture. 2015. Traverse City, MI: Ponemon Institute.

The IT Archipelago—The Decentralisation of Enterprise Technology. 2016. London: The Economist Intelligence Unit Ltd.

The Risk IT Framework. 2009. Rolling Meadows, IL: ISACA.

The U.S. Army Operating Concept—Win in a Complex World (TRADOC Pamphlet 525-3-1). 2014 Washington, DC: United States Army.

Transforming Cybersecurity. 2013 Rolling Meadows, IL: ISACA.

Trites, Gerald. *Information Integrity*. 2013. New York, NY: American Institute of CPAs and Canadian Institute of Chartered Accountants.

US Cybercrime: *Rising risks, reduced readiness*. 2014. Dover, DE: Pricewaterhouse-Coopers LLP.

Verizon. *2017*. "Data Breach Investigations Report." 2017.

Wang, Sichao. "Cloud Security Alliance Education White Papers and Educational Material White Papers" *in Are Enterprises Really Ready to Move into the Cloud?* February 2012. https://cloudsecurityalliance.org/wp-content/uploads/2012/02/Areenterprisesreallyreadytomoveintothecloud.pdf.

Weiss, Walter, and Carl Hovland. "The Influence of Source Credibility on Communication Effectiveness" *Journal of Abnormal and Social Psychology*, vol. 46, 1951. Reprinted in *Public Opinion Quarterly*, 1951–1952.

West-Brown, Moira J., Don Stikvoort, Klaus-Peter Kossakowski, Georgia Killcrece, Robin Ruefle, and Mark Zajicek. *Handbook for Computer Security Incident Response Teams (CSIRTs)*. 2nd ed. 2003. Pittsburgh, PA: Carnegie Mellon Software Engineering Institute.

"What's IT Automation?" RedHat. https://www.redhat.com/en/topics/automation/whats-it-automation.

Wheatman, Jeffrey. *"Gartner Security and Risk Management Summit" State of Security Governance*, 2016. 2016. Stamford, CT: Gartner Inc.

WhiteHat Security Web Applications Security Statistics Report 2016. 2016. Santa Clara, CA: WhiteHat Security.

Whitteker, Wes. *Leading Effective Cybersecurity with the Critical Security Controls*. 2016. Bethesda, MD: SANS Institute.

Wolak, Russel, Stavros Kalafatis, and Patricia Harris. "An Investigation into Four Characteristics of Services," *Journal of Empirical Generalisations in Marketing Science*, vol. 3, 1998.

Wrighton, Tyler. *Advanced Persistent Threat Hacking—The Art and Science of Hacking Any Organization*. 2015. New York, NY: McGraw-Hill Education.

INDEX